THEORY AND REALITY IN DEVELOPMENT

Paul Streeten

THEORY AND REALITY IN DEVELOPMENT

Essays in Honour of Paul Streeten

Edited by

Sanjaya Lall

Senior Research Officer, Institute of Economics and Statistics, and Fellow, Green College, Oxford

and

Frances Stewart

Senior Research Officer, Institute of Commonwealth Studies, and Fellow, Somerville College, Oxford

© Sanjaya Lall and Frances Stewart 1986

All rights reserved. No reproduction, copy or transmission of this publication may be made without written permission.

No paragraph of this publication may be reproduced, copied or transmitted save with written permission or in accordance with the provisions of the Copyright Act 1956 (as amended).

Any person who does any unauthorised act in relation to this publication may be liable to criminal prosecution and civil claims for damages.

First published 1986

Published by
THE MACMILLAN PRESS LTD
Houndmills, Basingstoke, Hampshire RG21 2XS
and London
Companies and representatives
throughout the world

British Library Cataloguing in Publication Data
Theory and reality in development: essays in honour of Paul Streeten.
1. Developing countries—Economic conditions
I. Lall, Sanjaya II. Stewart, Frances
III. Streeten, Paul
330.9172'4   HC59.7
ISBN 0-333-39824-6 (hardcover)
ISBN 0-333-39825-4 (paperback)

Transferred to digital printing 1999
02/790

Contents

Editors' Preface — vii

Note on Paul Streeten — ix

Notes on the Contributors — xi

1. Paul Streeten: An Appreciation — 1
   Hugh Stretton
2. Adam Smith's Prudence — 28
   Amartya Sen
3. Stagflation and the Third World — 38
   Wilfred Beckerman
4. Recession, Rent and Debt: Quasi-Ricardian and Quasi-Keynesian Components of Non-Recovery — 58
   Michael Lipton
5. Proposal for an IMF Debt Refinancing Subsidiary — 87
   Mahbub ul Haq
6. Alternative Approaches to North–South Negotiations — 95
   Frances Stewart
7. Extending Free Trade to Include International Investment: a Welfare Theoretic Analysis — 115
   Jagdish N. Bhagwati and Richard A. Brecher
8. The Third World and Comparative Advantage in Trade in Services — 122
   Sanjaya Lall
9. Outward Orientation, Import Instability and African Economic Growth: an Empirical Investigation — 139
   G. K. Helleiner
10. The Early 1980s in Latin America: The 1930s One More Time? — 154
    Carlos F. Diaz-Alejandro

Contents

11 Communal Land Tenure Systems and their Role in Rural Development 165
   Keith Griffin
12 World Food Security: National and International Measures for Stabilization of Supplies 192
   Nurul Islam
13 Bureaucratic, Engineering and Economic Men: Decision-Making for Technology in Tanzania's State-owned Enterprises 217
   Jeffrey James
14 East–South Trade 240
   Deepak Nayyar

List of Paul Streeten's Publications 270

Index 279

Editors' Preface

All of us who have been students or colleagues of Paul Streeten have benefited from his highly incisive and original intellect, but, more than this, we have gained from his courtesy and warmth and his vision of a better life for the poor of this world. In putting together this collection in his honour, we have been delighted to see how widely our feelings were shared across the spectrum of development economists (and others also).

Paul left Oxford many years ago, but in many subtle ways he is still with us, and we like to believe that he regards Oxford as his spiritual home. The fact that development economics is a thriving discipline at Oxford is due in no small part to the pioneering role Paul, together with the late Thomas Balogh, played in the early days of the subject. This collection is a token of our appreciation for Paul's achievements, not just in the past but also in the years to come.

A person like Paul Streeten has so many professional links that this volume could have been very much larger. Inevitably we had to be selective in inviting contributions. Also inevitably, a few people who wanted to contribute were unable to do so because of other pressing commitments. We are grateful, nonetheless, that so many busy academics found the time to prepare papers for this book. We are also grateful to Tim Farmiloe of The Macmillan Press for enthusiastically supporting the venture from its conception.

SANJAYA LALL
FRANCES STEWART

Oxford

NOTE   We should like to record our deep sorrow at the death of Carlos Diaz-Alejandro in July 1985. He combined brilliance and ebullience, warmth and wit, in a unique way. His early death has left an irreplaceable gap.

Note on Paul Streeten

Paul Streeten is Director of the World Development Institute at Boston University. He was a Consultant and Special Advisor to the Policy Planning and Program Review Department of the World Bank, as well as Director of Studies at the Overseas Development Council. Until September 1978 he was Warden of Queen Elizabeth House, Director of the Institute of Commonwealth Studies and a Fellow of Balliol College, Oxford. He was Acting Director and a Fellow of the Institute of Development Studies (and was Vice Chairman of its Governing Body), Professor at the University of Sussex and Deputy Director-General of the Economic Planning Staff at the Ministry of Overseas Development. He was a Member of the Board of the Commonwealth Development Corporation, of the Provisional Council of the University of Mauritius and the UK Royal Commission on Environmental Pollution. He was President of the UK Chapter of the Society for International Development (Co-chairman, with Mr A. Tasker, of the Committee that wrote a Report on the Strategy of the Second Development Decade), a member of the Council of the Overseas Development Institute, Vice Chairman of the Advisory Committee on the Social Sciences and a member of the UK National Commission of UNESCO, a member of the Africa Publications Trust, a Governor of the Dominion Students' Hall Trust, London House. He was an Associate of the Oxford University Institute of Economics and Statistics from 1960 until 1964, and editor of its *Bulletin*. He was editor of *Oxford Economic Papers* until 1961. He was a Fellow of the Institute for Advanced Studies at Wesleyan University, Middletown, Connecticut, in 1962, and a member of the Council of the Walloon Institute of Economic Development.

He is a member of the Society of International Development's North South Round Table, and on the Advisory Board of MIT's Center for Policy Alternatives. He has been visiting professor at several North and South American, Japanese, and European universities. He participated in the Conference on the future of science and technology in Austria in 1972. He led an ILO Mission on Basic Needs to Tanzania. He delivered the Montague Burton Lecture on International Relations at the

University of Leeds on 5 November 1974, and the Zahid Husain Memorial Lecture at the invitation of the State Bank of Pakistan in Karachi on 1 September 1979. He was on the faculty of the Salzburg seminar of American Studies, 1983. His developing country experience includes India, Pakistan, Bangladesh, China, Philippines, Malaysia, Sri Lanka, Israel, Mauritius, Malta, Egypt, Nigeria, Ivory Coast, Kenya, Kuwait, Tanzania, Panama, Trinidad, Barbados, Argentina, Brazil, Chile, Venezuela, and Mexico. He has worked for UNCTAD (Rapporteur of the Expert Group on the Link), for UNDP, UNIDO, FAO, UNESCO, WHO, WFC, OECD and UNICEF.

He has a DLitt., MA and BA from Oxford University and an honorary LLD and MA from the University of Aberdeen. He is an Honorary Fellow of the Institute of Development Studies at the University of Sussex.

His recent research has been on problems of direct private foreign investment, aid, trade, international monetary issues, basic human needs, agricultural price policies, and the social and human aspects of development. He is also interested in regional development, technology, education, the environment, alternative styles in development and interdisciplinary studies.

He has collaborated with Gunnar Myrdal on *Asian Drama*. His publications include *Economic Integration* (1st edn 1962, 2nd edn 1964), *Value in Social Theory* (editor), *The Crisis of Indian Planning* (co-editor with Michael Lipton and contributor), *Commonwealth Policy in a Global Context* (co-editor with Hugh Corbet and contributor), *Diversification and Development: The Case of Coffee* (with Diane Elson), *Aid to Africa*, *The Frontiers of Development Studies*, *Trade Strategies for Development* (editor), *The Limits of Development Research*, *Foreign Investment, Transnationals and Developing Countries* (with S. Lall), *Recent Issues in World Development* (edited with Richard Jolly), *Development Perspectives*, *First Things First*, as well as numerous articles. He is editor of *World Development* and on the board of other journals.

Notes on the Contributors

Wilfred Beckerman is a Fellow of Balliol College, Oxford.

Jagdish A. Bhagwati is Professor of Economics and Director of the International Economics Research Centre at Columbia University, New York.

Richard N. Brecher is Professor of Economics at Carleton University.

The late **Carlos F. Diaz-Alejandro** was Professor of Economics at Columbia University, New York.

Keith Griffin is President of Magdalen College, Oxford.

Mahbub ul Haq is Federal Minister for Planning and Development, Government of Pakistan.

Gerald K. Helleiner is Professor of Economics at the University of Toronto, Canada.

Nurul Islam is Assistant Director-General, Economic and Social Policy Department, at the Food and Agriculture Organisation of the UN in Rome.

Jeffrey James is Assistant Professor of Economics at Boston University.

Sanjaya Lall is Senior Research Officer, Institute of Economics and Statistics, and a Fellow of Green College, Oxford.

Michael Lipton is Professorial Fellow of the Institute of Development Studies at the University of Sussex.

Deepak Nayyar is Professor of Economics, Indian Institute of Management, Calcutta, and currently on secondment to the Ministry of Commerce, Government of India, as economic adviser.

Amartya Sen is Drummond Professor of Political Economy and a Fellow of All Souls College, Oxford.

Frances Stewart is Senior Research Officer at the Institute of Commonwealth Studies and a Fellow of Somerville College, Oxford.

Hugh Stretton is a Reader in History, University of Adelaide, Australia.

1 Paul Streeten: an Appreciation

HUGH STRETTON

Connoisseurs of Paul Streeten's style may remember that it did not develop, it appeared like Minerva from the head of Zeus, fully grown and armed. Here is a sample from its first year in print:

> We have found grounds to doubt that businessmen try to maximize profit. They have other aims too. Even if they tried, we would be sceptical that they could: they often do not know the relevant data. Even if they tried and could, it is doubtful whether they in fact would maximize profits: where there is uncertainty actual returns diverge from expected returns. This divergence is in the nature of things. The theory which we have been criticizing assumes that businessmen should, would and could behave in a way which may be undesirable, unsuccessful and impossible.

Seven unstated assumptions of the offending theory are then detected, six of them paired to show how three of them contradict the other three.
    That talent should have been timely. The Anglo-American synthesis of Keynes's macroeconomics with neoclassical microeconomics was just beginning its long post-war career. Its core was a master model of an inappropriately formal, determinate, unadaptable kind. It had internal inconsistencies, especially between its macro- and micro-theories. It misrepresented too many facts of economic life, and recommended too much bad economic behaviour. The real need was not to staple the *General Theory* to orthodox microeconomics like that, it was to replace the microeconomics with more open, observant, adaptable approaches to the facts of business life.
    Paul Streeten was born in 1917; he is two years younger than Paul Samuelson. Samuelson distilled the old and new orthodoxy with

spectacular success in books published in 1947 and 1948. In the two following years Streeten attacked much of the method and microeconomics of that orthodoxy in comprehensive papers on 'The Theory of Pricing' (*Jahrbücher für Nationalökonomie und Statistik*, October 1949, from which the sample above is taken), 'The Theory of Profit' (*Manchester School*, September 1949) and 'Economics and Value Judgements' (*Quarterly Journal of Economics*, November 1950). It is part of the tragedy of our times that so much of the world followed Samuelson, rather than Streeten and those like him.

Not that anybody was quite like him. Those first dense, laconic, lucid papers argued as he has argued on subject after subject since: too much of the orthodox theory is untrue, and unadaptable to changing life. It neglects its own self-verifying and self-falsifying effects on the life it misrepresents. It conceals values, many of which if explicit would be disagreed with. It is often self-loving, more concerned to be an enjoyable or saleable theory than to serve humankind. Trying for (1) a unanimous value-free science of (2) an isolable, internally determined economic system animated by (3) a single-purposed 'economic man' is a threefold mistake: a moral, political and scientific mistake. In real life, he argued, 'morality, politics and economics merge'. He had just graduated from the Oxford school of Philosophy, Politics and Economics, an exemplary product of its designers' integrative intentions. But whatever his broad mind owed to its many disciplined Austrian/Scottish/Anglo-Hungarian education, the wit and the puritanical self-scrutiny were individual. The first paragraph of 'Economics and Value Judgements' argued plausibly for making tacit assumptions explicit. The second paragraph exposed and criticised a tacit assumption of the first. Why that playful device? A footnote hints that one purpose may have been to show that he could sin as wickedly as Samuelson – a truly delicate way to approach the subject of another's vices. Whatever else, his writing is full of intellectual fun and surprise.

From 1948 to 1964, teaching at Balliol with occasional years in the United States, he attended to a very wide range of theoretical and policy problems. The range had to be wide as he took his pupils through most of the Economics curriculum. He taught long hours. As teacher and critic or collaborator his manner is cool, good-natured, gentle, generous. He is more than usually interested in how other people think. He is a skilful analytical philosopher and logician; no suppressed premises, logical leaps or *non sequiturs* escape notice. Before there were analogue computers I used to think his head contained one. It processed passages of reasoning, his own and others, impartially. Routinely as it did so (it seemed to me) it tried the effect of reversing each positive and each negative, running every model backwards as well as forwards and running it while varying each of its premises in turn, scanning every matrix for neglected boxes, and testing every proposition for truth, tautology, political realism, moral turpitude and (especially) undistributed middles. Those pernickety skills might have made him a terrible pedant if they had not been servants of strong social and moral concerns. But they were and are: when he draws attention to an unstated premise or an undistributed middle it is always one that *matters*, somehow to someone, substantially. Precision must not be sterile; imagination must not be impractical; they should join, he once wrote, to generate 'imaginative visions of alternative possibilities with close and precise attention to detail'.

The values that direct the combination are not simple, or anyway not stereotyped. They were developed in sometimes happy, sometimes endangered, sometimes tragic experiences of childhood, persecution, war, love, nationality and religion which are not the subject of this paper. Four reviewers of his work have called him respectively an Oxford radical, a Social Democrat, a neo-institutionalist, and a systematic sceptic. All true, but the last may mislead: there is nothing especially sceptical about his understanding of God, man or social institutions, he is only sceptical of economic theories that are blind to all three. The values apparent in his work are humane, egalitarian, democratic, personally generous and self-effacing. Together with his integrated understanding of economic life and how we think about it they made him a marvellous tutor, for all the students whose work he read and questioned, and for all the colleagues whose work he helped them write.

Through those tutorial years his own writing ranged nearly as widely as his teaching had to do. There was continuing criticism of neoclassical theory and positivist philosophy: he and Balogh attacked some assumptions and misuses of the idea of elasticity; 'Programs and Prognoses' appeared; Kaldor's contribution to 'objective' welfare criteria was dismantled in a chapter on 'Values, Facts and the Compensation Principle'. He wrote a prescient book about the problems of European economic integration. He also wrote about the history of economic thought, international trade and exchange, taxation and risk-taking, domestic and foreign investment, human capital, productivity and growth, wages and prices and inflation. Most of the papers are in one way or another about relations between theory and life in matters of social as well as theoretical interest. They detail the harm done to policy and practice by using inappropriate models, or models inappropriately; how beliefs both shape and are shaped by material interests; how analyses and predictions and purposes affect one another; how misleading the means/ends model can be for understanding or planning behaviour of which most items have both some value, and some effects. In one of the very few lines of self-description that anyone ever extracted from him he said that this early theoretical work emphasised 'discontinuities, asymmetries, irreversibilities, and indivisibilities': all qualities of life that resist formal modelling.

If with, or after, Myrdal he is the best philosopher and methodologist of social science, part of the reason is that he refuses the division of labour that treats methodology as 'a field' and methodologists as the specialists in it. Instead he writes about life with continuous attention to what his assumptions and methods are doing to his perception and understanding of it, or he writes about scientific methods with continuous attention to their social uses and abuses and effects.

It is convenient to relate Paul Streeten's early work on the relations between theory and life to his relations with Thomas Balogh and Gunnar Myrdal. It is especially interesting to do so because the three are alike in many of their beliefs but different in their styles and strategies as dissenters in a profession whose work they think very important, but many of whose prevailing ideas they think wrong and dangerous.

Thomas Balogh has been Paul's tutor, colleague, collaborator and friend. Paul has also taught Thomas, whose prefaces thank the man 'who did so much to help me towards anti-conventional views' with such 'patience and ingenuity in interpreting my intuitive doubts in a coherent and consistent language'. Thomas has diverse experience in Hungary, Germany and Britain as banker, broker and public servant; a formal education chiefly in law; wide reading in European and English economic writing; plenty of theoretical devices to use eclectically where they fit; practical expertise with the monitoring, accounting and statistical services of modern states and corporations; and a nose for what markets may do next, or in his own words 'economic flair, what the Germans call *Fingerspitzengefühl*, the most important qualification for economic advisers'. He brings any or all of that to bear on economic problems as they arise or (often) as he accurately expects they will arise. For analytical and policy purposes he makes his own selections, abstractions and simplifications, often brilliantly. He does not believe that complex, continuously changing economic life will ever be well understood by means of 'closed, determinate systems and models'. His record of perceptive diagnosis and prescient early warning is remarkable. Why not accept his understanding of how it is done?

Critics, including Streeten, see two objections. First, the practical wisdom may be wasted if it fails to persuade a theory-soaked profession. More conciliatory dissenters have found that unorthodox thought may nevertheless be accepted if it uses the orthodox language, is precise in detailing departures from orthodox expectations, and is economical in its suggestions for repairing or augmenting the theory. True believers may then accept a case of 'imperfection', 'distortion', 'market failure' or 'second best', happy that it is life, not holy writ, that has erred. (But dissenters may fear that this way of winning battles is helping to lose the war.)

The second shortcoming of the advice to 'keep an open mind and avoid formal determinate theories' is that it is negative. It doesn't tell us positively how to become, or to produce, good open-minded economists. If students should not learn the neoclassical master-model and methods, what *should* they learn? Balogh has two answers. Economists should know more than economics – he defends the Oxford requirement that they study other things as well. But for the economics itself he says regretfully that recruits nowadays had better learn the mathematical orthodoxy, if only to understand the enemy and compete for the jobs, but then unlearn a good deal of it, and study the actual working of historical processes and major economic institutions. It is not a very satisfactory answer, as if (say) chemists still had to begin by learning then unlearning alchemy. But if he is right about the nature of economic activity and the mental equipment required to understand it, there may be *no* satisfactory answer: no reliable economic education in the sense that there are reliable ways of educating competent chemists or dentists.

Meanwhile Lord Balogh acknowledges economic theory as a fact of life with which – until it can be eradicated, as witchcraft and smallpox and other plagues have been – institutional economists must learn to cope. In learning to cope with it himself, his pupil Streeten has been his best teacher. Anyone who suspects the lessons were not well learned should read Balogh's comprehensive review of orthodox theory in *The Irrelevance of Conventional Economics* (1982). Streeten agrees that recruits must learn neoclassical economics. 'While the world is as it is' he writes, 'you have to transcend it, you cannot bypass it.'

Gunnar Myrdal studied natural science, law and philosophy as well as economics, and soon applied the philosophy to the economics to identify *The Political Element in the Development of Economic Theory* (1930, 1953). From 1931 – 7 and 1942 – 7 as theorist, public servant, member of parliament and cabinet minister he helped to plan and direct Sweden's radical progress from poverty to wealth; he then gave ten years each to European economic organisation and Asian development. His biggest books, *An American Dilemma* (1944) and *Asian Drama* (1968) were written in English. His main philosophical work was translated or introduced to English readers by Paul Streeten, *The Political Element* in 1953 and *Value in Social Theory* in 1958. Streeten contributed methodological appendixes to *Asian Drama* (some of which are reprinted in *The Frontiers of Development Studies*, 1972) and a critical account of Myrdal's work to the *International Encyclopedia of the Social Sciences* (reprinted in *Development Perspectives*, 1981). He insists that he learned a great deal from Myrdal. What Myrdal learned from Streeten I don't know. But he never stopped learning – there is a radical progress from the simple separation of facts from values in *The Political Element* and the straightforward use of the values of the American creed in *An American Dilemma*, through the 1953 revision of *The Political Element*, to the different and complicated understanding of the texture of social thought in the later essays in *Value in Social Theory* written after Streeten's Economics and Value Judgements' and 'Programs and Prognoses'. In 'The Logical Crux of All Science' (1957) Myrdal relates facts and valuations as structurally interdependent, logically as well as psychologically. Value premises are no longer discrete, detachable items to be introduced into social research by some neat logical insertion. They come 'on the hoof', embodied in people and cultures. In a passage of Streeten's in which his own and Myrdal's contributions seem inseparable,

> The valuations [which] form the basis of social theories are more like the complex of attitudes that unify a personality or a style. The beliefs, moral principles, sympathies, preferences, ideals and actions that characterize a group cannot be deduced logically from a set of abstract premises, nor are they the mechanical product of certain interests. And they are never 'given' once and for all, but change under the strains and stresses to which their relations to each other and to experience give rise. Although many prognoses are formulated to justify programmes, the relation between them is not static but one of cumulative interaction.

Streeten adds a rigorous demonstration that

> The strict separation of *ought* from *is*, which dominates modern economic theory ... is not, as it claims to be, morally neutral, nor

simply a discovery of philosophical analysis. For no observation or logical analysis can *discover* that we *ought to* separate values from facts, or ends from means. No amount of description or deduction can show that we can fully analyse actual political and moral choices without introducing values into our analysis.

There are thus fully contentious, value-structured ideological elements in

a philosophy which denies the logical connection between facts and values and deduces from this denial its own moral neutrality (suppressing a series of necessary unwanted premises). (From the revised version in *Value in Social Theory* (1958) of 'Programs and Prognoses', *Quarterly Journal of Economics* (1954).)

Hence the institutionalist creed: it's no good trying to give societies full of conflicting interests an objective, unanimous economic science by abstracting an ideal economic system from 'whole life' and modelling qualities it might have in stable equilibrium. Economic behaviour needs to be understood in its social and political context. Its study is necessarily shaped by the values and purposes of the inquirer. And as societies and social purposes change, so must some of the moral and technical presuppositions, and the concepts and analytical frameworks and theories, with which their economic behaviour can best be studied.

Pragmatic, open-minded economists of the institutional kind arrive at their practical wisdom by various routes. Some are graduates of neoclassical or Marxist schools, but their temperament and values make them sceptical of received theory and eclectic in its use. Some, including many of the most famous, came to the profession experienced in business, government or other disciplines without formal training in economic theory. A few learned from institutionalist teachers. But why so few? Why don't institutional economists educate more of their kind, rather than asking recruits to acquire an orthodox professional education and then discard half of it?

It is worth digressing to explore a problem with which Paul Streeten has wrestled more persistently than any. For institutional economists there seems to be a dilemma: the distinctive qualities which make them most useful to the world are precisely those that get them rejected by the profession.

The dilemma is between what they can see and what they can sell.

On the one hand economic activity is conditioned by its political and social context, is partly wilful and irregular, and is subject to continuous (and plenty of discontinuous) historical change, so no general selector or simplifier – no one master-model of the system or its members' motivation – is appropriate equipment for understanding, forecasting or managing it.

On the other hand master-models and their accompanying methods seem to be inescapable in two ways. First, belief in such models affects economic behaviour, so the most sceptical economist still needs to know the fashionable models in order to understand and predict the believers' behaviour. Second, however a model may be discredited by hard facts or hostile critics, experience suggests that people will only give it up *for another like it*, i.e. for another with the same fatal allure, the same false pretences to sufficiency and universal application. Myrdal says 'facts kick', but however hard they kick, Streeten still finds that 'it takes a model to kick out a model'. The trouble is that the model it takes is usually another of the same kind, the kind that doesn't work. The real need is not to discredit this or that one, it is to cure people's longing for models of that overambitious, non-performing kind. But the addiction is obstinate. As one alchemic formula fails, addicts just yearn for another, for a magic that *will* turn the lead into gold: they won't settle for honest chemistry. While the addiction persists, economists must often choose between modes of failure: between best-selling models that don't work, and better methods that won't sell.

This is a recurring theme of Paul Streeten. In 1950 he and Balogh published the most acute criticism of Ohlin and Samuelson's developments of free trade theory (in articles in *Banca Nazionale del Lavoro*, reprinted in the *Bulletin of the Oxford University Institute of Statistics*, 1951, and in Balogh's *Unequal Partners*, 1963). But

> It is regrettable but inevitable that no single new method of analysis can be put into the place of the old approach. This limitation is imposed by the complexity of the problem which the customary method artificially, and mostly tacitly, assumes away.

They do proceed to replace the old approach. But their new analysis and policy advice have to be complicated, conditional, partly uncertain – much less simple and less alluring than the orthodox advice to open the frontiers and trust the hidden hand.

As with Balogh, so with Myrdal. In his account of Myrdal's work in the *International Encyclopedia of the Social Sciences*, Streeten describes how he criticised, and revised or replaced, traditional concepts of employment, consumption, investment and capital. But

> Myrdal has been less successful in this reformulation and reconstruction than in his critique of existing concepts. His critique is often not accompanied by the presentation of useful alternatives. He has often remarked that 'facts kick' against the hard crust of established models or paradigms. But the powerful hold of these paradigms, and the need to demolish established paradigms by providing alternative ones rather than simply by pointing to facts inconsistent with them, may explain why Myrdal's critique has not been more widely accepted by the profession.

Or Balogh's critique, or Galbraith's, or Streeten's ... What *do* institutional economists have to offer as 'useful alternatives' to the models and methods they criticise?

What I think the best of them do in their own practice is this: they know well that selecting, abstracting, simplifying and modelling are necessary for any effective understanding and government of economic activity. But complex and changing economic activity, studied with diverse and changing purposes, calls for a versatile and changing stock of concepts and models, subject to obsolescence and replacement. So the best economists *model as they go*. The continuous dialogue between the facts 'out there' and the social scientists' perception of problems, and development and choice of methods and models to organise observation and understanding of the facts out there, has been described well by Edward Hallett Carr in *What is History?* (1961), and by Paul Streeten often. Here are general and particular examples:

> There is an element of erosion in almost all growth of knowledge on social relations. A good deal of our behaviour is habitual, semi-instinctive, subject to taboos and conventions. Analysis, which is based on the assumption that people behave in this way, brings taboos and conventions into the open, increases people's awareness of them, and leads to the desire for conscious manipulation. But the manipulation destroys the fabric on which, according to the initial prognosis, it is supposed to work.
>
> In economics, the knowledge of the irrational, quasi-conventional character of competition led to monopolistic agreements; knowledge of the outwardly imposed rules of the gold-standard game led to a

desire of every nation to be master of its own fate; and generally, greater awareness of the network of economic relations led to a desire to manipulate it, and thus to its disintegration. Increased organization by individuals and groups led to increased disorganization at large. ('Programs and Prognoses', *Quarterly Journal of Economics*, August 1954)

Besides suffering from their own effects, models and methods of analysis may also be outmoded by historical changes 'out there', or by inappropriate choices and uses of concepts and models:

> The distinction between 'consumption' and 'investment' or between 'employment' and 'unemployment' may be useful in one setting but inappropriate in another. In the essence of ... the institutional approach to probe into the psychological, social, political and cultural justification for the formation of certain concepts. I have attempted to subject the concept 'capital output ratio' ... to such an institutional criticism ... The main conclusion ... is that the postulate of a fairly constant relationship between inputs of capital and the flow of production attributed to them is completely unwarranted, but, at the same time, supports strong vested interests which would suffer from the measures to which a deeper probe would give rise.
> (*The Frontiers of Development Studies*, 1972, p. 117)

Other examples are as follows: (1) Balogh, studying trade between unequals, replaces Samuelson's selection of supposed mutual interests of the traders with a selection of their actual conflicting interests, in a framework which invites attention to half a dozen likely determinants of their unequal productive and bargaining capacities. (2) Turning from Western Europe to Southern Asia, Myrdal and Streeten replace Western concepts of capital, saving, investment, consumption, employment and unemployment with new or altered concepts that are more appropriate for Asian use. (3) Experience leads Streeten and others to make less and less use of traditional aggregates of national output, income and effective demand, and more and more use of categories which separate certain basic human needs from other wants, and reclassify goods and services by their relation to those needs. (4) Whatever societies they are studying, none of the three is content to limit economic analysis by using the concept of 'revealed preferences' to take people's demands as given. Wherever the facts and the investigators' purposes require it they replace that concept by others appropriate for research into the social construction of wants, because societies affect their members' welfare (and interest institutional economists) 'as much by the wants they generate as by the wants they satisfy'.

Those and many others like them are theoretical choices and devices to fit particular times, places, problems and purposes of inquiry.[1]

Question: If institutional economists do not have a master model to give their work internal theoretical consistency and built-in criteria of economic efficiency and welfare, what do they have instead? Looking for order in life's complexity, how do they decide which elements of it to select, abstract, 'model as they go'? What gives their work intellectual coherence and consistent practical direction?

Answer: Their social purposes have to. For example:

Many confusing and complex issues become clearer and simpler if we remind ourselves of the purpose of development and the place of industrialization in a development strategy. In particular, questions about energy, the environment, pollution, appropriate technology, appropriate products and consumption patterns, markets, international trade and integration, and the transnational corporation can be answered more easily if we know where we want to go. Many apparently technical and separate problems are seen to be connnected and become amenable to a solution if we bear the basic objective in mind.

Development is not about index numbers of national income, it is not about savings ratios and capital coefficients: it is about and for people. Development must therefore begin by identifying human needs. The objective of development is to raise the level of living of the masses of the people and to provide all human beings with the opportunity to develop their potential. This objective implies meeting such needs as adequate nutrition and safe water, continuing employment, secure and adequate livelihoods, more and better schooling, better medical services, shelter, cheap transport, and a higher and increasing level of measured income. It also includes meeting nonmaterial needs, such as the desire for self-determination, self-reliance, political freedom and security, participation in making the decisions that affect workers and citizens, access to power, national and cultural identity, and a sense of purpose in life and work. Much of this can be achieved in ways that do not increase the measured output of commodities, while a high and growing index for national income growth can leave these basic needs unsatisfied.

If we approach development in these terms, the place of the private motor car, of heavy demand on sources of energy, of highly sophisticated luxury goods, of the transfer of inappropriate products and technologies, of the role of the trans-national enterprise, of urbanization, of the relation between industrial and agricultural policies, and of domination and dependency, all appear in a different light. (*Development Perspectives*, pp. 195 – 6)

Applied like that, economists' values can be both better considered and better related to the technics of the work than can the values concealed in neoclassical or Marxist master-theories. Case by case, problem by problem, economists who consciously 'value as they go' can look for the limiting conditions, the historical trends and processes, the institutional hindrances and opportunities, the usable social mechanisms and economic levers, the openings for invention and contrivance and persuasion, which offer or obstruct social improvement. What defines 'improvement'? Their values do, or the values of the clients and publics their own values move them to work for. However technical, quantitative and factually objective the detail of the work, somebody's social purposes have to select and shape it, and it can only be as truth-telling, moral and internally consistent as those purposes are. So it takes a good person to be a good economist, and the unity or consistency of institutional economists' work is chiefly moral. (Any Streeten pupil knows that orthodox economists' work is no less value-structured. But if instead of being thoughtful and explicit its values are unconsidered and concealed, and include valuing the formal qualities and academic sales of theory above its effects on society, Streeten parodists won't fail to observe that while the consistency of institutional economics is chiefly moral, the consistency of orthodox economics is chiefly immoral.)

Less frivolously, I think it is no accident that so many of the best institutional economists are men and women of the reformist democratic Left, and that they include the best analysts of the role of values in social science. Those particular values and social concerns dispose people to work in practical, socially productive ways, to be more concerned with the social usefulness of any theory they use than with its elegance or academic appeal. Working in that way, their values and social judgement have to guide their scientific choices so directly and consciously that an awareness of the irreducible role of valuation (whether direct or 'mechanised', conscious or not) in social analysis comes more easily than it does to people – now unhappily a whole generation of people – who have been taught to believe that their values are hostile or irrelevant to their science.

Of course, there are plenty of social reformers in other schools. But many of them believe in separating or distancing their social values from their scientific choices. Knowingly or not, they mechanise their morals, building values into the master-models in whose technical 'discovering power' they have such confidence. For neoclassicists and Marxists alike, building the morals into the machine makes the morals easier to conceal. Positivist ideals and illusions of value-freedom are easier to sustain. The means-ends model can look like a fact rather than a choice. Powerful professional and psychological barriers then hinder any self-searching exposure – *and therefore any deliberate improvement* – of the values and the role they play.

By contrast – to summarise this digression – institutional economists' methods compel them to refer to their social values and purposes as often and consciously as to the facts and technical considerations of the problems they study. The best of them know it, and know what their work owes to the quality and right use of their valuations. In controversy with more orthodox theorists of Right and Left they become expert (because as avowed valuers they have nothing to lose by this choice of weapons) at exposing the values, often less lovable or coherent or both, concealed in others' work. They need have no awe of, or vested interest in, 'mainstream' theory or 'cumulative' science; they expect most theories, models, concepts, analytical frameworks and other devices to need replacement sooner or later. And their values tell them (or should) that no quality of a theory is as important as its uses and social effects, or excusable if those are sterile or bad. Altogether it is not surprising that this school should have produced (or attracted – I don't know which causes which) the best investigators of social science itself.

That methodological work was prompted by confronting conventional economic theory with the changing realities of European and North American societies. A further round of theoretical originality was prompted when the same orthodoxy faced the different facts of undeveloped Africa and Asia.

Streeten had already collaborated with Balogh in writing about the potentially unequalising effects of trade and exchange between unequals. They were early and able critics of Samuelson's popular fantasy that free trade would allow the hidden hand to equalise the world's incomes. In the 1960s, with Gunnar Myrdal in the methodological work for *Asian Drama*, then with Dudley Seers in the practical work of the

Department of Overseas Development, Streeten turned full-time to development problems. In 1966 he moved from Whitehall to direct the Institute of Development Studies at Sussex, then in 1968 returned to Oxford to direct the Institute of Commonwealth Studies and Queen Elizabeth House. What to do with an Institute in danger of outliving its subject of study? Deftly and appropriately, he and his colleagues turned it into a centre of development studies, and turned its old imperial journal into the multi-disciplinary, institutionalist *World Development*. From 1976 he worked part- and then full-time at the World Bank, adding some distributional criteria to its project assessments and developing its interest in 'basic needs'. Since 1980 he has directed Asian and other development studies at Boston University. In 1984 he returned for a further year at the Bank.

Development theory in the 1950s was much concerned with capital accumulation: with the rates of saving and investment that would set poor countries on the path of economic growth. Some theorists looked beyond those economic variables to social and political conditions, but chiefly as they affected people's propensities to save and invest. The task of development might be hard but its principles seemed simple:

> The Harrod-Domar model, according to which the rate of growth of output equals the ratio of savings to income divided by the capital-output ratio ... added output-generation to the Keynesian income-generation of investment, and thereby provided the principal pillar for the analysis of development and for many development plans. Capital accumulation became ... the main strategic variable, and the propensity to save and the capital/output ratio became the basic equipment of development analysts, planners and aid officials.

For that simple programme,

> The existing body of economic analysis came in very handy. It neglected climate, it ignored attitudes and institutions as strategic variables, it regarded consumption as not productive, and it treated the state as exogenous. The conclusion: pour capital into the sausage machine, turn the growth handle, and out comes ever-growing output ... There is assumed to be a 'trade-off' between equality and growth, and therefore equality, which hinders growth, has to be sacrificed or postponed, and with it goes any deep analysis of land reform, education, corruption, social discipline, and the interest and efficiency of the state. (*Development Perspectives*, pp. 102, 426)

Myrdal, Prebisch, Singer, Hirschman, Baran, Balogh and others were already objecting in one way or another when Streeten joined in. How did he find the state of the art? It depends which page of *Development Perspectives* you read. A *Festschrift* tribute should seek credibility by including some criticism of its subject, so readers are invited to compare the above account from page 426 with this one from page 103:

> What is remarkable about those early discussions is the proliferation of ideas, criticisms, and qualifications which contrasts sharply with the monolithic view that a single paradigm existed. This view is an optical illusion created by looking back from later vantage points ... but it should always be borne in mind that the early days of development economics were a time of intellectual pioneering, of considerable excitement, of the opening of new geographical and intellectual frontiers, of optimism and confidence. 'Bliss was it in that dawn to be alive / But to be young was very heaven!'

Inconsistent? Perhaps not if the first passage really depicts *them in the prevailing darkness* and the second depicts *us bringing the dawn light*.

To sketch something of the breadth and depth of Paul Streeten's contribution to development economics we can notice in turn his continuing philosophical and methodological work; then studies of particular regions, problems and aspects of development; then debates about development strategies. But those separations are misleading. Critical and constructive, theoretical and practical, local and general strands of argument are woven together through a great deal of the work.

For example – to begin with some methodology – the criticism and replacement of concepts are directly related to new causal theory and analysis and to practical policy implications in the methodological appendixes to *Asian Drama*, of which he wrote later:

> [Myrdal] subjects the commonly used concepts of employment, unemployment, income, consumption, savings, investment, capital, output, capital/output ratio, etc., to close scrutiny and finds that in large measure they dissolve when applied to underdeveloped societies.
> Having dissolved them, the question arises whether they can be reassembled: whether capital, for example, cannot be given a new and wider meaning, including investment in forms conventionally accounted as consumption, or investment in a programme of family planning or in a land reform; and whether employment cannot be

replaced by a richer and more realistic concept of 'labour utilization'. (*Development Perspectives*, p. 422)

Here is another example of the 'whole cloth' of philosophy, theory and practice. Myrdal in 1933 and Streeten in 1950 and 1954 had criticised the logic of the means/ends model and its false pretence of value-freedom. Myrdal and Balogh and Streeten had often criticised 'mechanistic model thinking' in economics. Late in the 1950s, Hirschman, Lindblom and Streeten were criticising the version of sausage-machine development theory known as 'balanced growth'. Then in a decade of 'plan failure' and development pessimism Streeten brought those diverse themes together in a paper ('Programmes and Prognoses, Unbalanced Growth and the Ideal Plan', *Banca Nazionale del Lavoro*, June 1964, reprinted as Chapter 4 of *The Frontiers of Development Studies*) which connects the philosophical mistakes about ends/means and programmes/prognoses directly to the practical shortcomings of the national development plans and planning procedures of the 1950s. What use are plans that specify five years' worth of national 'ends' with instrumental policies to achieve them, when most 'ends' are subjects of conflict; what are ends to some citizens are means to others, and *vice versa*; one main purpose of planning should be the educational transformation of many of the people's ends; and ends achieved generate new wants, new problems, new interests and conflicts. Instead of separating ends (to be valued) from means (to be costed), alternative policies and social processes should rationally be valued 'whole' for all their effects and by-effects.

The logical critique leads to proposals for better practice. Sensible planning builds on some present social interests and values, and works to alter some. It may also work on itself, to change the conditions for planning. Its function is often 'to turn means into ends and ends into means where the development process requires this, and to improve itself by so doing'.

> To postulate a sharp means-ends or targets-instruments dichotomy is to ignore this process of transformation, and thus the political reality of a development Plan ... The Plan should be regarded as a steadily forward-moving pattern of policies, which have to be modified continually in the light of newly-emerging events, changing casual connections and modified valuations. The programes of the planners and the prognoses of social researchers are not two independent areas, but the programmes affect and alter the prognoses, and the prognoses

in turn alter and modify the programmes ... Planning aims not at an *optimum* but at *improvements* .... It contains a rough perception of the connections between conditions prevailing over a period of time and the possibilities of moving, through rationally co-ordinated policies, towards changing objectives. (*The Frontiers of Development Studies*, pp. 46-7)

There follow two pages of practical illustrations from Indian life and planning, to make the import of the theory clear to untheoretical readers. Then, characteristically, two more pages of theory defend the practical planning theme against predictable professional objections. Patiently, this time in the jargon of the profession, the philosopher/practitioner explains once again why fashionable 'instrumental' techniques, effective for other purposes, are no good for national economic planning, especially in poor countries. Thus analytical philosophy, technical economics and political common sense, with general and national and local applications, mix in one coherent paper to confound my poor attempt to deal 'in turn' with Streeten's contributions to methodology, then specific development problems, then national strategies.

I nevertheless persist. The criticism of orthodox (and some unorthodox) theory continued. He wrote on European development concepts (1968); further implications of the *Asian Drama* studies in 'An Institutional Critique of Development Concepts' (1970); methods of project appraisal (with Frances Stewart, 1972); old and new social indicators (with Norman Hicks, 1979). His short histories of development theory ('Development Ideas in Historical Perspective', 1977; 'Changing Perceptions of Development', 1977; 'Development: What have we learned?', 1980 'Development Dichotomies', *World Development*, 1983) were laced with criticism. There were also papers about interdisciplinary studies (1976) and about the moral aspects of development theories and programmes (1970, 1972, 1976).

Early in the 1970s the moral or political direction of research became a hot topic; it was especially troubling for institutionalists because they had always insisted that it *had* moral and political direction. Institutionalists argue that (1) all social theory and analysis are value-structured, and (2) the economic problems of different times and societies may well call for the use of different concepts and theories. Careless (or ardent) thinkers can conclude that (3) there can be no criteria of true-or-false economic analysis, and (4) when economists from rich countries study poor countries they are likely to do so as predators whose intellectual services will do more harm than good to the people studied. Africa should prefer African truths.

Paul Streeten had more than once attended to (3), resisting the idea that the necessary value premises of social science made all its conclusions arbitrary. Returning to the subject when Western economists were under attack from some of their Third World brethren, he grappled with those accusations in two careful papers in 1974: 'Social Science Research and Development: Some Problems in the Use and Transfer of an Intellectual Technology', and 'The Limits of Development Research'. Part of the latter paper does its best to distinguish the effects of the variable value structure of social science from its qualities of truth or falsehood. Truth is different from logical validity:

> If economics is equated with a form of logic ('the logic of choice'), it would follow that there is only a single, universal economic science from China to Peru and no separate economics for Africa, Asia or Latin America. Yet clearly, if we turn ... to the content of our work, it should be plain that very different propositions are likely to be true for different societies. In this sense, it is perfectly legitimate to speak of 'African', 'Asian' or 'Latin American' economics or politics or sociology. ... It is part of scholarship to recognize the limitations of the propositions established and possibly applicable to one region (or period) but not, or not without modification, to another ...
>
> Yet such limitation of excess claims, if it is legitimate, is such that it must be recognized as legitimate by scholars wherever they may be. There have been sociologists (like Karl Mannheim), anthropologists (like Lucien Lévy-Bruhl), linguists (like Benjamin Lee Whorf), and philosophers of science (like Thomas Kuhn) who have argued that the criteria of truth and validity themselves vary from time to time and place to place, according to their context. But I believe it can be shown that at least some criteria of truth and validity cannot be dependent on social, cultural, linguistic or other existential factors, indeed that even asking questions about differences between beliefs and theories presupposes logically universal and fundamental criteria of truth ...
>
> I conclude that, although the laws of logic and the criteria for truth must be universal, the concepts, models, premises, assumptions, paradigms, theories or questions in the social sciences are in some respects peculiar. *There may be an African economics, distinct from a European economics; there can be no African truth.* (*Development Perspectives*, pp. 68–70)

That paper was written under political pressures which threatened the international fraternity of scholars and their truth-telling creed. It reminds me strongly of Max Weber's much-misunderstood papers on *Wertfreiheit*. The crudest meaning of value freedom advises scientists to understand society objectively without any reference at all to their own values. That was not Weber's view. He knew as well as Myrdal or Streeten do that science must be shaped by the questions scientists choose to ask and the concepts they choose to use. Illiberal governments of Imperial Germany concluded to censor the science and apply political tests to academic appointments. In what I suspect were chiefly practical efforts to protect academic independence and free speech, Weber asserted the non-political character of social science by dwelling on the elements of the work – the factual and logical elements – which *are* subject to universal tests of truth and validity. Similarly Streeten, sixty years later, pressed by militants urging their governments to nationalise truth, argued for universal criteria of truth. But remembering how choices of question and concept may affect perception of even the hardest facts, and being perhaps freer, more subtle or more scrupulous than Weber, he hedged. The passage quoted above continues:

> By rigorous analysis, by accumulation of evidence and by bringing out explicitly value premises, errors and biases can be reduced. But there will always remain a residual of ideology. And this residual element may be particularly misleading if transferred from the experience of industrial countries to developing countries. It is for this reason that the assertion of the universality of the criteria for truth must be qualified, although the remedy cannot be found in 'indigenous' theory construction or in erecting a barrier against 'alien' doctrines.

Streeten meanwhile worked at a wide range of development subjects and problems. 'The Coefficient of Ignorance' (with Balogh, 1963) was the first of a number of papers on education and development. In the late 1960s he wrote about Indian planning and aid, in the early 1970s about African agriculture and aid. In 1971 he and Frances Stewart wrote 'Conflicts between Output and Employment Objectives', a paper which still offers developing countries the best advice on this subject, and has increasing interest (if they only knew it) for those developed countries' policy-makers who are troubled by the microchip and the percentage unemployed but also by falling behind the Japanese, and who grow schizophrenic about conflicts between growth and employment. In other papers Streeten did similar service in clarifying real and apparent conflicts between developmental and environmental objectives.

Another difficult subject was private foreign investment in the developing countries. Through the 1970s there was great practical, theoretical and ideological disagreement about its effects. Some economists and Third World governments welcomed the multinationals as unmixed blessings – agents of growth and international equalisation. Marxists and other 'dependency theorists' saw them as pure exploiters, replacing colonial rule as the main engineers of international inequality. Between the two, with cooler heads than either, Streeten and Sanjaya Lall and others studied what the corporations actually did, and worked to improve the necessarily imperfect methods of estimating their effects. A string of papers was followed by Lall and Streeten's *Foreign Investment, Transnationals and Developing Countries* (1977). The conclusions were that host countries tend to get the transnational treatment – anything from excellent to terrible – that their governments invite or permit. Both sides of the 'dependency' dispute misrepresent the problem. Sinning characteristically, as ideologists or as theory-lovers wanting a determinate science of a determinate world, Right and Left alike deny the people and their governments much capacity to think, invent or choose.

> A reconciliation between the two perceptions, namely, that development can be speeded up by the international 'system' and that underdevelopment is caused by it, is possible along the following lines. The advanced industrial countries emit a large number of impulses of two kinds: those that present opportunities for faster and better development than would otherwise have been possible, and those that present obstacles to development, those that stunt growth. ... The interesting question then is not 'do the developing countries benefit or lose from their coexistence with developed countries?' but: 'how can they pursue selective policies that permit them to derive the benefits of the positive forces, without simultaneously exposing themselves to the harm of the detrimental forces?' Looked at in this way, the question becomes one of designing selective policies for aid, trade, foreign investment, trans-national companies, technology, foreign education, movements of people, etc. (*Development Perspectives*, pp. 107–8)

This was true and wise, as Japanese and Swedes and Singaporeans and some other late succeeders had worked out for themselves on their way up. But for academic or ideological purposes, it was unexciting; Lenin and A. G. Frank on the one hand and Adam Smith and P. A. Samuelson on the other continued to sell more copies.

The debate about transnational corporations overlapped the debate about neocolonial dependency and proposals for de-linking. Both were part of the continuing 'great debate' about development strategy. In that debate Paul Streeten has been an exemplary institutionalist in two senses. There can't be one correct path or strategy: strategies have to fit economic and social and political conditions which vary with time and place. He has also been a sceptical critic of the assumptions and reasoning and practicality of most schools of thought, including his own. (For astringent treatment of some of those nearest to his own, see especially his and Frances Stewart's 'New Strategies for Development: Poverty, Income Distribution and Growth', 1976.) He has always argued for broadly conceived development, and never assumed that measured economic growth would suffice. He has generally been for unbalanced growth, somewhat self-reliant growth, and strategies to redistribute first and grow later – but with attention to the limits and necessary accompaniments of those principles, and to the conditions and ways in which they can easily be misapplied.

Streeten's own summaries of the post-war history of development ideas from the 1940s to the 1980s have emphasised these changes:

1. From thinking measured economic growth would suffice, people learned that it often wouldn't. Many elements of economic and social and cultural development need to be independently contrived, in workable proportion and order. Growth is as much an effect as a cause of development.
2. Similarly, from relying on capital accumulation as the main engine of growth, people learned that many other economic and social and cultural conditions needed to be contrived.
3. From 'growth will trickle down' or 'grow first, redistribute later', people have learned that countries which grow first don't easily trickle or redistribute, and that redistributing first often helps growth.
4. From expecting poor countries to follow the rich along a regular path of growth, people came to see more complex and variable relations between the developed and the underdeveloped. Those relations can both hinder and help late developers. Each successful modernisation alters conditions for the next, and continuing changes in the developed countries continue to change the forces they exert on the less developed.

5. From seeing fast industrialisation as a main agent of development, people have learned what problems it can create, and how important it is in most circumstances to improve agriculture, including small-scale and subsistence agriculture, and to modernise the services that agriculture needs and the local material and social conditions that rural people need.
6. From 'best' technology people have learned to look as well or instead, in many circumstances, for 'appropriate' technology; for example, technology that can improve output and/or distribution with least call on scarce capital or skills.
7. From arguing *between* outward-looking, specialised, heavy-trading development, and insulated, self-sufficient development, some strategies have come to be less doctrinaire and to base structural and trading policies on the facts and possibilities of time and place.
8. From arguing *between* (a) correct pricing, (b) radical redistribution, and (c) technical innovation as strategies to end poverty and reduce inequality, many now accept that attempting any one of the three by itself may do little good and in some conditions actual harm; they need to be applied together, in a right order and relation to one another.
9. From thinking of population control as a simple effect of income growth, then as a condition as well as an effect of income growth, people have learned that it is a more complex, changing and partly independent problem. For example, if food, safe water and contraception are available, primary education for girls may do more to cut both death and birth rates than a lot of growth in other forms may do.

The spirit of all nine might be distilled if that other Bostonian Tom Lehrer would write a ballad with the chorus '*Disaggregate! Disaggregate! Disaggregate!*' Paul Streeten has been a critical recorder of those intellectual developments, and a leading contributor to the first eight. Five or six of them are elements of a general shift from indirect to direct approaches to poverty: from expecting growth to trickle down, to acting directly to meet the poorest people's basic human needs.

Most development economists have always wanted those basic needs to be met. The question has been how, how quickly, how directly or indirectly, and whether as a welfare alternative to growth (as opponents of basic needs strategies fear) or as an aid to growth (as basic needs strategists intend and sometimes achieve).

From his earliest microeconomic papers Paul Streeten has distrusted unaided market or automatic distributions of wealth and income. He has not expected very much of redistribution 'after the event' to correct very unequal income and asset ownership. He has not supposed that any likely distribution of income would assure a satisfactory distribution of all the other things poor people need. To reduce poverty he has argued for structural changes to the primary distribution of assets, income, education and health services, and other necessaries both material and immaterial. Summarising three decades of post-war experience,

> it became clear that measured income and its growth is only a part of basic needs. Adequate nutrition and safe water at hand, continuing employment, secure and adequate livelihoods for the self-employed, more and better schooling for their children, better preventive medical services, adequate shelter, cheap transport and (but not only) a higher and growing level of measured income: some or all of these would figure on the list of urgently felt needs of poor people.
>
> In addition to these specific 'economic' objectives, a new emphasis was laid on 'non-material' needs that cannot be dispensed, but, in addition to being valued in their own right, may be the conditions for meeting 'material' needs, such as self-determination, self-reliance, political freedom and security, participation in making the decisions that affect workers and citizens, national and cultural identity, and a sense of purpose in life and work. (*Development Perspectives*, p. 10)

Similar passages appear in a number of his papers. The one above was drafted in the year (1976) in which an ILO Conference resolution first popularised the idea of a 'basic needs strategy' of development. Like Monsieur Jourdain who found he had been talking prose all those years without knowing it, Streeten welcomed 'basic needs strategy' as something between a collective label and a unifying principle for ideas many of which he and others had been recommending for twenty or thirty years. Singly and with collaborators he has since written a dozen papers on the subject and its relations with other development themes. He helped to persuade Robert McNamara of it; directed three years of World Bank studies of it; and reported their findings in *First Things First: Meeting Basic Human Needs in Developing Countries* (with Shavid Javed Burki, Mahbub ul Haq, Norman Hicks and Frances Stewart, 1981).

The theme will be familiar to most readers. The main reasons why a development strategy should include direct, detailed action to meet basic needs are three: (1) meeting those needs is the most valuable purpose and effect of development; (2) meeting them as quickly and directly as possible is quicker and surer than indirect methods have proved to be; and (3) it should possible to meet basic needs directly in ways which help rather than hinder the other aims of development, including the growth of productivity.

Most of Streeten's efforts have been concerned with (3): with making attention to basic needs a positive aid, rather than a poor alternative, to effective development, and with convincing people that it could be so. However good the strategy, it had to combat hostile interests and convince many doubters. Mahbub ul Haq listed some of them in his preface to *First Things First*:

> To some, the concept of providing for the basic needs of the poorest represents a futile attempt to redistribute income and provide welfare services to the poor, without stimulating corresponding increases in their productivity to pay for them.
>
> To others, it conjures up the image of a move toward socialism, and whispered references are made to the experience of China and Cuba.
>
> Yet still others see it as a capitalist conspiracy to deny industrialization and modernization to the developing countries and thereby keep them dependent on the developed world.

'It is amazing', he continued, 'how two such innocent five-letter words could mean so many different things to so many different people'. It was less amazing to Streeten. Knowing how neoclassicists, bankers and Marxists respectively tend to think, those three responses were to be expected. Mahbub ul Haq and his associates searched the recorded experience of undeveloped and developing countries for associations and functional links – or lack of them – between meeting basic needs, growth and development. Their conclusions are in one sense inconclusive: basic needs have been met both with and without growth; there has been growth both with and without meeting the basic needs of the poorest. On past experience, therefore, meeting basic needs is neither a necessary nor a sufficient cause of growth, and growth is neither a necessary nor a sufficient condition of meeting basic needs. But institutionalists assume we may learn to do better, and even if we don't, those conclusions still negate the objections to a basic needs strategy. Meeting basic needs early and directly has been, so presumably can be, consistent with successful development. Where it is, the best purposes of development are served soonest and best.

Good causes can need protection from their zealots as well as their enemies. Direct attention to basic needs is part of a good development strategy, not a substitute for one. If applied by itself without necessary supports it may not even succeed in meeting basic needs for long. *First Things First* is full of warnings. 'An effective basic needs program calls for action on five distinct levels, at each of which supply, demand, and institutions are relevant.' Besides delivering basic goods or money directly to the poor it may also be necessary to improve market supplies of wage goods, and public education and health and other services. It may be necessary to redistribute assets or change systems of land ownership, tenancy, debt and local government. Appropriate macroeconomic policies relating to employment, incomes, prices and rates of growth must prevent gains from the better human capital and productivity of the poor being creamed off by the non-poor. Domestic efforts may need to be supported and supplemented by international aid. Thus the theorists warn against sanguine misuses of the basic needs principle, as patiently as they cope with objections to using it at all.

It may well be through his work on basic needs that Paul Streeten has had most effect on the course of events: on the Bank's policies and project appraisals while he was there, and on other professionals and policy-makers then and since. If so, the success owes something to the quality of the research and the lucid, plain-language exposition of it; but it may owe most, in the professional and governmental world where it matters most, to the care and skill with which orthodox objections – neoclassical, Marxist and other – are understood, dissected, and either 'distinguished', as lawyers would say, or rebutted.

Personally I incline to the Balogh view of neoclassical theory: rather than continuing to argue with it we would do best to walk away from most of it, as the chemists did from alchemy, and start afresh on different principles. That is a bolder policy than Streeten's, but also lazier, and less productive in the world as it is. However unfashionable sentimental reminders may be in a book like this, it seems right to remember that there must be some number of children alive now who would otherwise have died, fed who would otherwise be hungry, strong who would otherwise have amoebic dysentery, clear-eyed who would otherwise have bilharzia; some number of women better able than they would otherwise have been to limit their families and then protect them from disease and malnutrition; some number of men and women who have lived longer and are healthier, more knowledgeable and more productive than they could otherwise have been, because of (among other causes) those long, painstaking, boring hours at the Bank and elsewhere, hours of persistent, conciliatory, expert argument, much of it in their own tedious languages, with trickle-downers, price-mechanists, technocrats, deja-viewers, bank economists, revolutionaries, reactionaries, Uncle Tom Cobley and all.

The basic needs movement has had some success, replacing bad theory and encouraging good practice, partly because the facts kicked so very hard against the old theories, and partly because the new theories were chiefly acknowledging what practical people had known and done for twenty years or more in the government of Taiwan, South Korea, Sri Lanka, Cuba and elsewhere. At the time, much of that good performance had to disregard much of the economists' 'best professional opinion'. If the best professional opinion has now shifted some way – much of it grudgingly and not as far or as fast as it should – that is partly because expert persuaders like Streeten have had such formidable support from the accumulating facts 'out there'.

The comparative success of basic needs must be set against what is so far a greater failure. 'Programs and Prognoses' and Myrdal's work on which it built offered an intellectual revolution to produce a social science which would, literally, know what it was doing. Nobody (as far as I know) has tried to refute that work. It tends to be respectfully disregarded. Its authors are honoured; there are fewer explicit positivists than there were; most professionals now acknowledge that values and social purposes shape social sciences to some degree. But very few economists have really grasped, and learned to apply in their work, the self-awareness and the accurate, discriminating eye for the divers sources of disagreement that 'Programs and Prognoses' and 'Value in Social Theory' offered to teach them. And it is in this, more than in development economics or even neoclassical microeconomics, that the educational production of crippling incapacity continues most relentlessly. Lipsey's textbook still teaches tens of thousands of students (as it earlier taught their teachers) a crude positivist distinction between 'positive' and 'normative' economics as separate activities, the one scientific and the other not. Samuelson, who shows on many other pages that he knows better, still tells hundreds of thousands of freshmen, in Chapter 1, that there is one true science: 'there is only one valid reality in a given economic situation, however hard it may be to recognize and isolate it. There is not one theory of economics for Republicans and one for Democrats, not one for workers and one for employers'.

Near the end of 'Development Ideas in Historical Perspective' Paul Streeten contrasts Keynesians who blame bad policies on wrong theories with Marxians who blame them on class interests. Neoclassical doctrine and its educational hegemony derive strength from both sources. Its class implications and intellectual attractions combine to give it outstanding ideological, commercial and academic appeal. It makes powerful friends by endorsing capitalist freedoms and inequalities while falsely pretending to be objective, uninterfering, not ideological at all. Almost alone among the social sciences it can package what it wants most students to know into a few textbooks. It has the intellectual attraction of a comparatively simple, apparently coherent system of thought applicable to all economic systems and problems. It has principles and procedures that all can learn, together with abundant mathematical and specialist elaborations for longer courses and cleverer students. No wonder it wins most of the time, however hard the facts kick.

Faced with such competition, Galbraith has managed to bypass it and sell some better simplicities directly to students and public. Myrdal and Balogh have done their work in their own ways, alternately ignoring the profession and exposing its errors and thundering at it. Only Paul Streeten has continued for nearly forty years to reason with it in its own language, a patient missionary who never quite loses heart however inattentive the heathen or algebraical their witchdoctors, talking to them always with wit, impeccable manners, and stunning skill at their own game. So the public knows less of him than of Galbraith and some other dissenters, but the profession could often have learned more from him. Many have done so, many more could and should.

This book is to thank him on behalf of all the grateful learners. Most of all, as one of them, I am grateful to have been a colleague and friend, when we were young, of such a 'verray parfit gentil knight'.

NOTE

1. I thought to call it 'modelling as you go'. Peter Mayer, who shares Paul Streeten's understanding of social science and also his semi-detached, semi-despairing affection for things British, suggests we call it 'modelling through'.

2 Adam Smith's Prudence

AMARTYA SEN

INTRODUCTION

Shakespeare did not say it, but it is true that some men are born small, some achieve smallness, and some have smallness thrust upon them. Adam Smith, the father of modern economics, has had to cope with a good deal of such thrusting. That conclusion is inescapable, reading some of the recent pronouncements of conservative extremism (especially in Britain), with persistent attempts to implicate Adam Smith in justifying the straight and the narrow. The invoking of Adam Smith and 'the invisible hand' is a widespread phenomenon, varying from explicit attribution to implicit use of Smith's authority (in, say, the spirited outpourings of the so-called 'Adam Smith Institute').

The Wealth of Nations is, however, a complex work. Tearing out particular sentences as slogans, e.g. the bit about 'the butcher, the brewer or the baker',[1] does little justice to Smith's views. Note also has to be taken of Smith's *The Theory of Moral Sentiments* as the broader work of Smith, one specific promise of which is 'partly executed' (in Smith's words) in the *Wealth of Nations*.[2] The latter-day 'Smithians' may have a simple enough message to enhance our wisdom on economic affairs, but Adam Smith was scarcely capable of such heroic simplicity.

The tradition of using Adam Smith for defending simple (and frequently obtuse) political decisions goes back a long time. As early as 1812, the Governor of Bombay turned down a proposal to move food into famine-affected Gujerat by citing the authority of Adam Smith:'The digression of the celebrated author of *The Wealth of Nations* concerning corn-trade ... and particularly as far as respects the *inland trader*, is forcibly and irresistibly applicable to every state of society where merchants or dealers in grain may be established'.[3] Adam Smith had in fact said little, directly or indirectly, on how to deal with a developing famine. But that name and that alleged argument were to crop up again and again throughout that century in India, in China and in Ireland – justifying costly inaction in the face of widespread death by starvation. The taking of Adam Smith's name in defence of policies on which Adam Smith had said little has been one of the unchanging features of the economic politics of the two hundred years since *The Wealth of Nations*.

In *The Frontiers of Development Studies*, published a dozen years ago, we find Paul Streeten rightly pointing out: 'Adam Smith, both a moral philosopher and an economist, considered education as fundamental to social peace, self-improvement and economic progress'.[4] That is scarcely the policy of seeing education in the extraordinarily narrow and restrictive terms in which the alleged followers of Adam Smith have been trying to refashion the educational structure of Britain. There is hardly less irony in the willingness of the present policy-makers to accept massive unemployment as a price for 'sound' economics in view of Adam Smith's discussion on the very first page of *The Wealth of Nations* of how the prosperity of the nation depends on two main factors, one of which is 'the proportion between the number of those who are employed in useful labour, and that of those who are not so employed'.[5]

I have started off polemically, but I have an ulterior motive: to go on to discuss academic matters. In particular, to discuss Adam Smith's treatment of prudence, an issue that also has some relevance to political economic debates on current policy as well as some interest from the point of view of the history of economic thought. It has, of course, been much discussed that Adam Smith seems to have sung the praise of both 'sympathy' and 'self-interest'. While a great deal has been said on the well-known 'Adam Smith problem',[6] and I can add little to that, I will try to discuss some elementary features of Adam Smith's approach to this question.

PLURALISM AND SYMPATHY

Adam Smith's claim to be building up his theory of moral sentiments on the basis of sympathy has been well discussed by Raphael and Macfie.[7] There can be little doubt that Smith saw sympathy as having a 'linking' role. But this emphasis on sympathy coexisted with admitting many virtues, rather like in Aristotle's system. In this sense, Smith's approach may justifiably be seen as a 'pluralist' one, and the part that sympathy plays appears to be one of providing a common 'measure' for this plural system.

In contrasting his own theory with that of an unnamed defender (almost certainly David Hume) of 'utility' as the basis of virtue, Smith had the following to say on the exact contrasts between the two theories:

> According to this [Hume's] system therefore, virtue consists not in any one affection, but in the proper degree of all the affections. The only difference between it and that which I have been endeavouring to establish, is, that it makes utility, and not sympathy, or the correspondent affection of the spectator, the natural and original measure of this proper degree.[8]

The 'measure' of sympathy does not, of course, deny the intrinsic importance of each of a plurality of virtues.

In fact, Smith was in general quite critical of trying to reduce all virtues into one ultimate virtue. For example, in discussing Epicurus's attempt to see virtue entirely in terms of prudence, Smith seized the occasion to chastise the philosophers for having 'a peculiar fondness' for the reductionist exercise:

> By running up all the different virtues too to this one species of propriety, Epicurus indulged a propensity, which is natural to all men, but which philosophers in particular are apt to cultivate with a peculiar fondness, as the great means of displaying their ingenuity, the propensity to account for all appearances from as few principles as possible.[9]

The basic pluralism of Smith's position comes out sharply in his discussions of various virtues – prudence, humanity, justice, generosity, public spirit, etc. – to all of which intrinsic importance is attached. Whether the claim of sympathy providing a common 'measure' is well established by Smith can certainly be debated, but in doing that debating it has to be borne in mind that Smith's objective was not one of reductionist monism in the way that, say, Benthamite utilitarianism can be taken to be.

Smith does, of course, provide powerful and novel analyses of the relevance of sympathy in a wide variety of judgments. He shows the importance of sympathising with the motive of the agent, and the relevance of sympathising with the beneficiary's gratitude as well as with the agent's benevolence.[10] He also provides a brilliant account of what it is like to place oneself in the position of another[11] – an account from which modern welfare economists and social choice theorists have much to learn. But despite the concentration on sympathy, Smith's essentially pluralist perspective stops him from denying the intrinsic importance of a multiplicity of virtues.

PRUDENCE AND COMMON MOTIVATION

George Stigler's enjoyable essay on 'Smith's Travel on the Ship of the State'[12] starts off with interpreting Smith's remark that 'though the principles of common *prudence* do not always govern the conduct of every individual, they always influence that of the majority of every class or order', as implying:'*self-interest* dominates the majority of men'.[13] The point is certainly an important one in understanding Smith's assessment of the real world – including the world of day-to-day economics, and indeed many authors have taken Smith to task for introducing this dubious generalisation in economics.[14] Certainly that generalisation got respectability from Smith's seeming championing of it. Nevertheless, it is not strictly accurate to identify 'prudence' with 'self-interest'. In fact, Smith saw prudence as 'the union of' the two qualities of 'reason and understanding' on the one hand, and 'self-command' on the other[15] – the latter being a Stoic concept of which Smith makes much use.[16] Self-interest and self-love form a substantially narrower motivation than prudence.

Furthermore, even if prudence were to be narrowly – and (I believe) wrongly – interpreted as the pursuit of self-interest, the idea that prudence does 'always influence' the majority cannot be interpreted simply as 'self-interest dominates the majority of men', since there are many other influences about which Smith himself speaks. The distinction is of particular importance in analysing Smith's understanding of social behaviour, and the policy implications that might follow from it. For example, he emphasises the importance of 'rules of conduct' in influencing people's behaviour and the positive role that such rules can play:

> Those general rules of conduct, when they have been fixed in our mind by habitual reflection, are of great use in correcting misrepresentations of self-love concerning what is fit and proper to be done in our particular situation.[17]

Adam Smith did emphasise the pursuit of self-interest as a principal influence on the behaviour of the majority, but he did not overlook other aspects of prudence that go well beyond self-interest maximisation; he also admitted influences other than prudence in the determination of common behaviour. The qualifications have to be borne in mind in examining Smith's approach to economic behaviour.

USEFULNESS AND VIRTUE

The questions as to (1) whether people typically behave in a self-interested manner, and (2) whether this is the right thing to do, are, of course, quite different from each other. The folklore of history of thought seems to see Smith as asserting *both* that actual behaviour is self-interested and that that is a very good thing too. I have already disputed the first of this pair of assertions, claiming that Smith's view was much more complex than that. In that context, reference was made also to Smith's pointer to the role of 'rules of conduct'. I shall come back to that question, but before that I would like to address the 'rightness' issue.

In so far as Smith thought that self-interest-based behaviour would be peculiarly successful in generating economic prosperity, should it not be automatically assumed that he was recommending such behaviour? A good action is surely one with good consequences, and a good person one who takes good action? Again, the picture is much more complex than that bit of 'consequentialist' reasoning would suggest.[18]

Usefulness, Smith thought, is a good way of judging a piece of furniture, but scarcely adequate for judging a person:

> it seems impossible that the approbation of virtue should be a sentiment of the same kind with that by which we approve of a convenient or well-contrived building; or that we should have no other reason for praising a man than that for which we commend a chest of drawers.[19]

Prudence is, of course, worthy of praise in Smith's pluralist system of virtues, but not just because it achieves results – economic or otherwise. A person must also be judged by what he *is* and not merely by the useful purposes he *serves*; by what his motives are, and not only by what his actions achieve. While what Smith calls 'the natural selfishness and rapacity' of the rich (who 'mean only their own conveniency' and pursue 'the gratification of their own vain and insatiable desires'[20]) might, under certain circumstances, achieve good results, that does not make them men of virtue. Nor do their inadvertent achievements, when these occur, make them in Smith's eyes admirable as persons.

Our sensibility to the feelings of others, so far from being inconsistent with the manhood of self-command, is the very principle upon which that manhood if founded. The very same principle or instinct which, in the misfortune of our neighbour, prompts us to compassionate his sorrow; in our misfortune, prompts us to restrain the abject and miserable lamentations of our own sorrow ... The man of the most perfect virtue, the man whom we naturally love and revere the most, is he who joins, to the most perfect command of his own original and selfish feelings, the most exquisite sensibility both to the original and sympathetic feelings of others.[21]

CAUSES AND EFFECTS

Did Smith think that self-interest would, in fact, achieve wonders? In some ways he clearly did. In many economic transactions self-interest would make people serve each other's interests as well as their own. The famous fact of our not expecting 'our dinner' from 'the benevolence of the butcher, the brewer, or the baker' but from 'their regard to their own interest' is undoubtedly an important part of Smith's thinking about the activities of exchange and division of labour.

But did Smith think that intelligent pursuit of self-interest and – more broadly – prudence are the most helpful motives that we can cultivate (quite aside from the question of whether prudence would be a marvellous virtue *if* it were most helpful)? There is very little evidence that Smith thought that to be the case. While he did think that prudence is 'of all virtues that which is most helpful to the individual',[22] he also thought 'humanity, justice, generosity, and public spirit, are the qualities most useful to others'.[23]

There is no puzzle here. Anyone dealing with immediate policy issues has good reasons to concentrate on the 'ills' that are diagnosed to be currently present, and Smith's involvements with current policy issues were deep and sustained.[24] The various feudal barriers and other restrictions of economic transactions were undoubtedly seen by Smith as terrible hindrances to productive efficiency. Smith wanted those 'ills' removed and he explained (as no one had done before him with such clarity) how the unhindered pursuit of self-interest can be very useful in certain types of economic activities. In this respect the specialist nature of Smith's praise of the achievements of self-interest is comparable to

Edgeworth's belief that 'economical calculus' was particularly relevant to two types of activities, namely 'war and contract'.[25]

This is, of course, a far cry from arguing that the pursuit of self-interest and prudence do, in general, produce the best, or even just efficient, results. Smith's emphasis on 'humanity, justice, generosity, and public spirit' being 'the qualities most useful to others' does not contradict his belief that in some spheres of economic activity, self-interest does very well indeed.

The issue is of a good deal of practical relevance today, since serious empirical doubts have been raised about the motivational efficiency of the pursuit of self-interest even in the most elementary workings of capitalist economies. For example, the industrial success of Japan seems to have drawn greatly on a different motivational regularity – what Michio Morishima has called 'the Japanese ethos'.[26] The unusual extent of loyalty, co-operation, sense of duty and public spirit that can be found in Japanese economic relations – including on the factory floor – can be traced to powerful historical roots, which also influence other aspects of Japanese life (such as an astonishingly low crime rate, remarkably little litigation, etc.) Given the nature of interdependences in production and the advantages from a co-operative as opposed to narrowly self-seeking attitude, it is not really surprising that even the success of capitalist economies depends on many motivational features other than prudence in general and the pursuit of self-interest in particular.[27]

I don't believe that there is any contradiction between this recognition and Adam Smith's general position about the usefulness of different motivations, including the roles of 'humanity, justice, generosity, and public spirit'. And the point is further strengthened by Smith's explicit discussion of the role of 'general rules of conduct' in 'correcting misrepresentations of self-love'. What is oddly out of line is not Smith's own analysis, but the peculiarly limited view of Smith's beliefs based on a breathtakingly narrow reading of what he wrote.

Perhaps one can say in mitigation (though not in defence) of these narrow interpretations that the enthusiasm with which Smith outlined some of his views of particular (and limited) cause-effect relationships did sometimes leave room for misunderstanding. David Hume had noted, in his congratulatory letter to Adam Smith after the publication of *The Wealth of Nations* (not to be confused with Hume's more famous letter regarding *The Theory of Moral Sentiments*), that Smith's new book was full of what Hume called 'curious facts'.[28] Smith did have a fascination for curious facts not well-known or obvious to others, and his enthusiastic discussions of possible implications, based on quick reasoning, often did have the appearance of grand generalisations.

For example, consider Smith's analysis of the nutritional value of potatoes. He noted that 'the chairmen, porters, and coalheavers in London and those unfortunate women who live by prostitution', typically come from 'the lowest rank of people in Ireland' and 'are generally fed with this root [potato]'. From the further observation that the former group – the porters and others – are 'the strongest', and the latter group – the prostitutes – are 'the most beautiful women perhaps in the British dominions', Smith came to the conclusion that 'no food can afford a more decisive proof of its nourishing quality'.[29]

No doubt there is something in that odd line of reasoning about the nourishing quality of the potato, and no doubt also there is much more in the line of reasoning about 'the butcher, the brewer, or the baker'. But it is not fair to Smith to identify particular arguments, with a fairly limited focus, with Smith's general position regarding motives, achievements and virtues. Certainly, there is little justification for wrongly attributing views to Smith about what qualities are 'most useful to others' and what 'virtues are most important' when he has himself discussed these questions in detail and expressed his own views in very clear terms.

A CONCLUDING REMARK

Smith was, to say the least, a complex thinker. He has suffered more than most from oversimplification and – sometimes – distortion in support of political positions very different from his own.[30] On the particular subject of prudence, to understand Smith's views, we have to:
1. distinguish between prudence and the pursuit of selfishness;
2. distinguish between the consequential usefulness of a motive and its being a virtue;
3. distinguish between the contingent success of prudence (including of self-interested action) in some spheres of activity and Smith's general beliefs (including that 'humanity, justice, generosity, and public spirit, are the qualities most useful to others');
4. distinguish between the claim of prudence to be a virtue and the basic pluralism of Smith's moral framework (with 'sympathy' as the common measure);
5. distinguish between Smith's analysis of self-interested reasoning on the one hand, and on the other that of following general rules of

conduct', which have 'great use in correcting misrepresentations of self-love'.
If smallness must be 'thrust upon' someone, there are no doubt more deserving candidates than the father of modern economics.

NOTES

1. Adam Smith, *An Inquiry into The Nature and Causes of the Wealth of Nations* (1776; Everyman's Library, London: Dent, 1910), Vol. I, Book I, p. 13.
2. See D. D. Raphael and A. L. Macfie, 'Introduction', in Raphael and Macfie (eds) *The Theory of Moral Sentiments* (Oxford: Clarendon Press, 1976), p.24.
3. See my 'Famine', *World Development*, 8 (1980), and *Poverty and Famines* (Oxford: Clarendon Press, 1981), Section 10.4; and S. Ambirajan, *Classical Political Economy and British Policy in India* (Cambridge: Cambridge University Press, 1978).
4. P. Streeten, *The Frontiers of Development Studies* (London: Macmillan, 1972), p. 129.
5. Smith, *Wealth of Nations*, Vol. I Book I, p. 1.
6. The useful and varied collection of papers on Adam Smith that can be found in A. S. Skinner and T. Wilson (eds) *Essays on Adam Smith* (Oxford: Clarendon Press, 1975) includes some discussions of this problem. See also Raphael and Macfie, 'Introduction', op. cit. See also Donald Winch, *Adam Smith's Politics* (Cambridge: Cambridge University Press, 1978).
7. Raphael and Macfie, 'Introduction'.
8. Smith, *The Theory of Moral Sentiments*, eds Raphael and Macfie, VII.ii.3.21., p.306.
9. Smith, *The Theory of Moral Sentiments*, VII.ii.2.14, p. 299.
10. On this see D.D. Raphael, 'The Impartial Spectator', in Skinner and Wilson, *Essays on Adam Smith*.
11. Smith, *The Theory of Moral Sentiments*, VII.iii.1,4, p.317.
12. In Skinner and Wilson,*Essays on Adam Smith*.
13. Stigler, 'Smith's Travel on the Ship of State', p.237; italics added.
14. See, for example, Albert Hirschman's discussion of 'passions and interests': 'But by the latter part of that century [the eighteenth], the passions were collapsed into interests by Adam Smith who pronounced "the great mob of mankind" to be safely programmed: From the cradle to the grave its members were to be exclusively concerned with "bettering their conditions", (*Essays in Trespassing*, Cambridge: Cambridge University Press, 1981, p. 288).
15. Smith, *The Theory of Moral Sentiments*, IV.2.6, p. 189.
16. On this see Raphael, 'The Impartial Spectator', and Raphael and Macfie, 'Introduction'.
17. Smith, *The Theory of Moral Sentiments*, III.4.12, p.160.
18. On some limitations of 'consequentialist' reasoning, see Bernard Williams, 'A Critique of Utilitarianism', in J. J. C. Smart and B. Williams,

Utilitarianism: For and Against (Cambridge: Cambridge University Press, 1973). See also A. Sen and B. Williams (eds) *Utilitarianism and Beyond* (Cambridge: Cambridge University Press, 1982).
19. Smith, *The Theory of Moral Sentiments*, IV.2.4, p. 188.
20. Smith, *The Theory of Moral Sentiments*, IV.1.10, p. 184.
21. Smith, *The Theory of Moral Sentiments*, III.3.34-5, p. 152.
22. Smith, *The Theory of Moral Sentiments*, IV.2.6, p. 189
23. Smith, *The Theory of Moral Sentiments*, IV.2.9, p. 190.
24. See Winch, *Adam Smith's Politics*.
25. F.Y.Edgeworth, *Mathematical Psychics: An Essay on the Application of Mathematics to the Moral Sciences* (London, 1881), p. 52.
26. M. Morishima, *Why Has Japan 'Succeeded'? Western Technology and the Japanese Ethos* (Cambridge: Cambridge University Press, 1982).
27. Some of these general issues have been discussed in my 'The Profit Motive', *Lloyds Bank Review* (1983); reprinted in my *Resources, Values and Development* (Oxford: Blackwell, and Cambridge, Mass.: Harvard University Press, 1984).
28. Cited in *Encyclopaedia Britannica*, 11th edition (1911), Vol. XXV, p. 225.
29. Smith, *Wealth of Nations*, I.I.xi, p. 147.
30. See also Winch, *Adam Smith's Politics*.

3 Stagflation and The Third World [1]

WILFRED BECKERMAN

INTRODUCTION

It has generally been accepted that the economic prosperity and growth rate of the Third World is heavily dependent on the growth rates in the world's main industrialised countries taken as a whole.[2] This is not surprising given that, even after considerable expansion of intra-trade among non-OECD countries, 'industrial countries' absorbed 63.6 per cent of the total exports of non-oil LDCs in the period 1973–80.

Hence, one might have expected the sharp slowdown in the growth rate of OECD countries in the 1970s to have been mirrored in an equally sharp slowdown in growth in the Third World. Yet this does not seem to have been the case if one takes the last decade or so as a whole. But an important distinction needs to be made between the general trend during the period 1973 to 1980, when there was merely a slowdown of growth rates in the OECD countries (albeit accompanied by a recession in the mid-1970s), and the subsequent two or three years, when there was a much more marked recession in the OECD countries. For these two years witnessed a collapse in commodity prices, which led, in turn, to an abrupt swing in the prices of exports from the LDCs (to the OECD countries as a whole) from an increase of about 40 per cent between 1978 and 1980 to a fall of about 15 per cent – i.e. a turn-round of over 50 per cent.[3]

The main theme of this chapter is that the significant reduction in inflation that was achieved in the industrialised countries during the years 1980–3 was the result less of a weakening of real wage resistance on account of the unprecedented (in post war years) rise in unemployment than of the sharp fall in commodity prices. In short, the costs of curbing inflation in the advanced countries cannot be measured merely in terms of the massive unemployment and slowdown of growth potential inside the advanced countries themselves, but has to be attributed largely to the impact on the prices of commodities exported by the Third World countries.

In more formal terms, the hypothesis advanced here is that the analysis of the linkages between the industrialised countries and the Third World needs to be conducted in terms of the now familiar distinction (attributable to Hicks and Okun) between flex-price and fix-price markets. The prices of internationally traded primary products (i.e. 'commodity prices'), which are the main exports of the Third World, are determined in flex-price markets. By contrast, nearly all other prices in advanced countries, including real wages, are determined in fix-price markets.[4] In so far as this is the case, it has important implications for many aspects of economic policy, such as the scope for individual countries to influence their own inflation rate independently of how far commodity prices are being affected by changes in activity in other advanced countries, or the role of commodity price stabilisation schemes in contributing to greater price stability in the world as a whole and hence alleviating the need to resort to more painful and economically wasteful methods of curbing inflation.

In later sections of this chapter, some statistical results will be presented in support of the hypothesis and some of the obvious components of a rough and highly simplified model will be sketched out verbally to highlight the crucial role of the various key parameters in determining an individual country's degree of policy autonomy. First I shall summarise what seems to have happened during the last decade.

THE SLOWDOWN IN GROWTH

How much slowdown?

There is no dispute about the extent of the slowdown in economic growth in the industrialised countries since the 1973 'oil shock'.[5] During the period 1960 to 1973 the average annual (real) growth rate of the industrialised countries (weighted or unweighted) was about 5.2 per cent. Over the next ten years the growth rate fell to only 2.1 per cent.[6] But this overall figure conceals quite a significant further slowing down during the last four years. The more detailed figures are shown in Table 3.1.

As might be expected the slowdown in the output growth rate was mirrored by a sharp slowdown in the productivity growth rate. Various

TABLE 3.1 GDP growth rates of industrialised countries (% p.a.)

Time period	Growth rate of GDP
1960–73	5.2
1973–79	2.7
1979–83	1.1
1973–83	2.1

estimates of this are summarised by Lindbeck[7], of which the following (attributed to Kendrick) are perhaps the most relevant to the present paper:

TABLE 3.2 Trend growth rate of labour productivity

	1960–73	1973–79	Difference
Western Europe	5.9	3.2	-2.7
Japan	9.9	3.8	-6.1
U.S.A.	3.1	1.1	-2.0
All countries	5.8	2.8	-3.1

Why the slowdown?

Most commentators place the emphasis on the adverse demand impact of the oil price increase (equivalent to a loss of about 2 per cent of the OECD GDP), and on the policy response of some governments to the oil price increases with its associated sharp acceleration of inflation and of inflationary expectations, plus, in most cases a sharp deterioration in their external balances. However, several governments reversed policy in an expansionary direction in 1974 or 1975, and in the second half of 1975 the economies began to expand again. But the second oil price shock in 1979 struck before the inflationary spiral effects of the first shock had been fully absorbed. Together with other developments, notably the reaction against growing budget deficits which were increasingly seen as the cause of the continued inflation, the policy response of governments in 1979 was more firmly and persistently deflationary.

Thus, as William Cline puts it 'One of the most serious negative effects of world inflation on the developing countries may arise from the policies that industrial countries adopt to control their own inflation. Typically those policies lead to domestic recession and a stagnation of demand for developing countries exports, which stunts economic growth in those countries'.[8]

The productivity slowdown is seen by most commentators as having been chiefly – though not necessarily exclusively – the effect of policy measures designed to reduce inflation, rather than an exogenous change in the economic climate. Of course, as Lindbeck points out, there may well have been a fading away of a number of uniquely favourable circumstances promoting productivity growth in the 1950s and 1960s but, as he adds, if the latter had been the dominating force behind the productivity slowdown one would have expected the slowdown to have been gradual rather than abrupt as it turned out to be.[9]

It is true that during the whole of the post-1973 period there had also been a slowdown in investment. Various factors may have contributed to this. These would include the poorer expectations concerning the determination of governments to maintain full employment, the additional uncertainty generally associated with faster inflation, the emergence of excess capacity following the 1974–75 recession, the rapid growth of capital per head over the preceding twenty years or so, and the fact that the growth of real wages did not fall off as fast as productivity so that profit shares and profit rates fell substantially.[10] But Lindbeck reports various statistical results that appear to show that the output slowdown explains far more of the investment slowdown than does the fall in the profit rate.[11]

The precise pattern of events varied somewhat between individual advanced countries, partly in accordance with different economic situations and partly in accordance with different political preferences. In particular, faced with a trade off between inflation and unemployment, right wing governments will tend to give more weight to reducing inflation than will left-wing governments. This is because, on the whole, inflation hits the wealthier more than does unemployment. In an inflationary situation most tax regimes discriminate against income from capital (on account of inadequate allowance for the cut in 'real' wealth), whereas the only capital that workers have is human capital, which is what unemployment threatens most. Secondly, after over two decades of more or less full employment in the industrialised countries, the upheaval following the oil-crisis seemed to be a good context in which the balance of power in the labour market could be tilted back a bit in favour of the employers. Finally, economic doctrines that blamed inflation on excessive monetary expansion and government deficits naturally fitted a political environment in which there was pressure to reduce the role of the State in general and move towards a non-interventionist government posture in economic management.

Of course, not all governments shared these political attitudes, which were probably most acutely perceived in Britain after 1979. But governments that tried to 'buck the trend' with expansionist policies, such as France, failed to overcome the constraints imposed by the generally deflationary external climate and after about two years the expansionary experiment was more or less abandoned. This degree of constraint on the scope for independent action is one of the main implications of the model developed later in this chapter and that arises out of the impact on commodity prices of the pressure of demand in the industrialised countries as a whole.

Before coming on to that part of the story, however, it must be noted that not all commentators would subscribe to the explanation of the 1970s stagflation summarised above. Some commentators, for example, believe that in 1973 some mysterious event took place, presumably originating in Outer Space, which induced an exogenous fall-off in productivity growth simultaneously in all the industrialised countries of the world, as well as in the desire to be gainfully employed. And those who still felt like working – not being well informed about these supernatural forces – continued to claim the same increase in real wages to which they had become accustomed, so that real wages rose more than was 'warranted' by the now slower growth of productivity (aggravated by a deterioration in the terms of trade of the industrialised countries immediately following the first oil-price shock). Hence, firms, moving back up their neoclassical demand curves for labour, cut employment until marginal products had risen to match the higher real wages. This seems to be what is implied by the widespread view that workers have 'priced themselves out of the market'.

It would be out of place here to try to adjudicate between these two contrasting explanations of the slowdown in economic growth in the post-1973 period, and I must leave it to the reader to make up his own mind. The only point that needs to be made here is that the latter view usually relies on figures showing the rise in the share of wages in national income, which is identically equal to an excess of the rise in real wages above the rate 'warranted' by the increase in productivity (and the change in ther terms of trade). The view that workers have 'priced themselves out of the market' has been summarised frequently in *The Economist*[12] and recently in an article claiming that the view was now accepted by all economists.[13] But most economists, particularly in

Europe, would probably subscribe, instead, to the contrary conclusions in the 'Dornbusch Report'.[14] If, however, the slowdown in productivity is not exogenous and is, instead, as many commentators seem to think, the result of the deliberate policy decisions by governments designed to curb demand as a means of reducing inflation, then the data do not justify the above conclusion. The direction of causality would have to be reversed. The cut in demand and rise in unemployment may have led to the slower growth of productivity which, cet. par., led to a rise in the share of wages in total value added.

The impact of slowdown on the LDCs

As indicated at the outset, the usual view would be that the slowdown of growth just summarised would have serious effects on the growth performance of the LDCs. But it turns out that even after making the crucial distinction between the oil-exporting LDCs and the others, the adverse impact on the latter has not been as serious as might have been predicted – at least until 1980. The salient facts are summarised by Morris Goldstein and Mohsin Khan as Table 3.3.

As Goldstein and Khan say (p. 1), the comparison between 1968–73 and 1973–80 suggests that
(i) the growth rate of real GNP in the industrialised countries can be exceeded by the growth rate of their total imports;
(ii) industrial countries' overall import growth rate may be exceeded by the growth rate of their imports from non-oil developing countries;

TABLE 3.3 *Summary of main changes in growth rates in industrialised countries and in LDCs, 1968–80*

	1968–73	1973–80
Growth in real terms of:		
GNP of industrial countries	4.5	3.1
Imports of industrial countries	9.9	4.2
Ditto fron non-oil LDCs	7.7	5.6
Total exports of non-oil LDCs	9.3	7.2
GNP of all non-oil LDCs (excluding China)	5.8	5.2

SOURCES: M. Goldstein and M. Khan, *Effects of Slowdown in Industrial Countries on Growth in Non-Oil Developing Countries*, IMF, August 1982, Table 1, p. 2.

(iii) the growth rate of industrial country imports from non-oil developing countries can be exceeded by the growth rate of total exports of the non-oil developing countries; and
(iv) this export growth rate may, in turn, be quite different from the real output growth rate of the non-oil developing countries.

Of course, as the authors add, there has been tremendous diversity of growth experiences among the non-oil developing countries, reflecting to a large extent the dependence of individual countries on manufactured exports or on particular primary products. For example, the prices of metals, minerals and cereals were particularly badly hit in the second of the two periods shown above, whereas those of beverages and timber performed much better.

Overall, however, the Goldstein and Khan conclusion is supported by the aggregative data and by other commentators, notably Michael Michaely, who notes that the industrialised countries imports rose as a share in their combined GNP between the two periods, so that their non-oil imports rose during the 1973–79 period at almost twice the rate of their GNPs. In fact, the volume of imports of the industrialised countries from non-oil LDCs rose much faster than the volume of their *total* imports. However, this owes much to increasing imports of manufacturing imports from the LDCs, and the share of primary imports in the total imports of the industrialised countries fell.[15]

For the mid-1970s Cline also finds that the impact of disturbances in the advanced countries on the LDCs was less than one might have expected. He also refers to regressions results that show that, for the period 1960–77, the growth rates of the LDCs in any particular year were only 'moderately' affected by the growth rate on the industrial area in the previous year.[16]

THE COLLAPSE OF COMMODITY PRICES, 1980–82

Between 1972 and 1980 the IMF's 'All commodities price index' rose nearly threefold, by 167 per cent. Over the same period the export unit value index of non-oil LDCs rose more than threefold, by 223 per cent.[17] Of course, over this period, the prices of manufactured goods imported by the LDCs from the industrialised countries also rose and the price of energy imports rose even faster. Hence, although the terms of trade of industrialised countries deteriorated between 1972 and 1980 by about 20 per cent, the terms of trade of the non-oil LDCs also fell below their 1972 level (by about 8 per cent).[18]

But the progression was far from smooth. After the sharp rise in commodity prices from 1972 to 1974, there was a fall during the mid-1970s and then another very sharp rise from 1978 to 1980 accompanying the 1979 'second oil-shock'. The following table shows various indicators of the changes in commodity prices and in the indices of unit values of exports from the LDCs and of imports into the industrialised countries as a whole. The latter are relevant partly because it would have been impossible for changes in commodity prices to have been greatly attenuated in final trade prices as a result of changes in exchange rates, exporters' margins, commodity control schemes, and so on. But, as can be seen in the table, all the indices moved in a similar manner over the period in question. The 'swing' in the final column is the sum, ignoring signs, of the chages between 1978 and 1980 and between 1980 and 1982. As can be seen, whichever index one uses, the change from a sharp rise in the first two years to some fall in the second two years gives a total 'swing' of around 50 to 60 per cent.

Although the econometric results discussed below relate wages to changes in import prices (and other variables), not to commodity prices, so that it is necessary to put them against the background of the changes in import prices into the OECD countries as a whole, concentration on

TABLE 3.4 *Selected price indices (1980 = 100)*

	1978	79	80	81	82	'Swing'
1 Export unit values of non-oil LDCs	70	81	100	95	88	55
2 Unit value of imports into developed market economies	69	82	100	98	93	52
3 IMF 'all commodities' price index	78	91	100	92	83	45
4 UNCTAD commodity price index (SDRs)	78	87	100	93	83	45
5 UNCTAD commodity price index ($US)	76	87	100	84	71	61

NOTE
The IMF commodity price index in row 2 "includes 34 wholesale price series chosen as representative of the 30 commodities export by primary producing countries", the weights corresponding to average export earnings excluding industrial and major oil-exporting countries (oil is excluded from the commodities selected) (see IMF *International Financial Statistics, Supplement on Price Statistics*. No. 2, 1981, pp.1.19 and 24, and monthly issues of *IFS*). The UNCTAD commodity price index is an index of market prices of the principal commodity exports of developing countries, its weights being 'proportional to the value, in terms of US dollars, of exports from developing countries in the year 1975 to 1977' (see UNCTAD Monthly Commodity Price Bulletin, May 1983, Annex. p. 25). These indices are shown in US dollars and SDRs in the quarterly *National Institute Economic Review*.

the prices of imports from non-OECD countries would, of course, underestimate the full role of falling commodity prices in the deceleration of inflation. For, excluding oil, most of the OECD's total supplies of commodities are produced inside the OECD area, and many of them are important in intra-OECD trade. Apart from those protected under the European Community's CAP, prices of indigenously produced commodities will tend to move sympathetically with world prices. Coal, natural gas, and even oil prices are obvious examples. But in order to take full account of all commodity price movements it would be necessary to have an input-output table for the OECD area, which is, of course, not available.

This is one reason why we have concentrated here on the import prices of commodities. The other reason is that the prices of total imports into individual countries – which we postulate to have a significant influence on their rates of inflation – have varied by different amounts largely on account of changes in their individual exchange rates, thereby providing a much more varied data set for purposes of statistical verification of the relationship between inflation and import prices. If, at the level of the individual country, it is established that import prices rather than unemployment significantly affects the inflation rate it is legitimate to conclude that, for the industrialised countries taken as a whole, the prices of imports – which happen to be mainly commodities – influences the inflation rate. The chief difference is that, for the industrialised countries as a whole, import prices are not exogenous but are largely determined by changes in the level of economic activity and hence provide the mechanism by which aggregate unemployment does have an effect.

Although the share of imports of commodities from non-OECD sources in the total GDP of the OECD countries is only about 5 per cent (in 1981), imports of commodities from all sources, (including intra-OECD trade) represent 8 per cent of the total OECD GDP and 11 per cent of the GDP of OECD Europe.[19] Given these figures, and without even allowing for the primary commodities produced inside the OECD area and not entering into intra-OECD trade, the turn round in the prices of imported commodities into the average OECD country between the two-year periods 1978–80 and 1980–82 of about 50 to 60 per cent could be expected to have a *direct* effect of slowing down the rate of increase in the prices of total final expenditures by about 5 to 6 per cent (over a two year period). If allowance could be made for sympathetic movements in the prices of the non-traded commodities produced inside the OECD area the impact could be much greater. After all, the 'swing' in the OPEC oil price was considerable, and this certainly was reflected in the prices of all domestically produced OECD sources of energy.[20]

How much deceleration has taken place depends on the precise time period over which comparisons are made. Comparing 1978–80 and 1980–82 consumer price inflation slowed down by only 2.1 per cent, and wage inflation by 3.3 per cent. Comparing 1979–81 with 1981–83 consumer price inflation slowed down by 9.8 per cent and wage inflation by 8.8 per cent. But since real wages had already been rising faster than prices, they continued to rise, if very slowly, in the post 1980 years, in almost all OECD countries, including Britain, where unemployment was particularly high. In fact, given that our econometric results show that money wages are significantly correlated with import prices, the rise in money wages after 1980 was checked less than our equations would suggest. This may simply be because what our equations measure, of course, is the average relationship over the time periods on which the measurements were based (1961 through 1983 and 1972 through 1983), and so cannot be expected to apply exactly to every individual subperiod or country. But this 'excess' rise in money wages and continued strength of real wages certainly does not suggest that the mass unemployment was having a significant depressing impact on wages on top of the effect of the slower rise in import prices.

If hitting the labour force over the head with mass unemployment merely forces them to accept further increases in real wages it does not appear to be a potent threat. Of course, the fact is that however much those employees who have retained their jobs may fear unemployment, there is nothing they can do to ensure that their real wage moves in line with every change in world commodity prices, exchange rates and so on, let alone in line with the *real product wage* in their particular industry, which is some instances has fluctuated violently. The best they can do is to bargain over money wages, and our evidence strongly suggests that, in the last three years, the increases they have obtained have been moderated even less than the fall in commodity prices would have implied given the average relationship that we have found to exist between the variables in question.

COMMODITY PRICES AND STABILISATION IN THE OECD AREA

As indicated at the outset of this chapter, the link between economic fluctuations in the industrialised world and the prices of the commodities that form the bulk of exports from the LDCs reinforces the point recently made by Kaldor to the effect that

> it is necessary to disaggregate economic activities more than is generally done in macro-economic analysis ... by distinguishing between the primary sector of the world economy on the one hand and the 'secondary' and 'tertiary' sectors on the other hand ... In the field of primary production the market price is given to the individual producer in the classical manner described by Adam Smith. Industrial prices (in contrast ...) are not 'market clearing'. This means that the burden of any maladjustment between the growth of manufacturing activities is thrown almost entirely on the commodity markets.[21]

Unemployment equilibria and/or large fluctuations in the quantity (output or employment) dimension are obvious characteristics of most simple fix-price macro-models. Clearly, if a flex-price sector can be grafted on to the fix-price part of the model there is scope for mitigating the quantity implications of the fix-price assumptions. An elementary text-book example is the model of a two sector labour market – a unionised sector with fixed wages and a non-unionised sector with flexible wages. Labour displaced from the former on account of the high real wage goes into the latter and forces down wages therein, so there is no unemployment – merely a differential between unionised and non-unionised wages.

One might expect that grafting on a flex-price 'commodity' sector to fix-price industrialised country sector would similarly facilitate the achievement of certain policy objectives. In the context of the current major policy pre-occupations one would expect the price flexibility of the commodtiy sector to assist countries in the pursuit of a preferred combination of employment and price stability in one of two ways (or some combination of them). Taking the industrialised countries as a whole, this would appear to operate in the following manner.

First, in so far as real wages are fairly rigid the mechanism postulated above would operate: the fall in commodity prices, which has been reflected in a slowing down in the rise in import prices in most advanced countries, would imply a slower rise in money wages and would be the mechanism by which deflationary policies have worked. This means that the Phillips curve is as flat as many commentators have long believed; but inflation has slowed down because the fall in commodity prices caused the Phillips curve to shift downwards (inwards) rapidly. Thus the fall in commodity prices presented governments with the option of either reducing unemployment at the cost of a slower cut in the inflation rate, or keeping unemployment high in order to squeeze inflation out of the system as rapidly as possible (the option notably selected in Britain).

Secondly, in so far as money wages do not respond fully and rapidly to the slower growth of import prices so that real wages rise somewhat, there would be an automatic increase in purchasing power and in consumption that would, by itself, tend to help economic recovery. After all, it has long been widely believed that one of the factors contributing to economic recovery in the 1930s was the rise in real wages caused by the fall in commodity prices. In addition, in so far as one believes that neoclassical demand curve for labour is also relevant, the rise in real wages would be accompanied by a fall in the real *product* wage (since the fall in commodity prices implies a rise in the value added price). Hence, the direct demand for labour would rise as well as the demand for goods. However, this effect might be offset by a fall in export demand from the LDCs.

The point is that whatever the debates about the policies adopted by most industrialised countries in the last few years directed at reducing inflation – such as how exactly monetary policy works, whether the costs are excessive, what effects there will be on longer-term growth and so on – there seems to be a widespread agreement that the policies did at least achieve their objective. There is fairly general agreement that the mass unemployment has at least succeeded in moving economies out on to a downward sloping segment of the Phillips curve – albeit still with a rather flat slope so that the amount of unemployment needed to curb wage increases had to be very large indeed. This was in contrast with some earlier results on both sides of the Atlantic to the effect the changes in the pressure of demand or unemployment had a negligible impact on the rate of wage increases or price increases. Of course these results were contested, but even the authors of some of them would now accept that wage rigidity has been broken and that, at the current levels of unemployment, what they had previously held to be a virtually flat Phillips curve starts to bend down.[22]

The econometric results summarised below, however, suggest that they were right all along, but that the Phillips curves have been shifting downwards (inwards) on account of a slower rise in import prices (in turn largely the result of falling commodity prices). Of course, it is difficult to separate the relative impact of changing import prices and changing levels of unemployment on wages within individual countries using time series data. For in so far as the two variables are postulated to be highly inter-related one is faced with the usual more or less intractable problems of acute multi-collinearity, on top of the usual serial correlation problem. But the estimates referred to below have been based on techniques that incorporate cross country data, as well as time series, in a manner the minimises the severity of these problems.

Before describing the statistical results it should be pointed out that the contribution of falling commodity prices to the deceleration of inflation in recent years should come as no surprise. In the first place, it had already been widely accepted that the acceleration of inflation in the 1972–4 period was largely caused by sharp increases in commodity prices, so there is no reason to reject, *a priori*, the reverse impact in 1980–2. Secondly, various other studies have reached similar conclusions already, mainly in connection with the deceleration of inflation before the second oil-shock.[23]

STATISTICAL VERIFICATION

One obvious starting point is to use cross country data on rates of changes in import prices and domestic prices and *levels* of unemployment in each country in specific time periods, particularly the period 1980–2 under special investigation here. In this way one would hope to avoid the usual econometric difficulties of time series.[24] However, this approach could be very misleading and the absence of any cross-country correlation between unemployment and inflation could understate seriously the 'true' role of unemployment. For it is highly likely that – even without taking account of statistical incomparabilities – the 'natural' rate of unemployment differs between countries in line with differences in labour market conditions, social security provisions, and other factors. At the same time changes over time in unemployment within individual countries could still have an impact on wage inflation. If this were the case, the apparent absence of any correlation between international differences in unemployment *levels* and in inflation rates could also mean that too much of the variation in inflation rates would be caught up by the import price variable.

Hence, it seemed desirable to use rather more sophisticated econometric techniques in order to preserve the advantages of cross-country data without sacrificing the advantages of time series data for estimating the role of the unemployment variable within individual countries. The details of the methods are set out elsewhere in a paper by the present writer and Tim Jenkinson and only the main details will be reported here. The main feature of the estimates is that they are based on the familiar wage and price equation models, but the structure of the model is such that

1. The resulting reduced form wage equation expresses wage changes in any period as a function of (a) import price changes in the same period (b) a 'catch-up' term, representing the catch-up of real wages in any period corresponding to the extent to which, in the previous period, real wages had been affected by changes in prices; (c) the unemployment level and (d) a productivity variable.
2. Cross-country and time series data for most of the industrialised countries are combined in a way that makes allowance for differences between countries with respect to their auto-correlation structures. This is a major difference between the estimates shown here and such previous estimates of which we are aware that apply combined cross section and time series data to the particular problem in question here (such as the Bruno contribution referred to above).

The basic wage and price equations used are as follows:

$$W_t = a_0 + a_1 P_t + a_2 P_{t-1} + a_3 W_{t-1} + a_4 f(U_t) + a_5 o(Z_t)$$

$$P_t = b_1 W_t + b_2 M_t$$

where W = hourly earnings in manufacturing;
M = unit value of imports
U = percentage of labour force unemployed
Z = output per man hour (normalised for cyclical variations)

Making the homogeneity assumption that

$$a_1 + a_2 + a_3 = 1.$$

and $b_1 + b_2 = 1$ (i.e. constant profit margins)

After various substitutions and transformations, a reduced form equation can be obtained as follows (lower case variables indicate logs):[25]

$$dw_t = c_0 + c_1 dm_t + c_2(m_{t-1} - w_{t-1}) + c_3 U_t + c_4 z_t + e. \ldots \ldots (3)$$
where $c_1 = a_1 b_2/(1 - a_1 b_2)$
$c_2 = (1 - a_3)/(1 - a_1 b_2)$
$c_3 = a_4/(1 - a_1 b_1)$
and $c_4 = a_5/(1 - a_1 b_1)$

The main results are summarised in the Appendix. To note their chief features:
1. Whatever variants of the basic model are investigated the coefficient on import prices in the same period (c_1) is always highly significant statistically, and has a value of about 0.25.
2. The 'catch-up' coefficient (c_2) is significant in the period 1973–83, with a value around 0.12, and taking the whole period 1960–83 it is significant with a value of 0.04, but it is not significant durang the period 1960–7 taken by itself.
3. The unemployment variable is statistically insignificant in all variants of the basic model.
4. The application of ordinary least squares methods to the combined cross-country and time series data produces very poor results, by comparison with the other methods, particularly the 'variance components' method.[26]

The values of the coefficients correspond closely to the values that one would obtain by simulating the coefficients in the basic wage and price equations on the basis of the orders of magnitude of the share of imports in total GDP in most individual OECD countries (averages about 0.4), and alternative assumptions concerning the relative sizes of a_1 and a_2.

INTERNATIONAL LINKAGES AND ANTI-INFLATIONARY POLICY

One of the main conclusions that emerges from the above discussion of the impact of deflationary policies in the industrialised countries on commodity prices is that there is much less room for manoeuvre by an average individual country to combat inflation through any direct impact on its own internal demand levels – *other than through the exchange rate effect*. Apart from the effect on its exchange rate, a rise in unemployment in any given country is likely to be futile, as a means of slowing down inflation, if the OECD countries as a whole are not following similar policies. If they are not deflating, then commodity prices are not likely to fall, so that there is almost no limit (certainly we have not yet reached it) to which unemployment in an individual country would have to rise in order to dampen internal inflation. Indeed, if the rest of the world is expanding, individual countries will be unable to avoid inflation even at the cost of mass unemployment. This implies that it is absurd for governments to set themselves price stability targets as if they could control world commodity prices.[27]

Of course, one should not exclude the exchange rate from the picture. A country that deflates *relative* to the rest of the OECD area – which may mean simply expanding less strongly – will, *ceteris paribus* tend to experience a strengthening of its exchange rate, so that, *ceteris paribus* its import prices will fall (or rise less steeply). (This is one of the well-known scenarios concerning the effectiveness of restrictive monetary policy under conditions of flexible exchange rates).

But, at the same time, the greater is the *absolute* rate of expansion of the other countries taken together the greater will be the rise in world commodity prices and hence the danger of importing inflation. The precise impact on its own inflation of any change in the pressure of demand in any country will depend, therefore, on the change in its pressure of demand relative to other countries, and obvious parameters of a more extended model, such as the relative marginal propensities to import (influencing the amount of exchange rate response to differential rates of expansion), and the elasticity of supply of commodities (influencing their price response to the aggregate expansion of the industrialised countries taken as a whole), and the particular coefficients of wage and price adjustment and the speed of pass-through in the given country. Thus, even taking the exchange rate into account, it is still not necessarily true that the link with the flex-price system of commodity output always makes it easier for a given country to attain its preferred inflation/employment combination.

For the world as a whole, of course, the above analysis implies that the full cost of recent policies to combat inflation in the industrialised countries cannot be measured without taking account of the impact on the LDCs via the fall, between 1980 and 1982, in commodity prices. But, secondly, it has depressing implications for the prospects for economic recovery in the industrialised countries – as Lord Kaldor has emphasised. A revival of demand in the industrialised world runs the risk of setting off renewed inflation and checking the expansion of demand – for goods and for labour – through the reverse of the effects outlined above in the case of falling commodity prices. In this situation economic expansion cannot be reconciled with price stability by resort to incomes policies, since it is difficult to conceive of incomes policies that will hold back the prices of primary products![28] Instead, one is thrown back on the need for commodity price stabilisation policies. And, at this point, one has to face the fact that these have been as difficult to implement as have the more conventional incomes policies in the industrialised world.

NOTES

1. I am indebted to Tim Jenkinson who, as indicated in the text, is collaborating with me on the econometric aspects of the hypothesis maintained in this paper.
2. For a succinct summary of the conventional wisdom, see Flemming Larsen, John Llewellyn and Stephen Potter. 'International Economic Linkages'. in OECD, *Economic Studies*, No. 1. Autumn 1983, pp. 47 and 49.
3. OECD, *Economic Outlook*, July 1982, pp. 134-5.
4. Sir John Hicks, *The Crisis in Keynesian Economics* (Oxford, Oxford University Press, 1975), pp. 23-4, and Arthur Okun, 'Inflation: Its Mechanics and Welfare Costs" in *Brooking Papers on Economic Activity*, 1975, No.2. The application of the flex-price versus fix-price distinction to the topic under discussion here is, in fact, fully spelt out by Lord Kaldor in 'Inflation and Recession in the World Economy', *Economic Journal*, December 1976. See also his return to this topic in the *Lloyds Bank Review*, May 1983.
5. The definition 'industrialised countries' adopted here follows that used by the IMF (and other bodies) and corresponds to the OECD countries less Greece, Portugal, Turkey and Yugoslavia.
6. See OECD, *National Accounts 1952-81* p. 22, and *National Institute Economic Review*, November 1983, Table 1, p. 26.
7. Assar Lindbeck, 'The Recent Slowdown in Productivity Growth', *Economic Journal*, March 1983, p. 15. The estimates extracted here are those attributed to John Kendrick, in 'I1 1983, p. 15. The estimates extracted here are those attributed to John Kendrick, in 'International comparisons of recent productivity trends',*Contemporary Economic Problems* (ed. W. Fellner), Washing 1981. They refer to real value added per man hour.
8. William Cline and Associates, *World Inflation and the developing countries*, Washington D.C., Brookings Institution, (1981), p. 243.
9. Lindbeck *op. cit.*, pp. 13 and 18. Other commentators, such as Worswick in R.C.O. Matthews (ed) *Slower Growth in Britain*, (London, Heinemann, 1983) take the same view.)
10. See, for example, John Llewellyn, 'Resource prices and Macroeconomic Policies: Lessons from two Oil Price Shocks', in *OECD Economic Studies*, No. 1 Autumn 1983, pp. 197ff; and Douglas Purvis 'Perspectives on Macroeconomic Performance in the 1970s', OECD, *Economic Outlook, Occasional Studies*, June 1983.
11. Lindbeck, *op. cit.*, p. 20.
12. For example, November 27th 1982, December 18th 1982.
13. Ibid. March 3rd 1984. It has also been advocated, in the U.K. by Sam Brittan in *How to end the monetarist controversy* (IEA, London, 1981), and

in papers produced by some members of the L.S.E. Centre for Labour Economics, such as D. Grubb, R. Jackman and R. Layard, in 'Causes of European Stagflation', *Review of Economic Studies*, 1982.
14. 'Macroeconomic Prospects and Policies', report by a group of economists for the Centre for European Policy Studies, Brussels, (CEPS Paper, No. 1, 1983).
15. Michael Michaely, 'Trade in a Changed World Economy', *World Development*, May 1983.
16. William Cline and Associates, *op. cit.*, pp. 241 and 243.
17. IMF, *IFS Supplement on Price Statistics*, *op. cit.* pp. 19 and 24.
18. *Ibid.*, pp. 22 and 24.
19. In 1981 the combined GDP, in US dollars at current prices and exchange rates, for total OECD and OECD Europe respectively was $7,619 billion and $3,101 billion, imports of commodities were $587 billion and $340 billion respectively, and imports of commodities from non-OECD sources were $357 billion and $171 billion respectively (the latter figures have been based on the corresponding distribution by area of origin of commodity imports into EEC plus EFTA countries – which account for 93 per cent of the imports in question). The shares of total imports into these two groups including intra-OECD trade is, of course, very much greater, amounting to 26 per cent for OECD Europe, and 16 per cent including the other OECD countries. For the average OECD industrialised country, 45 per cent of total imports consist of 'commodities' (data from OECD *Economic Outlook: Historical Statistics*, 1960–81, pp. 17, 114, 120 and 122).
20. In this connection, *The Economists* index of commodity prices is very appropriate since it is weighted according to the value of imports into the OECD countries (net of intra-EEC trade in those commodities the prices of which are stabilised on account of the operation of the Common Agricultural Policy). This index shows that the behaviour of commodity prices during the period in question does not differ significantly from that described above in terms of indices based on the commodities exported by the LDCs.
21. Lord Kaldor *Economic Journal*, *op. cit.*, pp. 704–5.
22. See, for example, George Perry, 'Inflation in Theory and Practice', in BPEA, 1980, No. 1; *Economic Policy Review* (Cambridge). March 1978, No. 4, p. 3, and *Cambridge Economic Policy Review*, April 1981. p' 34.
23. See, for example, Philip Turner, 'International Aspects of Inflation in OECD *Economic Outlook: Occasional Studies*, June 1982, p. 7; Michael Bruno, 'Import prices and stagflation in the industrial countries: a Cross Section Analysis', *Economic Journal*, September 1980, p. 487; *The Economist*, 'Inflation is Down – but Not Out', 7 May 1983; and Larsen, Llewellyn and Potter, OECD, *op. cit.*, p.50.
24. This is similar to the approach used by other commentators, such as the OECD estimates by Philip Turner, *op. cit.*, June 1982, pp. 15ff.
25. See W. Beckerman and T. Jenkinson, 'Commodity prices, Import Prices and the Inflation Slowdown: a Pooled Cross-Section Time Series Analysis' (forthcoming).
26. See W. Beckerman and T. Jenkinson, *op. cit.* (forthcoming) for details.

27. Of course, a dedicated monetarist would argue that provided one keeps the money supply constant it is impossible to 'import' inflation, but this is not the place to go into that story.
28. Nevertheless, incomes policies in the industrialised countries would still serve a purpose of making it easier for governments to achieve their price stability objectives with less resort to deflation.

APPENDIX: COEFFICIENT OF W_t ON VARIABLES INDICATED*

All variables are in logarithms except u.
  VC = Variance Components method
  LSDV = Least Squares Dummy variables method
  OLS = Ordinary Least Squares method

Period 1962–83 (t-values in parentheses)

Method	$\dot{M}_t$	$(M-W)_{t-1}$	$\dot{U}_t$	$\dot{Z}_t$	C_0
VC	0.23	0.04	−0.002	0.56	0.05
	(6.73)	(3.74)	(−0.66)	(3.04)	(4.24)
LSDV	0.26	−0.01	−0.001	0.82	—
	(9.47)	(−1.35)	(−0.98)	(4.24)	
OLS	0.29	−0.002	0.002	0.78	0.04
	(10.6)	(−0.19)	(0.70)	(5.84)	(5.71)

Mean square error
VC   0.00085148695   31 per cent less than LSDV
LSDV 0.001225701   —
OLS   0.001455804   19 per cent higher than LSDV

Period 1973–83

Method	$P\dot{M}_t$	$(PM-W)_{t-1}$	$\dot{U}_t$	$\dot{P}_t$	a
VC	0.22	0.12	−0.001	1.03	0.05
	(5.71)	(3.90)	(−0.29)	(3.54)	(3.19)
LSDV	0.21	0.14	−0.005	1.33	—
	(7.60)	(5.18)	(−3.77)	(5.21)	

Mean square error
VC   0.00085838
LSDV 0.00085206

Period 1962–73

Method	$P\dot{M}_t$	$(PM-W)_{t-1}$	$\dot{U}_t$	$\dot{P}_t$	a
VC	0.25	−0.02	−0.003	1.06	0.02
	(3.88)	(−1.55)	(−0.96)	(5.62)	(2.07)
LSDV	0.26	−0.05	−0.010	0.037	—
	(5.15)	(−5.81)	(−3.37)	(0.125)	

Mean square error
VC   0.00056047
LSDV 0.00048868

* (a) See equation (3) earlier for explanation of model estimates.

4 Recession, Rent and Debt: Quasi-Ricardian and Quasi-Keynesian Components of Non-Recovery[1]

MICHAEL LIPTON

POLICY AND BANK FLOWS, EPIPHENOMENA: DEEP CAUSE, SHIFT TO RENT

The UK Development Studies Association bravely took as its theme, for its September 1983 conference, 'the continuing recession'. Then, and even more than a year later, the organisers may have appeared foolhardy.The main US indicators, especially real GNP, apparently signalled a strong and prolonged recovery. Many world commodity prices – their record lows of mid-1982 the despair of development experts[2] – were moving upwards. For a while, even inflation seemed to be recovering; but at the September 1984 Bank-Fund meeting the IMF reported that 1984 was the best year for the world economy since 1976, anticipated 5 per cent real growth in industrial countries' real GNP, and applauded the apparent containment of inflation, and even (outside Europe) of unemployment.

Nevertheless, the idea behind the words 'continuing recession' remains correct. This is not because Babylonian numerology of long-wave cycle theory – if such a mechanistic account can be called a theory – somehow keeps the world economy crawling along the floor, with at best fitful and temporary lurches upwards, until Kondratieff's magic clock strikes. The recession continues, and recovery is elusive, for three reasons: one, in the area of public policy; a second, connected with monetary flows; and a third, in the real economy.

The arguments presented here will concentrate on the last reason. They place it in the context of the Ricardian concern that the increasing share of differential rent – whether on farmland in British GNP in 1810–13, or on oil-land in world GNP in 1973–2000 – would reduce profits, accumulation, and therefore progress. Although rent on oil-bearing land is not precisely analogous to rent on corn-bearing land – mainly because oil is not obviously and directly a wage-good, whereas for Ricardo corn is the wage-good – an international shift of world income towards oil-land rents does depress profits and progress today, rather as a shift to corn-land rents did in Ricardo's model.

However, to explain 'continuing recession' in today's world, the Ricardo effect has to be analysed together with more topical demand-side worries. Can 'sudden changes in the channels of trade' ever mean, as Ricardo denied, that long-run real output is 'materially impaired'?[3] Is there a problem of recycling, real demand, or debt? These worries seem quite remote from Ricardo's model, where Say's Law applied,[4] and long-run 'general glut' – inadequate aggregate demand with the consequence of below-full employment and reduced accumulation – was ruled out. Yet even on the demand side, as we shall see, Ricardo's exposition of the effects of profit-to-rent transfers – especially in his earlier work – offers useful hints about current recycling problems, even though such problems appear strictly short-term in his world, governed as it was by Say's Law. In today's world (unlike Ricardo's) it is plausible to revive profits after the shift to rent, by compressing 'psychological subsistence', i.e. wage expectations; but the inoperability of Say's Law, indeed the very process that Ricardo left out (but which Malthus and Keynes put in), renders that approach to recovery unpromising, even though it is currently popular among governments in OECD. The shift to rent, and the destabilising effects of the 'recycling' procedures for that rent, will need to be tackled more explicitly.

Before going further, we must look briefly at the other two components of the 1980s' possible 'continuing recession': changes in public policy and in monetary flows. This is because these components interact with the quasi-Ricardian real-resource shift, since 1973, to oil-land rent in the real economy; and the interaction itself may impede recovery. It is central to the argument of this chapter that the large rises in the average *and marginal* ratios of oil-land rent to world production – rises which began in 1973, continued in 1978, were stalled (though hardly reversed) by the recession itself in 1982–4, but surely which were long-term phenomena[5] – would have sufficed to ensure that, even without fundamental change in the 1960s styles of monetary management or public policy-making, recession became longer, deeper and more difficult to reverse. For any 'energy-neutral' reflationary act in OECD, the shift to rent on oil-land increases the ratio of inflation to real growth.[6]

However, *public policy* has helped to make recovery more difficult. The inflationary aftermath of the 1975 – 7 reflation led to an overriding concern among OECD governments to destroy inflationary expectations. This concern has led governments since about 1978 to remove 'traditional' (1945–78) private sector expectations that *public* investment would limit the fall in aggregate demand consequent on an initial or induced fall in *private* investment. Those terrified by inflation – and not 'only fools' – 'will not let sleeping accelerators lie'.[7] There is plainly a recession-maintaining impact from this deliberate (counter-inflationary) withdrawal of a public sector 'floor' for investment.[8]

The second incidental problem of non-recovery, incidental to Ricardo's rent demon but interacting with him, is the problem of *monetary flows*. This concerns the tendency of banks – faced with large new deposits from enriched (oil) rentiers, rather little effective control (at least in Euromarkets) on their use,[9] and recession in developed countries – to vent their cash surpluses in a few developing countries, and/or developed-country sub-sectors, thought to be immune. Each bank tends to pick the same countries and/or sectors, leading to overexposure by banks, over-borrowing by sectors or countries, and high risk from undiversified portfolios. Given 'continuing recession' (especially combined with high real interest rates), this means eventual defaults, open or disguised. These defaults then contract the cash base of the banking system. Lending – dramatically to the 'few developing countries'[10] and over-borrowed sectors, but ultimately even to prime borrowers[11] – is reduced, and the recession feeds on itself.[12] Big banks seldom go broke; but, when forced by bad debts to contract lending, they cause *firms* to go broke, or at least to contract.

We must return to this issue; but both the monetary flows and the public policy responses are secondary causes of the prolonged recession, and the abortive nature, so far, of recovery. The prime cause is the sharply increased *transfer of Ricardian rent* from entrepreneurs to rentiers – overwhelmingly to Saudi Arabia, Kuwait and the UAE, which own the best (most intra-marginal) oil-bearing land. For Ricardo, GNP transfers to rents on (corn) land had to be at the expense of profits, because full employment and (psychological subsistence) wage-rates were given (see below). For us, too – except to some extent in the USA and Japan – real wages (and other components of the labour share) in OECD countries have until fairly recently been rather inflexible downwards, so that profitability, and hence the inducement to invest, have borne the brunt of the shift to rent on oil-land. Each sharp recovery, moreover, is threatened by the risk that, in raising demand for energy, it may induce a repetition of the 1973 and 1979 oil-price transfer effects.

Thus the consequences of the 1975–7 demand reflation – the second oil shock of 1979–80, renewed inflation, and growth first sluggish, then aborted – were systematic. They were rooted in the transfer of world income from profits to rent on oil-bearing land. For Ricardo, while right about the recessionary nature of a shift to rent, was not right in claiming that any resulting 'general glut' had to be very brief. To Ricardo, we must add not Say but Keynes on effective demand. The shift of GNP to rent, by reducing the profitability of production, in 1977–81 made Western output price inelastic (and investment sluggish) when demand recovered. Falling Keynesian marginal efficiency of capital was induced by rising Ricardian rent. Sustained recovery could well be aborted as this process is repeated.

RICARDIAN RENT AND STAGNATION – THEN AND NOW

Let us consider the precise form of Ricardo's pessimism about long-term growth prospects. Each owner of land – of 'the natural and inexhaustible powers of the soil' – draws rent, reflecting in value the difference between the productivity of the land he owns, and that of the piece of land that is only just worth using, i.e. that just produces enough to pay the subsistence wage, normal profit, and no rent. Now, as output and income rise, so does demand for the product of land. Hence worse land is drawn into use. The gap between the productivity of good land and of land just worth using goes up; and so, therefore, does rent. With the wage-rate fixed – by custom, subsistence, unions or whatever – the pushing out of cultivation on to worse marginal land (i.e land earning no rent) cannot lead to lower wage-rates on that land; it is the profit rate, there and in every other use, that must fall. 'Rents ... are enjoyed necessarily ... at the expense of the profits of stock'.[13]

The forces that, for Ricardo, push down profit *rates* as rents rise, are reinforced by considerations – for today's economists, though not for

Ricardo, plausibly reduced to price elasticities and accounting identities[14] – that push down profit *shares*. In Ricardo's Britain, most landowners were not entrepreneurial farmers (these were tenants); and in Ricardian models, long-run average wage-rates, being fixed at subsistence, cannot fall if rents rise as a share of GNP. Therefore when growth pulls up the share of rent and thus of landowners, the same process (by drawing into cultivation ever worse intra-marginal land)[15] must pull down the share of GNP enjoyed by both manufacturers and (tenant) farmers. This reduction in the *share* of profit in GNP, and hence (relative to GNP) in the ability to self-finance investment and subsequent growth, accompanies the fall in the *rate* of profit, the inducement to invest; both cut the growth rate. 'Cultivation is extended, and rents rise – and profits then fall ... Profits are the fund from which all rent is derived'. But for this shift to rent, 'greater profits would lead to further accumulation ... [and] ameliorate the condition of the labouring classes'.[16]

There are, in fact, three ways in which accumulation is squeezed, in Ricardo's model, as growth pushes up differential rent. The first way is by the direct erosion of profits, because, given GNP, the extra rent cannot come out of (subsistence) wage-rates of (fixed full) employment levels; we, like Ricardo, have concentrated on this. The second way is that a growing labour-force, working on worse and worse new farmland, needs ever more labour time per unit of corn produced. On the marginal unit of land, where differential rent is zero by definition, profitability is therefore cut by the need to pay the subsistence wage to more man-hours per unit of corn grown, leaving a smaller part of that unit as profits.[17] The rate of profit on capital being everywhere equal, this downward pressure on profitability in marginal farming is communicated to all other sectors also. The third force squeezing accumulation is that the first two effects, apart from reducing the *funds* available for it, also reduce the *incentives* to undertake it; with profitability lower, the capitalist is encouraged to use a larger proportion of his surplus to acquire land (and claims upon rent), or to consume, rather than to accumulate productive assets.

If we move from a British to a world scale, this surely sounds surprisingly like the experience of 1973–81. So clear, indeed, was Ricardo that rents on land for *mining* were governed by a 'principle precisely the same as that which we have already laid down respecting land' for *farming*, that two pages are all he devotes to the upward pressure of growth upon the rent of mining land (at the cost of profits overall) in the *Principles*.[18]

What does the analogy tell us about the recession now? Before we answer, the Ricardian fear that growth would be choked off by income transfer from profits to rents, must be decomposed into two parts: the supply part, described above; and a set of fledgling worries about demand, tempered in the *Principles* by an increasingly firm belief in the long-run operation of Say's Law. Ricardo's main concern, however, was always supply side: that growth of output and income would at best fall, perhaps to a rate below that of population growth, and at worst to zero, as the shift to rent choked down the rate (and share) of profit, and thus the incentive (and capacity) to invest.[19] While Ricardo was not a stagnationist, his view of the effects of the threefold squeeze on profits was quite gloomy. 'Only improvements in machinery' can check the 'tendency for the profits ... to fall' until the fall has 'arrested all accumulation'.[20] The 'motive for accumulation will diminish with every diminution of profit'.[21] Growth swells rent; extra rent reduces profit; reduced profit reduces the incentive and capacity to supply. This triple squeeze on profits – Ricardo's supply-side fear about the effects of rising differential rent – needs both a Marshallian and a Keynesian gloss. Only then can it be clearly related to the (possible) continuing (albeit interrupted) recession since 1973.

The Marshallian gloss is that the realism of the fear depends on the lowness of two elasticities. First is the price elasticity of supply of land; if the supply of land were very price elastic, then extra land could be drawn into cultivation (or oil-bearing) that was only little worse than land already used, so that growth would not raise rent much. Second is the elasticity of substitution between land and (a) labour and (b) capital; unless that is low, growth in demand for the products of land – food or oil – could be satisfied, with a slight deterioration in the average returns to inputs, by operating existing land (in farms or oilfields) with slightly more (a) workers of (b) equipment. Indeed, those who do *not* believe in a long 'Ricardian' post-OPEC recession argue against either or both of the elasticities. They thereby claim, by implication, that price responsiveness since 1973 has rendered the growth of income in oil-importing countries much less oil-intensive.[22]

The Keynesian gloss is that Ricardo's account is a prototype of Keynes's discussion of the dependence of the inducement to invest upon the marginal efficiency of capital. For Keynes 'the *expectation* of yield' as a proportion of 'the *current* price of the capital-asset', as compared to the market rate of interest, determines the rate of accumulation.[23] Of course, Ricardo did not believe that a reduced 'expectation of yield' could produce general glut, or recession for long – merely temporary distress due to 'sudden changes in the channels of trade'. Ricardo believed in Say's Law. We don't; do we?

* * *

Ricardo's first reason, then, for fearing that a shift to rent would reduce growth related to the effects via the supply of output. The fall in the normal *rate* of profit reduces the entrepreneur's *incentive to supply* output, and to accumulate capital for that purpose. The shift to rent in the *share* of output reduces his surplus and hence *ability to supply* output, and to accumulate capital for that purpose. Ricardo's second reason is on the side of *demand* for outputs.

At least in his early work, Ricardo's attachment to Say's Law cannot silence his fears that farm (or oil?) land-rentiers may be less entrepreneurial, more conservative, less prone to recycle, than the farmers or manufacturers from whom they gain income as rents are raised by growth plus diminishing returns to land. Even 'if the demand for home commodities should be [increased] because of the [rise] of rent on the part of the landlord, it will be [diminished] *in a far greater degree* by the [diminished] opulence of the commercial classes'.[24] If income is redistributed from rentiers to capitalists, however, 'the same capital would employ more hands'.[25] Because of Ricardo's faith in Say's Law, however, any diminution of growth via such demand-side effects must for him be short-run;[26] we cannot share that confidence.

It is therefore important to ask how income redistribution (from profit to rent)[27] affects demand. Rentiers in England in 1780–1820 seemed to be much more likely than capitalists to lock up their surpluses into the 'improvement' of stately homes or demesnes. Today's oil rentiers seem to some, relatively likely to put surpluses into property also – and into luxurious airports such as Lagos, or into the tables of Monte Carlo. More seriously, suddenly enriched rentiers are much more prone than entrepreneurs to embody their surpluses in ultra-conservative, relatively unproductive, yet unstable forms of saving or recycling, i.e. seven-day bank deposits, and to over-concentrate recycled resources into familiar, individually safe-looking, yet cumulatively overcrowded and *unsafe* forms of assets. (The alleged 'import surplus of OPEC' since 1982 is a statistical illusion as regards the main oil exporters).[28]

The supply-side aspect of Ricardo's fear – the discouragement of investment and output by reduced profit rates and shares, following the shift to rent – is a deep threat to global recovery. The deterrents to expansion, constituted by the ever-present *danger* of oil (and oil-derivative) price rises whenever Western or Third World GNP accelerates, are unlikely to be overcome until we learn to expand GNP at a much lower unit cost in terms of fossil fuel.[29] Yet industrial market economies' imports of commercial energy rose from 1.4 per cent of GDP in 1960 to 5.8 per cent in 1980 – proportions probably about doubled if energy embodied in other imports is included. For middle-income oil importers, the proportion rose from 1.9 per cent to 7.8 per cent. On top of that, such economies as the USA and the UK had to divert further GNP to oil-land rents (and to high-cost drilling) domestically. By volume, the proportion of oil in global energy use was the same in 1980 as in 1960 – 45.8 per cent.[30]

It is, however, the demand-side effects of a shift to rent – for Ricardo, mere short-term adjustment problems, albeit aggravated by such policy errors as the Corn Laws – that for us, after 1973 – 84, must appear as the immediate (as opposed to the deep) threat, posed that shift, of prolonged or deepened recession. This is despite the fact that the delays and distortions in the transmission of extra monetary demand, caused by the shift of income from entrepreneurs to conservative rentiers, are more amenable than the supply-side problems to intelligent intermediation.[31] However, these demand-side problems of the shift to rent have been exacerbated, since about 1978, by a series of banking and policy decisions and indecisions, culminating in the failure – even in the aftermath of quasi-defaults across Latin America and Eastern Europe – to set up clearly specified lender-of-last-resort facilities for banks in respect of their international operations.[32]

FARMLAND RENTS DIDN'T STIFLE GROWTH: WHY SHOULD OIL RENTS?

Why, you may wonder, is there all this fuss about rent? If the oil-lords' gains since 1973 do no more harm to growth than did the farm-lords' gains after 1815, then surely we have nothing to fear? Indeed, twenty-three years after Ricardo died, his persuasion bore fruit in Britain's repeal of the Corn Laws.[33] At least until the 1880s, the westward expansion of the North American land frontier brought into use – to meet the growing demand for food and fibres, generated partly by European economic growth – new land almost as productive as the old. Rents in Europe and North America therefore showed little or no tendency to rise relative to profits.[34] From the 1880s to the 1980s, as the *extensive* margin of land became costlier to push out, two new factors exorcised Ricardo's rent demon. First, the supply of farmland in efficiency units was raised by a series of dramatically land-saving techniques that cheapened the process of pushing out the *intensive* margin: first, guano; then, fertilisers; later, improved seeds.[35] Second, growth in demand for farmland was slowed down by a steadily falling marginal propensity to consume food and fibres, and by non-land-based replacements for many fibres (and now perhaps some foods, e.g. sugar?)[36]

So neither British nor Western growth was anything like as hard hit by shifts from profit to farmland rent as Ricardo feared. If Britain could outwit the farm landlords in the short run by freeing the importation of grain from the USA, and if the West could do the same in the long run, as new science came on stream and generated technologies that responded to incentives to save land,[37] cannot transfers of rent from entrepreneurs to oil landlords be restrained by analogous or other procedures? Of course, the very fact that this question is interesting in itself confirms the contemporary power of Ricardo's analysis, despite the fact that Ricardo's successors for 150 years avoided its worst predictions.

To seek remedies in *simple* analogies to post-Ricardian experience, however, does not work. Britain could repeal the Corn Laws; the world cannot usefully reduce tariffs on oil imports from Mars. Eleven years after the first oil shock, there is no really convincing sign of a new energy science that might produce a stream of land-saving inventions that could be used by innovators to stem the rise in rents to oil-bearing land, as Mendelian plant genetics has stemmed the rise in rents to farmland. However, exploring similarities and differences between the transactions (and transactors) – in farmland rents as possible 'limits to growth' in Britain then, in oil-lands rents in the world now – will help us to grasp the reasons why durable recovery from the current recession is likely to prove difficult. That will avoid false solutions, such as 'breaching the OPEC cartel' (if events do not achieve that anyway). In 1973 and 1979, OPEC merely caught up with market realities. The shift to rent on oil-land as a consequence of growth, and the problems generated by oil landlords' limited propensities to consume do not depend for their profit-squeezing power upon the vagaries of market structure, although these can indeed make things even more difficult.

GENERAL ANALOGIES: SCALE AND TRACTABILITY OF FOOD VS OIL THREATS

In what respects are the dangers of 'continuing recession' more (or less) serious, with regard to the international shift of income to OPEC oil-lands since 1973, than with regard to the *intra*-national shift of income to UK farmland that Ricardo feared between 1813 and 1823? That is really three questions. First, in *general*, do we face a bigger or smaller, more or less tractable threat? Second, is the *logical* structure of that threat different? Third, are the *specific* parameter values, affecting the production-side and demand-side recessionary impacts, more or less favourable?

In three *general* ways, we are misled into thinking the new oil-rent threat is smaller or more tractable than was the old food-rent threat. First, we do have Ricardo's powerful analysis of real transfer effects to alert us to the danger. We seem, however, to be making rather little use of that advantage. Most of the monetarist – Keynesian controversies about stagflation totally ignore Ricardo's prescient analysis, in 1813–23, of a situation analogous to that confronting most non-oil entrepreneurs world-wide since 1973.[38]

Indeed, most Keynesians *and* monetarists deny that the sevenfold rise in real oil prices in 1972–81 (reduced in 1982–3 to about sixfold)[39] had anything 'fundamental' (blessed word!) to do with stagflation. Even many factual accounts of Western inflation,[40] profit erosion, and unemployment grossly underplay the sharp *discontinuities* of late 1973 and 1979–80, as real income transfers to oil landlords at once deflated Western monetary demand and inflated costs of production. The general and rather confused view is that in 1968–74 – *à la mode de* Joseph Heller – 'something happened' to turn Phillips curves vertical, worsen inflationary expectations, reduce the marginal efficiency of investment, and lower the price elasticity of supply of real output in the West. By some unexplained black magic, the Keynesian policies of 1945–68 are supposed to have stopped working, and those who see oil price rises as crucial are dismissed as naive by most professional economists. Yet obviously these rises *both* transferred effective demand from the rest of the world to OPEC, *and* pushed up production and consumption costs and derived wage costs: stag and flation respectively.

The second respect in which we *ought* to be better off than in Ricardo's day in handling a rent-induced recession is in the greater scope and sophistication of public policy. Rents should be channelled more smoothly to investible funds now than then; since Bagehot, central banks are somewhat more acceptable as supervisors of recycling processes. And, upto a point, Sweden and Austria have shown than even 'distributional coalitions' can be got to bargain centrally in order, in effect, to agree the allocation of a fall in real income.[41]

However, many developed countries have worsened their stagflations in an endless attempt to pass those falls among interest groups. And international organisations, in offering temporary accommodation to a less developed debtor country, often impose conditions that compel it to meet obligations by severe contraction that further reduces world demand, including demand for exports from *other* debtor nations.

Our third apparent advantage over Ricardo's contemporaries, in handling a rent-induced recession, is arithmetical. In the early nineteenth century, even the richest country, Britain, spent perhaps 40 per cent of income on land-based food and fibres; but below 10 per cent of Western GNP, and below 6 per cent of GNP in low-income countries, is even now spent directly or indirectly on energy imports.[42] Surely, growth of income *now* will be much less significantly diverted to them than was growth of income *then* to food and fibres?

Unfortunately, the arithmetic is much less favourable than it seems, for three reasons. (1) Then, large parts of extra income, spent on food and fibres, went not to rent but instead (a) to extra farm profits (even if the profit *rates* fell as Ricardo predicted, or at least did not rise), (b) to pay extra farm *workers* (even if one believes in a constant psychological subsistence wage-*rate*), since marginal farm output was still very labour-intensive; but today almost all OPEC income is presumably rent. (2) Then, the US land frontier meant that the freeing of trade in agriculture goods, e.g. by Britain's 1846 Corn Law Repeal, could permit acquisition of such goods for many years with only very slow rises along any given curve of marginal cost. Now, no such cheap options have been apparent for oil purchases since 1973. (3) Then, massive technical progress in agricultural production and marketing – fertilisers and refrigeration respectively – was in 1870–1913, by pushing the marginal cost curve sharply down, to justify even further Ricardo's belief that the rentiers could be made to disgorge their gains, if only free trade were put to work upon medium-term supply elasticities. Now, neither nuclear nor non-conventional power sources as yet appear to offer such prospects.

LOGICAL STRUCTURE OF OIL THREAT VS FOOD THREAT

So we do not seem to have general advantages in handling oil rent, related to the size or tractability of the threat to non-rent incomes, that the post-Ricardians did not enjoy in their encounter with the threat of recession from rising farm rent. There is, however, another possible sort of overall advantage or disadvantage we might have (as opposed to the question of whether 'our' specific parameter values are more or less favourable than theirs: see the next section). The logical structure of the problems might differ, in three possible ways.

First, food from farmland is the basic wage-good, but farm output is not a *major* direct input into 'Western' output; conversely, oil and its derivatives are not such important wage-goods, but are a key direct input into most other 'Western' production. Second, the class relationships between farm-lords, entrepreneurs and workers in nineteenth-century Britain – and hence the potential flows of funds among classes – were structually different from the relationships and flows between oil-lords, entrepreneurs and workers in the world since 1973. Third, a huge group of nations with differently structured demands and supplies from *either* farm and oil-land rentiers on the one hand, *or* Western entrepreneurs on the other – the oil-deficit LDCs – complicates today's OPEC-DC relationship. Conversely, the colonies were a *relatively* unimportant factor in the relationships between farm-lords and entrepreneurs within the leading nineteenth-century industrial nations.

* * *

We have seen (note 17) that Ricardo is fully aware that there are many wage-goods, and does not structure his model on the assumption of a pure corn-wage. However, he does sometimes seem to regard the role of food as the archetypical wage-good as crucial to the operation of the rent squeeze on growth. 'There are *no* causes which will for any [substantial] length of time make capital less in demand, however abundant it may become, but a comparatively high price of food and labour ... *Demand for capital [is only] checked by* the rise in the price of food, and *the consequent increase in the value of labour'*.[43] If that were so, 'rent of mines', including oil-wells, could not cause recession for any long period. However, Ricardo's remark must surely be read as to some extent rhetorical. If *only* dear food can cause recession, and that *only* by making it less attractive for capitalists to employ labour, then on Ricardo's own account rising rents cannot cause recession; for Ricardo insists that high rent is entirely the effect of a high price of food, and in no way a cause of it.

In Ricardo's Britain – and much more in, say, rural India now – it was perhaps plausible to define a subsistence corn-wage-rate, dependent wholly on the price of corn. Not only does growth push up the land cost of marginal corn production (causing higher rent), but this rising cost then pushes up the amount of cash needed to pay a subsistence wage-rate. The latter effect lowers profitability, because the money wage-bill absorbs a larger share of the value of sales. So the need to give up profits, just to maintain real wages after corn gets dearer, is an *extra* squeeze on investment in the non-corn sector. But it is not the *only* squeeze. Reduced profit rates and profit shares, caused respectively by the rising rent-per-acre and rent/GNP ratio as cultivation is expanded, would squeeze the incentive and the capacity to invest, even if the products of land were brought only by capitalists and thus did not, by getting dearer, drive up money wages. That is crucial now: oil is closer to being a producer good than a consumer good.

Indeed, the fact that oil is 'less of a wage-good' than corn does little to exorcise the rent demon, for three reasons. First, just as there was a Ricardian double squeeze on investment when profitability fell (with a shift to farm rents) *and* money wage-rates rose (because of dearer food), so there is a 'Yamanian' double squeeze when profitability falls (with a shift to oil rents) *and* input costs of future production rise (because of dearer oil). Second, oil does enter into the costs of wage-goods. Third, real wage-rates have proved almost incompressible in many developed countries during the oil squeeze, not because they are at 'subsistence', but because the real wage-rates of major groups of workers are for various reasons (state employment, social security cushion, non-competing groups) not highly responsive to generally rising unemployment. Hence the rise in oil rents consequent on the rise in the price of oil – the archetypical producer good, but something of a wage-good too – has compressed profits in a two-sided squeeze, just as Ricardo analysed out for a rise in farm rents consequent on a rise in the demand for food, the archetypical wage-good.

* * *

The class relationships in Ricardo's England were perhaps more special than Ricardo made explicit, in respect of their interaction with his rent theory. To what extent does the danger of rent-induced recession rest on assuming what are *contingent* facts: that – with regard indeed to farmland in Ricardo's England, but much more dubiously to oil-land in today's world – landowners, capitalist (tenant) land-users, capitalist manufacturers, land labourers, and industrial labourers are largely separate, immobile groups?

Certainly, integration of these classes reduces the risk of prolonged recession. For example, in nineteenth-century America and much of continental Europe, farming entrepreneurs were much more often also landowners than in England. Hence, when land-rent rose, each farmer-entrepreneur would have both the extra cash and the inducement to invest in land improvement. Similarly, rising oil prices impinge on oil landlords who are also – increasingly with the takeovers of company interests, or increases in royalties, by OPEC countries – oil entrepreneurs too. However, if the fact that many oil landlords are also oil entrepreneurs eases the financing of the new exploration on existing oil lands, it also eases the construction of monopolies, combining oil landlord and oil entrepreneur interest, to restrict output. So the class unity of landlord and entrepreneur can do more harm (by *preventing* more land-intensive output) than good (by *financing* it).

This is made worse in three ways. First, despite all the propaganda, oil has turned out to be price inelastic (given buyers' income!) in the medium term – much more so than food was in Ricardo's England. (Oil prices in real terms are substantially higher now, for oil importers weighted by import volumes, than in the alleged peak of 1980; dollar appreciation, plus the denomination of oil prices in dollars, has hidden the real impact of, in effect, a 'third oil shock' in the wake of the 1983–4 boomlet.)[44] Second, obviously, a few oil landlord-entrepreneur-countries have found it easier to act together in restraint of output than thousands of farm landlords could ever do. Third, the 1973–4 and 1979–80 'oil shocks' were worse than the gradual 'rent shocks' that troubled Ricardo and Malthus, because the more recent experiences were compounded by (a) a high degree of landlord cartelisation, (b) sudden catch-ups by the cartel of gradual, but unrealised, rises in *potential* differential rent, combined with (c) rising entrepreneurial incomes for the landlords themselves, who increasingly also managed the oil wells.

So the unification, to some extent, of oil landlords and oil entrepreneurs, and the small number of the former, make class relations in the 1973–85 world sequence *more* conducive to the stifling of growth via a shift of GNP share away from non-oil profits, than were class relations in the 1776–1846 British sequence to the stifling of growth via a GNP shift away from non-farm and farm profits.

A second major difference in the relative importance of classes between two sequences also appears to worsen the prospects of revived growth now. Certainly after 1846 – some would argue even sooner – the assumption, shared by Malthus and Ricardo, that growth in real demand could not raise wage-rates above a set 'psychological subsistence' (PS) clearly began to break down. In particular, extra demand for food 'leaked' into higher derived demand for a supply of farm labour that was not, as the classical economists had assumed, infinitely price elastic at the set PS wage-rate. Increasing proportions of these rising wages, during growth, were used to buy non-farm products (Engels' Law). This, in turn, increased the fixed capital that it was profitable to accumulate in non-farm production. This process of reviving the profit share, and hence growth, by dropping the PS assumption and allowing farmworkers' demand for non-farm output to rise as more food is produced, must in practice have been quite a powerful 'cure' for the damage done to non-farm profits, by the fact that growing this extra food implied a shift to differential rent. Of course, in today's world, the growth in differential oil rent to OPEC is vastly in excess of growth in the wages of oil labour. (Indeed, it is more often argued that the 'continuing recession' will be cured by OECD profit recovery due to real-wage *falls* in OECD – a declining PS – than by wage-demand *rises* (from a rising PS in OPEC) transmitted to OECD products. We return to this former argument later.) Clearly, however, oil and most of its substitutes are produced with little labour per unit of output. Recirculation of demand via extra labour income is far less important in modifying the oil rent story now than it was in modifying the farm rent story then.

The final class relationship to consider is that between rentiers and *non-land-based* entrepreneurs. In 1850–1900 Western landowners – British 'pure landlords' as well as Prussian Junkers – reinvested much of their landed income into industrial entrepreneurship.[45] Such class integration is much rarer for today's oil landlords. To the large and, since 1970, greatly increased extent that oil-land rents are retained by bargaining OPEC governments, the reflux into entrepreneurship is small and indirect. It is limited at home by the size and absorptive capacity of oil-producing nations. Most seriously, the reflux is limited, destabilised, and perhaps made inefficient abroad by the fact that banking intermediation (for all its luxuriant growth) is not developed to meet the drastically new requirements of diversified 'recycling', from a highly localised class of almost pure rentiers, to finance world-wide entrepreneurship. It finances largely expanded consumption backed by 'sovereign risk guarantees'.

* * *

So two of the structural differences between Then and Now – wage-goods vs producer goods and the balance among classes – are not very favourable to our prospects of escape from Ricardo's trap. The third structural difference, *if intelligently handled* (it is hard to see how it can be 'left to the market', whether or not that would be a good thing), gives more reason for optimism. This difference is the emergence of Third World demand as a far more independent force, in the response to rent-related and other price changes, than was 'colonial' demand in Ricardo's day.

Extra income in developing countries is, in several respects, less likely to trigger further rises in rental incomes from oil-lands than is extra income in rich countries. First, a much larger proportion of extra LDC income is spent on food, producible (largely by entrepreneur-farmer workers owning their own land) within LDCs even now by non-oil-intensive means, compared to extra production of food in DCs, or non-food in LDCs. Second, even extra non-food demand is normally met in a more labour-intensive, fossil-energy-extensive way within LDCs than within rich countries.

Third, it is plausible (though not proven) that, inasmuch as the extra LDC income generates extra demand for DC products, such extra demand is more likely than is extra DC demand (domestic or foreign) to be for producer goods – and, therefore, to concentrate in ultra-deflated, accelerator-prone producer goods sectors and regions of DC economies. This has always been the main argument, that Brandtian 'massive transfers' are more acceptable than 'any old' demand reflation. The claim is that the first-round effects of extra DC demand, induced during recession by extra LDC orders, are likely to embody a higher ratio of extra real output to extra price inflation than are the first-round effects of general monetary or fiscal expansion. Also, because they draw on spare capacity rather than on new investment, the energy requirements of such marginal demand may well be smaller.[46]

In default of empirical work, it is not easy to see how high these three cats will jump. Clearly, however, they give the international economy *further degrees of freedom* in escaping a world, neo-Ricardian trap of oil rent-induced 'limits to growth': a trap considerably tougher than the farmland rent trap that once seemed to face Britain. LDC demand expansion – certainly if internal, probably if devoted to imports (substantially from the most depressed suppliers in DCs) – has great potential for reflating the world economy in ways that transfer relatively less of the extra income to oil-lords' rent.

Of course, if LDC demand expansion is in inappropriate sectors – either because of price incentives (market or 'fixed') or because of grandiose planning – this transfer could happen after all. The extremely oil-intensive leakage of extra GNP to 'defence' spending – or even to war-making – is a clear-cut example. Less familiar is the imbalance between transport and production growth. For example, sub-Saharan

Africa produced 14 – 15 per cent less food per person in 1980–3 than in 1970–3.[47] Massive investments in African smallholder agricultures, water development and economically tested biological and chemical research are clearly indicated – not only, of course, because relatively little oil would be used in producing current output from such investments. They are not happening. Instead, in the context of ECA's 'Transport and Communications Decade' for Africa, during 1980–3 $6.7bn was secured for trans-African 'super-highways'. These link places currently with low aggregate supply elasticities, more readily and more petrol-intensively to each other, and subsidise access to them by the oil-intensive and capital-intensive mass-producing agricultures and industries of Europe (and white South Africa). A further $33bn is scheduled for the African super-highway spending by 1988.[48] *Quem deus vult perdere, prius demetat.*

SPECIFIC PARAMETER VALUES

So we seem to have no general advantage in the 1980s, as compared to 1776 – 1846, in handling the recessionary impact, feared by Ricardo, of a shift from profit to rent. The logical structure of the problem is less favourable, except in the important respect that LDC demand expansion provides new degrees of freedom for forms of recovery that may reduce, per unit of extra output, the extra demand for oil. But those new options are not being intelligently used. Are the *specific* parameters, then, more favourable to world growth with oil rent-avoidance now, than to British growth with food rent-avoidance then? This discussion can do no more than throw out, for empirical research, a few suggestions.

On the production side, there are five relevant comparisons.
1. What is the impact of 'typical' extra income and output on the demand for oil now, compared with demand for food and fibres then?
2. What is the share of rent in *initial* incomes of oil factors of production now, compared with the share for food-and-fibres producers then?
3. To what extent, in the two situations, would *extra* world demand swiftly call forth, in the marketplace or via managed research, improved ways of obtaining the extra products of 'the natural powers of the soil' without significantly transferring income to rent?
4. How adaptable are production and energy (or in 1776–1846, food) technologies, to cut the energy (or food) costs of growth?

5. Could downward adjustability of the wage share in GNP (in response to a given rise in rent) modify the normal decline in profitability?

1. First, oil exporters may keep rather less of the fruits of growth now than did food-growers then. Admittedly, the income elasticity of direct and derived demand for oil is typically above unity, whereas, for food and fibres in 1815–46, it could hardly have exceeded 0.7 world-wide. On the other hand, the proportion of world GNP spent on oil now is much lower than that spent on food and fibres then, even in Britain, certainly world wide. On balance, world growth diverts a smaller proportion of extra demand to oil factors now than it did to food-and-fibre factors then. However, the oil suppliers are cartelised (albeit imperfectly) as the food-and-fibre factors were not. Moreover, the great mass of world GNP – and therefore of the absolute value of its growth – is and was concentrated in countries that, as a whole, produce a large proportion of their own food and fibres, but a much smaller proportion of their own fossil fuel energy. Hence, if growing world demand led to windfall gains by landowners (or other agricultural factors) due to some residual monopoly power, those gains could to some extent be taxed (e.g. on Henry George lines), or otherwise removed, by action within *national* borders against domestic food-lords then. That is infeasible against *foreign* oil-lords now.

2. Second, rent is a much larger part of oil producers' income now, than of food-and-fibre producers' income then. Far smaller parts of the earth's surface can produce oil than crops. The proportionate gaps between unit production costs on average land in current use, and on marginal land, are much greater for oil. And, partly for these reasons, oil producers are much better able to act together to curtail production and maintain rent. It is fallacious (note 22) to see an 'easy way out' for countries such as Britain that, after 1973, could develop alternative oil sources; the GNP costs of such development, even if less than those of paying the differential rent to OPEC, were substantial still.

3. Third, these differences favour oil producers now (over food-and-fibre producers then) even more sharply in respect of the rent response to *expanded* demand, notably during recovery from recession. Even given the technology, nineteenth-century food output could expand – in North America and Australia – with very slow, if any, rise in average cost of production, or fall in efficiency of land; but marginal cost, as oil output shifts from (say) Saudi Arabia, through the North Sea, to the Athabaska tar sands, rises in steep, discontinuous steps. OPEC's extra

growth-induced income consists overwhelmingly of rent, which must press upon world wages or profits. It is quite wrong to infer from technical responses to dearer oil which permit a lower *average* ratio of oil rent to GNP, that the *marginal* propensity to consume oil (or increasingly costly substitutes) as income grows has fallen similarly.

4. The question of technical adaptablity is the most speculative. As Popper has pointed out, if we could correctly predict technical progress we could make it sooner. If we cannot predict it, how can we predict its speed of impact?[49] Ricardo, and indeed Malthus, proved too gloomy in the long run because – in face of impending scarcity of food-land – science proved more inventive, and technology more responsive, than had seemed remotely possible. Today (despite all the talk of conservation), it remains to be seen whether the requirements of extra fossil-fuel energy, per 1 per cent of extra *full capacity* GNP generated, are indeed significantly less than in 1972. Third World industrialisation (and agricultural energy intensification) may or may not be offset by conservation, fuel substitution, and fuel efficiency improvement in developed countries, and world growth at near capacity, which we have not experienced since 1973, would accelerate both these Third World processes. Despite all the talk of new energy sources (or of, for example, replacing fossil fuel by atmospheric nitrogen in fertilisation), it is not clear that there has been any major shift from oil or from fossil fuels in general, in the way that full capacity growth is related to extra energy demand. Yet with real oil prices still over six times 1972 levels, a large shift seems to be required to offset price rises on the 1979–80 pattern sufficiently to maintain future full capacity growth, i.e. to avoid its self-destructive leakage into oil rent. Of course, if the extra world demand were itself restructured towards production and income (especially for self-consumption) by the LDCs' rural poor, that would itself reduce the impact of growth on oil rents. But this is not happening.

5. One plausible route towards restoration of the rate and share of profits, whose reduction through higher rents renders future investment for growth, respectively, less attractive to undertake and less feasible to pay for, is by variations in wage-rates. Ricardo assumed that no wages were saved; relaxing that assumption (and in policy matters seeking to raise the savings/wages ratio) is more plausible at 1980s than at 1810–20 wage-levels, but would in most rich countries still do little to replace the lost *capacity* of entrepreneurs to finance investment, and nothing to restore the *attractiveness* (profitability) of doing so.

More plausibly, we can drop Ricardo's other, central wage assumption: that the wage-*rate* covered a psychologically non-compressible return to labour time, and was to be multiplied by normal ('full') employment level, to estimate the wage *share*. The notion of 'psychological subsistence' is much less credible today than in Ricardo's time, at least in OECD countries. Hence it is commonly argued that market systems will — or that governments actively should — seek to restore both the rate and the share of profits by so operating as to reduce either the (real) wage-rate or the wage share, thereby restoring both the profitability and the 'affordability' of investment.

In this context, comparisons are commonly made between the USA, where a declining real wage-rate since 1973 has allegedly permitted a response to recession that involves only brief and small rises in unemployment, and Western Europe — particularly the UK — where 'union power' is supposed to have led, via real wage rigidity, to substantial rises in unemployment. This is a naive view. Higher US employment rates owe much to reflationary policies, especially after 1979–80, which European countries chose to avoid. The impact of higher money wages upon aggregate demand, while outside Ricardo's universe, cannot be dismissed so readily. Probably, too, the scramble to restore oil-squeezed profits by compressing the wage share — with public subsidies to technologies and research that might 'help' — bears considerable blame for the upsurge in unemployment in OECD since 1979.

DEMAND PARAMETERS, REFLUX AND DEBT

Whatever rent-receivers do with their extra share of GNP, the fact that they receive it suffices to erode the entrepreneur's *incentive to invest profitably*. However, if rent-receivers promptly place their extra incomes, via smoothly functioning capital markets, where entrepreneurs can borrow them, then at least those entrepreneurs — although still discouraged from investing by a lower, rent-drained, rate of profit — do not lose any *capacity to invest*. In this sense, the demand of rent-receivers for different sorts of asset is critical.

As we have seen (note 24), Ricardo explicitly feared that — apart from the erosion of profit incentives when growth raised rent — the way that surpluses were used *after* transfer to the rentier would mean that they supported less investment, and less demand for labour, than when those surpluses had stayed with the entrepreneur. I doubt that this was a major barrier to growth in nineteenth-century Europe or North America.

Growth happened anyway. Therefore, either the shift to rent was not very big, or the rentiers reinvested (or lent to those who did), or investment was not greatly constrained by finance: the answer is probably a bit of each. Today's debt mess, while worsened by the incomplete response of *central* banking to internationalisation of *commercial* banking,[50] is, in essence, a sign of the absence of sufficient, appropriate channels (and/or will) for the reflux of rentiers' extra demand into the supply of risk capital to entrepreneurs.

European receivers of farm rents, after all, were much less isolated from general commerce than Ricardo's demand-side fears might suggest. They lived in the same local communities as businessmen; they kept their money in the same banks from which local businessmen borrowed; in England, those banks 'branched' to connect the rentiers' savings with distant businessmen. Of course, banks made errors, contracted lending or even went bankrupt, and spread recession. These grave consequences were not much ameliorated, despite successive 'banking crises', until the 1870s in England (in the aftermath of Bagehot's *Lombard Street*) and the mid-1930s in the USA (in the aftermath of the response, via the Federal Deposit Insurance Corporation, to the wave of bank failures in the Depression). The point, however, is not that recycling from land rents to investment finance was perfectly managed, but that errors were, in time, handled.

In 1976 or so, it might have been argued that this also applied to the recycling of oil rents. Yet the seeds of today's debt crisis – the reliance on sovereign repayment, the concentration of lending on a few countries, the general unconcern for the embodiment of loans in productive projects – were already there. So, most basically, were (a) the lack of direct liaison between the new sources of surplus and the areas and activities where banks placed their money, (b) the lack of international lender-of-last-resort facilities, and (c) above all, the high risk of new oil price rises, and new stresses on the recycling mechanisms, once sustained recovery began. All these chickens came home to roost after 1978, and are still depositing guano over all and sundry.

We should not be taken in by claims that the debt crisis is not in its scale historically new. The debt service ratio for *all* developing countries was 20.7 per cent at the end of 1983.[51] It was 28.3 per cent for low-income Africa, and 53.2 per cent for oil importers in Latin America at the end of 1982. Yet in 1965–76 even a 20 per cent ratio, for any *one* developing country, carried a four in ten risk of repayment difficulties.[52]

It is hard to accept denials that this debt expansion was needed largely because of the increased extraction of oil rent, and financed substantially by the placement of such rent. The data are obscure, largely because several billions of dollars in OPEC interest receipts are unaccounted for.[53] But it speaks for itself that of $86 bn current account deficits among oil-importing LDCs in 1981, $68 bn comprised the oil deficit in 1981, as against 'only' $27 bn (of $33 bn deficit) in 1978.[54] Of course rising real interest rates – in large part the result of an attempt by developed countries to control money supply without restraining government demand for money – worsened the LDCs' repayment difficulties (hence the sharp fall in new lending to them); so did the persistently low prices of some commodities, the rising dollar (the main unit of repayment), and the embodiment of lending to some LDCs in unviable investment, or in consumption. However, the loss of confidence by banks in their power to retain and attract deposits, if these are on-lent to developing countries, is shown by the virtual collapse of commercial bank lending to most of these countries.

In 1981, the latest available year, three high-income oil exporters – Saudi Arabia, Kuwait and UAE – had current account surpluses totalling over $60 billion. To allow for unrecorded flows of investment income,[55] perhaps $10 – 30bn should be added. Since 1981, oil prices have continued to rise in real terms, alongside rent to OPEC as a share of (non-US) gross entrepreneurial income, although this is concealed by the 'dollar effect'.[56] Moreover, these three 'rentier nations' remain the biggest single potential source of private finance for the balance of payments deficits of developing nations. The allegedly 'vanished oil surplus' is an artefact of unreported OPEC incomes, and of inappropriate aggregation of countries with war deficits (Iran and Iraq), true deficit oil-producers (Mexico) and, remaining, nations in substantial true surplus. Any recovery, after a while, will probably increase the inflow of rent to this surplus group. The banks clearly believe that depositors will not wish them to intermediate the use of such rents, unless they reduce their exposure to LDCs. Drastically, they have done so, despite strong pressure from the IMF, and despite the obvious risks that such action may promote overt default.

Meanwhile, the extreme concentration, among banks as well as countries, of 'development debts' has highlighted the weaknesses and dangers inherent in the current methods of recycling – and de-cycling. Massive flows, or bubbles, of sovereign debt have been massively retrenched. Dramatic claims are often made that two or three countries could destroy, by overt default, large parts of Western banking. The truth is less acute, but more chronic. An unanticipated rescheduling, even if agreed with smiles, erodes the cash base, in the same way as an open default does. In the West as well as the Third World, bank lending has not only become more conservative for any *given* cash base. Also, unanticipated *erosion* of the banks' cash base leads to a multiple reduction in bank lending and in overdraft facilities, compared to what could otherwise have happened. Recovery in activity by firms, not survival by major banks, is the main victim. Domestic monetary policy is fixated upon domestic aggregates (however doubtfully measured); central banks' attitude towards international lender-of-last-resort facilities involves deliberate vagueness (lest over-confidence should cause commercial banks to lend more riskily); and hence no safety-net is in place. Thus recovery is impeded, not only by the shift to rent itself, but by money-multiplier repercussions through the banks (which receive and on-lend the extra rent) if their loans are defaulted or rescheduled unexpectedly.

* * *

Can the world economy resume steady growth? Can we renew the experience of 1950–70, now fashionably mocked as the age of *dirigiste* illusions of demand management, yet in the retrospect a period of outstanding and widely shared economic success – in development, employment and inflation control, not just in growth?

For any durable return to rapid growth, the rent problem must be recognised and tackled. Some reductions in the energy intensity of growth may have been achieved since 1973, but they are probably small ones. They are, moreover, probably due more to the build-up of spare capacity (which means that growth requires less investment) and of unemployment (which enables growth to rely more upon human than on fossil energy) than to conservation, or to innovations in energy. If so, then *full capacity* growth may not have become significantly less oil-intensive, nor therefore, if achieved again, more sustainable in face of Ricardo's demon. Also, the role of oil and natural gas in energy use has not fallen significantly.

Not being a scientist or a prophet, I can't predict the likelihood that future growth will transfer less rent to oil-lords than growth in 1973–84. Perhaps the best hope – and among the most neglected – is the possibility that a larger share of the *initial* demand stimuli may come from non-oil-developing countries. Food production by small farmers there, in particular, is not oil-intensive in respect of beneficiaries' extra demand, nor – compared to alternatives, and despite fertilisers and all that – on the supply side either. And the 'Brandtian effect', of a relatively high ratio of growth to inflation when Third World demand leads to spending in depressed producer goods industries, may be significant.

However, the short-run problems need urgent attention, too, especially if the latter demand pattern is to be initiated. A steady stream of reschedulings, without compensatory monetary policy and without clear international lenders-of-last-resort, must render both banks and depositors not just increasingly reluctant to lend to LDCs, but decreasingly able to expand lending to anybody.

Nor is this excessive reliance on short-run tourniquets of concern only to industrial and middle-income countries. If official flows must go to rescue the Brazils, or even to 'bale out the banks', then – if such flows, concessional plus non-concessional, are restricted in total by aggregate monetary policy – there is less of them for others.

In a sense, Bangladesh is the international lender-of-last-resort.

NOTES

1. This paper is a substantially revised version of a plenary lecture to the Development Studies Association conference at the Institute of Development Studies, Sussex University, in September 1983. I am grateful to David Evans and Donald Winch for helpful and incisive comments. Responsibility for errors remains my own.
2. Shortly after the 1973 oil shock, Paul Streeten, with characteristic economy, remarked to me: 'Economists have high elasticity of expectations, i.e are hysterical'. His own debunking of the commodity-price bandwagon appears in 'The Distribution of the Gains from Trade and Technical Progress', in *The Frontiers of Development Studies* (London: Macmillan, 1972), especially pp. 459–61 and 466–8.
3. D. Ricardo, *Principles of Economics* (ed. D. Winch) (London: Everyman, 1973), Ch. XIX, p. 177. Ricardo stressed that 'temporary periods of distress should not be confused with secular stagnation' (Winch, 'Introduction', pp. xv–xvi).
4. *Ibid.*,Ch. XXI, pp. 192–3: 'M. Say has, however, most satisfactorily shown that there is no amount of capital which may not be employed in a country, because demand is only limited by production. By producing [a man] necessarily becomes either the consumer of his own goods, or the purchaser and consumer of the goods of some other person'.
5. Evidence purporting to show that growth has become less oil-dependent will be discussed below. Pointing the opposite way, the partial recovery of 1983–4 pushed oil prices substantially above the alleged 1980 'peak'; the illusion to the contrary is created by failure to allow for the rising dollar exchange rate, plus the fact that oil is denominated – though not, except by US users, paid for – in dollars. Even if the evidence for a sharp fall in the

marginal propensity to use oil became convincing, a *long-run* rise in the price of fossil fuel, as extraction costs increase – and hence the shift of world product towards rent on the intra-marginal oil-land – seems more than likely. Only a sharp fall in the price of alternative energy sources could offset the Ricardian effects of this. Cross-elasticity of *demand* between fossil fuel and other energy sources, however, is positive. There is little evidence that this is adequately offset by the positive effect on *supply* of non-fossil sources of the higher oil price, e.g by speeding up cost-cutting technical progress in obtaining these sources, or in devising energy-efficient ways to produce or consume.

6. It is not claimed that the shift to oil-rent – and the higher *marginal* oil-rent/profit ratio as GNP rose – was the *only* factor rendering extra production less profitable in response to extra demand. Other factors, notably the increasing strength of *employed* labour, have also tended to reduce the profit share, via both private and 'social' wages. Upward (non-oil) pressures on state expenditure have also tended to reduce post-tax profit shares. But these were gentle trends; OPEC's implementation of its dormant power to extract higher differential rent was sudden, though the rise in that power must have been continuing throughout the post-war boom.

7. T. Balogh, 'Productivity and Inflation', *Oxford Economic Papers*, 1958. For one model with autonomous investment creating a 'floor' below which activity cannot fall in the downswing, See J. Hicks, *A Contribution to the Theory of the Trade Cycle* (Oxford: Oxford University Press, 1950).

8. Charles Cooper has usefully analysed this impact in an unpublished paper to the 1983 (Brighton) Conference of the Development Studies Association. Two comments may be added. First, the built-in stabilisers, especially unemployment insurance, have preserved Western countries from much deeper recession (but made inflation even harder to reverse). However, defence expenditure – because it is capital-intensive and probably oil-intensive – has not had a stimulative effect comparable to that of the former 'floor' on public investment. Second, we are in a fine muddle about interest-rate policy. Probably the US experience in 1982–4 (that very high government deficits plus very high consequent real rates of interest were on balance powerfully inflationary) shows that private investment demand is highly and positively responsive to expected aggregate demand (and hence is 'crowded *in*' by government deficits), but rather inelastic to the cost of borrowing.

9. S. Griffith-Jones and M. Lipton, *International Lenders of Last Resort: Are Changes Required?*, Occasional Papers in International Trade and Finance, Midland Bank International, March 1984.

10. Bank lending to non-OPEC developing countries peaked at about $40bn in 1981 (about $31bn to Latin America), fell in 1982, and in 1983 fell to about $12bn ($9bn). Bank of International Settlements, cited in *The Economist*, 22 September 1984, p. 56.

11. The money multiplier, together with the identity of assets and liabilities, ensures that a contraction in the cash base leads to a multiple contraction in advances.

12. M. Lipton, 'World Depression by Third World Default?', *Bulletin of the Institute of Development Studies*, Vol. 12, No. 2, April 1981.

13. D. Ricardo, Letter to Malthus of 6 February 1815, in P. Sraffa, *Works of David Ricardo*, Vol. VI (Cambridge: Cambridge University Press, 1952), p. 173.
14. We simply write $wL + pK + rA = Q$: wage-rate *times* employment, plus profit-rate *times* 'capital', plus rental *times* area of land in use, equals GNP. If r increases, with w fixed at subsistence, L at full employment, K at capital in use, A at farmed area, and Q at GNP, then p must fall. If r increases because A has risen less than in proportion to K and L, and has pulled up differential rent, the same applies.
15. (a) All this is discussed with reference to the *extensive* margin; Ricardo, of course, made explicit the possibility of similar effects due to expansion at the *intensive* margin. (b) If there is population growth (or, relaxing the full employment assumption, absorption in manufacturing of spare labour time) to raise the requirement for corn, then (pK) in note 14 is squeezed even more.
16. Ricardo, *Notes on Malthus*, in P. Sraffa (ed.), *op. cit.*, Vol. II, 1951, p. 157.
17. In terms of gold, 'increasing labour-cost of producing wage-goods' leads to a falling rate of profit (Winch, *op. cit.*, p. xiv). Oil is unlike corn in that it is not directly a wage-good. Today, however, oil enters heavily, Leontief-wise, into the production of most wage-goods and services (not least corn). 'The mixed wage basket is conspicuous in all the illustrative examples of the central distribution chapters' of Ricardo's *Principles* (S. Hollander, *The Economics of David Ricardo*, London, Heinemann, 1979, p. 257; see also pp. 685–6). It is incorrect to confine Ricardo's analysis of the rent squeeze to effects on corn prices; Ricardo recognised the existence of other wage-goods.
18. Ricardo, *Principles*, pp. 46–7.
19. Ricardo's unfortunate faith – at least in the *Principles* – in the 'law' of Jean-Pangloss Say enabled him to see this as only a 'temporary period of distress' (Winch, *op. cit.*, p. xv). Ricardo is not clear, however, about just how long the adjustment period lasts. He states that it is longer, and the distress deeper, in 'rich and powerful countries, whose large capitals are invested in machinery [difficult or] impossible to divert . . . to the purpose of another' activity than that for which demand has shrunk (*Principles*, p. 177).
20. *Ibid.*, pp. 71–2.
21. *Ibid.*, p. 73.
22. Optimistic popular discussions seldom distinguish between (a) *real* and (b) *money propensities* to consume energy (which have indeed fallen); (c) *price elasticities* of demand, for *energy* and (d) *oil* (probably still low, except perhaps in the long run); (e) *elasticities of substitution between oil and other fuels*; and (f) between *energy and other factors* of production, upon which depend, not only (c) and (d), but also the (crucial) (g) *income-elasticities of demand* for *energy* and (h) for *oil*. See, for example, *Newsweek*, 12 September 1983, p. 58. The US real propensity to consume energy – 'the amount of energy used to produce \$1 of GNP' – 'dropped by almost one-quarter' in 1973–83, though the price rise would convert this into a large rise, at least a doubling, in the money APC of energy. The US oil/energy ratio, while not completely stagnant, as was the world ratio (see note 30), dropped only from

47 per cent to 43 per cent. Similarly, the alleged agreement by 'most analysts' upon 'near-flat demand [for oil] for the rest of this century', even if justified, carries no assurance that the crucial income elasticity of demand for energy – and hence, largely, for oil-land – has declined at all.
23. J. M. Keynes, *General Theory of Employment, Interest and Money* (London: Macmillan, 1936), pp. 136–7.
24. D. Ricardo, *Essay on Profits*, in P. Sraffa (ed.), *Works*, Vol. IV, 1951, p. 36, my italics. I have put the words in square brackets in place of Ricardo's 'diminished', 'fall', 'increased' and 'increased', respectively.
25. *Ibid.*, p. 35.
26. Ricardo held the 'sophisticated' version of Say's Law, which precludes only a glut that is both long-term and general, as argued by A. Heertje, *Economics and Technical Change* (London: Weidenfeld & Nicholson, 1977), pp. 20–5, and as proven by the words I italicise from *Principles*, pp. 192–3: 'No man produces but to consume or sell ... By producing, then, he necessarily becomes either the consumer of his own goods, or the purchaser of the goods of some other person. It is not to be supposed that he should, *for any length of time*, be ill-informed of the commodities which he can most advantageously produce ... and, therefore, it is not probable that he will *continually* produce a commodity for which there is no demand'.
27. The rise in rent must be at the cost of profits, because the wage-rate is already at psychological subsistence; there is long-run full employment; and additions to the labour force resulting from population growth (or to employment, if the full employment assumption is dropped) on average work more hours on worse land to grow the same amount of corn, further eroding profits-per-hour, after subsistence needs are met via wages-per-hour.
28. See IMF, *World Economic Outlook 1982*, p. 142, on the world's apparent approximately $60bn annual deficit on the current account of the balance of payments! Much of this is attributed to interest, etc. paid to high-income oil-exporters, recorded as a minus item on the current BoP accounts of the payers (mostly OECD countries), but often with no corresponding plus item on those of the recipients (mostly Saudi Arabia, Kuwait and UAR).
29. See note 22 above for an untypically intelligent, but still fallacious, popular claim that we have learnt to do this.
30. World Bank, *World Development Report 1983*, pp. 29, 156–7, 162–3.
31. This is shown by the recycling of 1974–6, and by its simultaneous support (gearing) and diversification through a large increase in aid, especially from OPEC countries.
32. Griffith-Jones and Lipton, *op. cit.*
33. These variable levies, to raise imported corn prices to (UK) domestic levels, were a prototype of the CAP of the European Community. Also, corn levies (to worsen the effects of a shift to cornland rent during domestic expansion) are analogous to restrictions on imported coal (similarly worsening the effects of a shift to oil-land rent during domestic expansion).
34. Conjecture: the *share* of true land-rent in GNP probably fell, in most of Western Europe and North America, from the 1840s to the 1890s.
35. Near or on the horizon are further breakthroughs: male-sterile wheats,

permitting hybrids to be grown (1984–5); biological nitrogen fixation on a commercial scale (1990?); genetic engineering of major varietal change (2000?).
36. There is major potential, too, for 'health-induced' land-saving shifts in the structure of food demand from animal products to cereals. Overall, upward pressure on rents in twentieth-century developed countries has been due mainly to demand for *urban* land, and to renewed protection of agriculture. The long-term rent-raising effect of growth on derived demand to expand the land frontier into inferior lands, as predicted by Ricardo, has been outweighed by the rent-reducing impact of land-saving innovations.
37. Y. Hayami and V. Ruttan, *Agricultural Development: an International Perspective* (Yale University Press, 1971).
38. Why? (a) Ricardo's theory of the shift to rent, in the *Principles*, was in essence an appendage to his case against the Corn Laws. (b) He believed that prolonged general glut was impossible, and by this belief rendered his demon less threatening.
39. World Bank, *op. cit.*, p. 8.
40. 'In the second half of 1973 – before oil prices shot up – consumer prices in OECD countries rose at an annual rate of 10.3 per cent' (*The Economist*, Schools Brief, 22 September 1984).
41. M. Olson, *The Rise and Decline of Nations* (Yale University Press, 1982).
42. 'Newly industrialising countries' appear to be close to Western levels. 'Whereas in 1972 crude oil represented 10 per cent of [Brazil's] import bill, a decade later it made up over half' (*Financial Times*, 14 September 1983).
43. Ricardo, letter to Malthus, 17 October 1815; Sraffa, *op. cit.*, Vol. VI, p. 301, my italics.
44. From 1975 to 1982, fuels as a proportion of total imports to the EC 'ten' increased from 31.4 per cent to 33.0 per cent: EUROSTAT, *Energy Statistics Yearbook 1982*, p. 31. On dollar appreciation, see note 56 below.
45. L. and J.C.F. Stone, *An Open Elite? England 1540–1880* (Oxford: Clarendon Press, 1984).
46. Each of these two points has the defect that is the other's virtue! The reduced claims on *new* investment mean less reflation (not just less extra demand for energy and less inflation). The likelihood that the initial extra LDC demand will draw real, unemployed DC resources into use may mean higher marginal claims on energy than mere monetary reflation would imply.
47. World Bank, *Accelerated Development in Sub-Saharan Africa: An Agenda for Action*, World Bank, Washington, DC, 1981; FAO, *Monthly Bulletin of Agricultural Economics and Statistics*, April 1984.
48. A. Ellis, *Financial Times*, 12 September 1983, p. 12.
49. The development of Hicksian innovation theory into a testable theory of induced *invention*, responsive in its balance of factor-saving to changing relative factor scarcities (as in Hayami and Ruttan, *op. cit.*), does not alter this fact. The speed and nature of energy-saving innovations depend on the speed and extent to which the supply side – of research as well as of energy provision and use – can respond to changes in relative prices.
50. Griffith-Jones and Lipton, *op. cit.*
51. World Bank, *World Development Report 1984*, Washington, DC, 1984, p. 31.

52. M. Lipton, 'World recession by Third World Default?', *Bulletin of the Institute of Development Studies*, Vol. 12, No. 1, April 1981, note 10.
53. IMF, *World Economic Outlook 1982*, Washington, DC, 1982, p. 142.
54. IMF, *World Economic Outlook 1983*, Washington, DC, 1983, p. 70.
55. World Bank, *World Development Report 1983*, Washington, DC, 1983, p. 175; and see note 53.
56. See note 5, and 'Oil Prices and the Dollar', *Financial Times*, 22 October 1984, p. 16.

5 Proposal for an IMF Debt Refinancing Subsidiary[1]

MAHBUB UL HAQ

Reviewing the current international economic scene, it is tempting to slide into a luxurious defeatism and to sound the final alarm. It takes a good deal of courage to remain calm and constructive in a general mood of mass hysteria.

Of course, no one can review the current scene without rising concern. When we lift our eyes from individual events and specific crises, a disturbing trend is increasingly clear. It lies in an erosion of confidence in our collective ability to find solutions for our international problems; a gradual retreat from that previously fashionable but new-dreaded word 'internationalism'; a slow turning away from the spirit of the mid-1940s. Frankly, if the underlying currents were in our favour, I would have worried a little less about the individual waves. But we seem to be turning away from multilateralism to bilateralism; we appear to be losing that promising spirit which gave birth to the United Nations and the Bretton Woods. This is a cause for regret but certainly no time for rhetoric. If anything, this is a time for a quiet soul-searching since such profound changes in the international mood cannot be traced merely to the folly of a single nation or a single leader.

Nowhere is the need for this quiet soul-searching more obvious than in the present disorganised chase for some viable proposals for the mounting debt problems of the developing countries. What should have required a collective international approach has been left – with some reluctance and many prayers – to the mercy of isolated, *ad hoc devices*. It is as if we were afraid of our own collective capacity to address this problem. Surely, our founding fathers 40 years ago would have least expected that when an international problem of such a serious magnitude arose, we should all be found trembling on the brink.

I intend to focus here on the debt problem. This is not because I regard this as the most serious threat to the stability of our international fabric. It is in fact for two specific reasons. First, the debt problem is a symptom, not a cause, of international irrationality – an irrationality that is manifest in restricted world trade, high interest rates and declining capital transfers at a time when exactly the opposite policies are needed for world economic recovery. When fundamental solutions elude us, it is sometimes necessary just to chip away at the margin and to keep the patient alive. Second, humanity responds generally to a sense of crisis. In many ways, the debt issue offers us an opportunity to open some new windows of international understanding, to demonstrate once again that all nations can gain from a collective approach to restoring the economic health of some of its ailing members.

SOME COMMON FALLACIES

I believe that a calm and professional approach to the debt problem must avoid some common fallacies:

1. We must avoid the fallacy that the current debt problem reflects the irresponsibility of some major indebted nations. We must remember that only a few years ago, Mr McNamara applauded the same nations for their courageous borrowing and for their successful recycling of petro-dollars, which contributed to a higher growth rate of the world economy. We must remember that as late as 1981, many of these nations were upheld by the international financial institutions as the very model of economic management, precisely at a time when they had already accumulated vast debts. We must finally remember that the fragile international banking edifice rests today on the responsibility, not the irresponsibility, of indebted nations which have preferred to pay their bills – often with trembling hands and with silent prayers – despite falling real wages and rising domestic discontent. If we must find a scapegoat, though the very exercise is useless, it must be found as much in the deep world recession, reduced petro-dollars, rising interest rates and greater trade protectionism as in domestic mismanagement.

2. We must avoid the fallacy that many indebted nations are insolvent. They are merely illiquid. Their development potential is still enormous. Their unsold wheat or cotton or meat or manufactured goods can be converted into repayable foreign exchange both through widening world markets and through counter-trade. The eventual solution lies in exploiting their development potential, not in frustrating it. And let us

not forget that it is only through non-action or wrong action or indifferent action that we can convert the illiquidity of the indebted nations into insolvency.

3. We must avoid the fallacy that present debt renegotiations, which essentially postpone payments of interest and principal while the debt continues to accumulate, are a lasting correction of the basic imbalance. Total external debt liabilities of developing countries (including short-term debt and credits from the IMF) amounted to $810 billion in 1983, up from $766 billion in the previous year. By recycling debt, essentially on a short-leash basis, some time is definitely being bought. This time may prove valuable, but no permanent solution is being provided.

4. We must avoid the fallacy that the debt problem requires only a financial response. It requires a developmental response. It is linked with a restricted world trade market: over one-half of world trade is subject to some form of non-tariff barriers. It is linked with the net transfer of medium- and long-term lending from private sources to developing countries which fell dramatically from $16 billion in 1981 to minus $21 billion in 1983, or a violent swing of $37 billion in just two years. It is linked with high interest rates on floating debt which raised the cost of annual debt service by over $4 billion between February and May of this year alone. It is linked with declining official assistance: for instance, the International Bank for Reconstruction and Development (the World Bank) disbursed $12 billion last year to achieve a net transfer of only $1 billion, while IDA-7 has been replenished at a lower real level than in the past. It is also linked with development restructuring in the indebted nation that reflects lowered imported consumption but higher levels of future development activity. In short, any debt renegotiation is only the beginning of a process which must be backed up by complementary policies in trade, resource transfers and investment planning.

5. We must avoid the fallacy that the current debt crisis can be resolved either exclusively through a case-by-case approach or primarily through a collective approach. An adequate solution will combine elements of both. A case-by-case approach is needed to address the unique problems of each country. But this neither precludes, nor would it be successful without, a collective approach to easing trade protectionism, reversing declining trends of resource transfers, strengthening the financial resource base of the IMF and enforcing a more responsible code of ethics on future commercial bank lending. Let us frankly recognise that the case-by-case approach is a carry-over from the days when debt problems could largely be regarded as an aberration arising from the behaviour of an individual country. It has the advantage of familiarity

with techniques that have been applied in the past. However, the debt problem covering a number of large debtors at the same time is an unusual and a new phenomenon. It requires evolution of general guidelines which would give cohesion and consistency to the case-by-case approach. Let me also say candidly that those who are currently polarising the entire discussion between the start alternatives of a case-by-case or a collective approach are rendering no real service to the practical problem we face.

6. We must avoid the fallacy that costs of adjustment should be borne entirely by the indebted nations. There could never have been any overborrowing by these countries unless there was overlending by the banks. Any financial transaction requires delicate judgements by both sides. It is the collective judgement of the world community that has been proved wrong by unforeseen developments – particularly by a deep world recession and a reduced supply of petro-dollars for recycling.

Moreover, the industrial nations are already bearing some involuntary costs of adjustment. Imports of developing countries – mostly of indebted nations – were forced to be cut down from $85 billion in 1982 to $48 billion in 1983, thereby imposing a heavy penalty not only on themselves but on industrial countries which rely on exporting 28 per cent of their total exports and 6 per cent of their national income to developing countries. This continuing penalty could only be worsened by a banking crisis. It is preferable by far to share voluntarily the costs of adjustments of an agreed solution than to bear involuntarily the costs of adjustments of a continuing problem.

7. Finally, we must avoid the fallacy that the solutions to the debt problem will be costless or that they can come out of adroit international gimmickry. The costs will be heavy for permanent solutions, though heavier still for lingering non-solutions. It is because of these costs and reluctance over their sharing that permanent solutions have eluded us so far. There is, in fact, no dearth of thoughtful proposals. The proposals advanced by Peter Kenen, Felix Rohatyn, Charles Schumer, William Cline and some others have several common and overlapping features. They would stretch out maturity dates of short-term loans. They would reduce future interest costs to developing countries by imposing a once-for-all penalty (10 per cent under the Kenen Plan) on commercial lenders. They would limit future interest payments by developing countries to a defined percentage of their total export earnings (generally a ceiling of 25 per cent). They rely on intermediation through an IMF with augmented resources or through an entirely new institution. The reason why so many good proposals remain unimplemented so far is not

because of what they contain but what they omit. They generally omit a proper sharing of costs. They show little concern with new lending, in their preoccupation with rolling over old lending. They are not entirely convincing on additional sources of funds for their preferred intermediaries. They are not generally linked to broader trade, resource transfer and development policies in their anxiety to seek a purely financial solution. And they have unfortunately got mired in the sterile debate over the country-by-country approach vs sweeping reforms. However, I believe that, despite some shortcomings, they provide many essential blocs for an eventual solution – blocs on which we must build and build constructively and expeditiously.

ESSENTIAL ELEMENTS IN A SOLUTION

Let us first identify the essential elements in an acceptable solution. They are principally three:

First, in terms of accounting, the commercial lenders should not be made to appear carrying the risk of present illiquidity or potential insolvency. It is not important that they are paid back immediately – but they must have the assurance of getting back *what is due to them*, when and if they need the funds. In fact, such an institutional assurance is enough for them to leave the funds where they are.

Second, the developing country debtors can only pay in reality what their trade surpluses allow them to pay. Their surpluses would be the reverse of the deficits of the industrial nations. But these large trade surpluses of the developing countries are neither possible nor desirable over the long run. They would also require adjustments not only by these developing countries but by the industrial nations in their trading patterns, for otherwise the circle cannot close.

Third, the difference between the first and the second element must be bridged through an institutional advance – an intermediary that is willing to lengthen maturities to make the immediate servicing of debt manageable, to provide extra liquidity to the creditors against lengthened maturities so as to build trust in the financial markets and to ensure that the domestic economic management in the debtor countries continues to guarantee that the problem of illiquidity is overcome in due course without degenerating into a problem of insolvency.

From these three elements, let us try to put together a viable institutional solution.

AN IMF DEBT REFINANCING SUBSIDIARY

I believe that a constructive search for an institutional solution must begin with the selection of an intermediary. The logical choice is the IMF or a subsidiary of the IMF. This is not for any infatuation with the role that the IMF has been playing recently in debt negotiations in Latin America, though I must frankly state my conviction that the IMF is often being criticised not for the constraints its staff or management desire but for those imposed on it by its *original charter* or by its *dominant members*. My reasons for advancing the selection of the IMF are clearly practical. The Fund is already in this business; it will have less difficulty in winning a new mandate from powerful creditors than any new organization; it can negotiate additional resources more easily than any alternative we can think of, including the possibility of a special SDR issue. Thus, the search for new institutions like a Debt Discount Corporation proposed by Kenen or a world-wide Municipal Assistance Corporation proposed by Rohatyn – while useful as a pressure point – may not be very rewarding when consensus is likely to be reached more quickly on a modified role for IMF.

But I would like to advance a step further. It is not fair to burden the normal machinery of the IMF with this additional and awesome task without creating a special window or even a subsidiary with its clearly defined mandate. We are dealing here with a widespread, long-term problem with its several links with the policies of the indebted nations as well as of international community, with major additional costs requiring additional resources and more equitable sharing of adjustment burdens. It requires a special approach with expertise in debt problems. It may even require a different cast of characters on the IMF Board, reflecting the interests of commercial lenders as well as of official debtors and creditors. It would certainly require more day-to-day coordination with the World Bank, UNCTAD, GATT and other institutions which are the part custodians of the related policies in development, resource transfer and trade fields, which must also become essential ingredients in any viable solution. In fact, a joint subsidiary of IMF and World Bank may be even more appropriate so that there is a proper blend of short-term financial issues and long-term developmental considerations. It is for these reasons that I am persuaded that the time has come for the establishment of an IMF Debt Refinancing Subsidiary for the creditworthy, middle-income countries – in much the same way that the IDA had to be established in the World Bank in 1960 to look after the interests of the poorest, less creditworthy nations.

Such an IMF subsidiary may have to be funded by a special SDR issue. A smooth resolution of the debt crisis requires more world liquidity, in one form or another. This can be created by additional SDR allocations in the Fourth Basic Period which should be in two parts:

1. direct allocations to countries which should be used substantially to improve reserves or reduction of debt; and
2. a part to be allocated to the new subsidiary to provide the resource backing for its debt reorganisation efforts for individual countries.

The basic task of this IMF subsidiary will be to find a country-by-country settlement within the framework of an enlarged consensus on a viable long-term solution. Such a solution must (a) stretch out maturities; (b) reduce interest costs to a defined ceiling of export earnings; (c) apportion adjustment costs between the indebted nation and its external creditors; (d) protect new lending levels; (e) ensure more markets, sometimes even through counter-trade; (f) reverse declining resource transfers; and (g) reach a new equilibrium in the balance of payments at a higher, not a lower, level of development activity. It will not be easy to reach such a solution in each case. It would require moving one two fronts simultaneously – the indebted country's domestic front, which is the current preoccupation, and on overall external policies which are being ignored in practice. It would also provide more resources and more breathing space so that the present short time periods allowed for adjustment can be suitably lengthened. It would provide a built-in functional co-ordination with other international institutions, both at the management and staff levels.

It is not necessary at this stage to sketch out the role and the mandate of the new IMF subsidiary in great detail. What we need initially is a consensus – however fragile – to travel down this path, a consensus that must be sought between now and the annual meeting of the IMF's IBRD in September this year and the meetings of the Interim and Development Committees which will precede. From these deliberations, let us hope, there will be the birth of a new initiative, a reaffirmation of he commitment that the founding fathers made some forty years ago.

In focussing exclusively on the debt issue and in advocating a partial solution, I do not wish to disappoint those who fervently believe in fundamental solutions and in comprehensive global negotiations. The pressure for such negotiations must continue. In fact, I see a complementarity, not a contradiction, in the two approaches. The destination can only come nearer with each confident step.

But while we pursue the idea of an IMF Debt Refinancing Subsidiary, there are at least two other urgent issues on the international timetable which must not be ignored:

First, we urgently need a fresh round of global trade negotiations, under the joint umbrella of GATT and UNCTAD, to address current restrictions on world trade. The prospects for such negotiations may improve with the current faint hints of a world economic recovery. These trade negotiations must cover agricultural protectionism and restrictions on trade in services (including international migration), besides the usual preoccupation with manufactured goods.

Second, careful and professional preparations must be undertaken now to make possible the holding of a new Bretton Woods Conference in 1985 or 1986.

Let me conclude by reminding you that the stakes are awfully high in finding a viable solution for the deepening debt crisis of the developing countries. What the world needs today is not elegant analyses but a few practical steps, a few workable solutions, however modest, however short of our ultimate ideal. We must start here a process, a process of responsible change, whose logic proves irreversible and whose momentum is carried over to finding more fundamental and basic changes in the international order. Let me respectfully suggest that while many of us in the developing countries are bruised and battered today, and while the bitterness of our immediate experience may sometimes overwhelm the calmness of our analysis, let us at least try to win respect in the international forums by the force of our arguments, not by the force of our language. It is in that spirit that we must address the international economic issues.

NOTE

1. This paper constitutes the text of an address given to the United Nations Economic and Social Council at Geneva in July 1984.

6 Alternative Approaches to North-South Negotiations[1]

FRANCES STEWART

Over the last thirty years, growing attention has been paid to North-South issues. At a political level this was a natural development following many Third World countries' political independence, and their increasing recognition of the gap in per capita incomes between North and South. While this gap may not have widened in relative terms, it has certainly widened in absolute terms over this period. The questions at issue relate to the 'rules' of the game – whether these are biased, how they might be reformed, and how best to operate within them. Despite much talk, there has been very little progress in terms of changing the rules. This chapter is concerned to analyse why this is so, and within the perspective this analysis gives, to make suggestions for more fruitful approaches to North-South negotiations. Paul Streeten has been a leading analyst of these issues, and much of what follows has been inspired by his thinking.[2]

There has been rather remarkable agreement on the content of proposals to reform the international economic system so as to improve the development prospects of the Third World. Thus the proposals for reform for the UN Development Decades are similar to those launched by the Group of 77 (G77) in their claims for a 'New International Economic Order'. These proposals in turn contain the same main elements as those advocated by the two Reports of the Brandt Commission. Despite the consensus among those concerned with development at an international level, and despite the fact that most of the main proposals have been around now for quite a time, there has been almost no progress in realising the changes. The document on an International Development Strategy for the Third United Nations Development Decade began with the statement that, 'The goals and objectives of the International Development Strategy for the Second Decade remain largely unfulfilled' (para. 3).

The main elements of the reform proposed by the G77, the Brandt Commission and the United Nations for the Development Decades are:

1. A substantial increase in concessional resource flows from North to South towards (and beyond) the achievement of the 0.7 per cent target.
2. Enlarged flows of non-concessional (private) finance.
3. The restructuring of debt and some debt relief among poor countries.
4. Improved access for exports of LDCs to the markets of developed countries, including both manufactured and primary products.
5. The stabilisation of commodity prices through the Common Fund and the Integrated Programme for Commodities.
6. The reform of the International Financial System so as to increase the participation of LDCs in decision-making; to increase the role of SDRs; to reform IMF conditionality.
7. Improvements in the behaviour of multinational companies through a Code of Conduct.
8. Other proposals, including policies towards the development of energy; towards population; towards food security; and towards arms reduction.
9. Recent reports, notably the International Development Strategy for the Third Decade and the Brandt Commission, have stressed the mutual need for sustained growth – in the North to increase markets for Southern goods, and in the South to increase markets for Northern products.

These proposals have been justified in two ways. It has been argued that they are necessary to promote development in the Third World and therefore they have a *moral* justification for those concerned with development. However, this argument has been challenged from two points of view. First, it has been contended that some (at least) of the changes are not necessary to promote development and may indeed actually impede it. (See, for example, the debate about aid.) Secondly, it has been argued that development can only impose a moral obligation if the fruits of growth are going to the most deprived. Since many of the proposals would, at least in the first instance, help governments of LDCs, or middle-income groups, rather than the deprived, it is suggested that there can be no moral case for the proposed changes. (See Lal's recent pamphlet (1983) and Seers (1984).) The second way that the proposals have been justified is by appealing to mutual interests. It is argued that interdependence between North and South is such that both have *mutual interests* in the proposals. For example, free trade should increase incomes in both North and South as resources move to more efficient uses; commodity price stabilisation, it is suggested, will help consumers of commodities as well as producers; acceptance of the Code of Conduct for MNCs would increase the stability of the environment for MNCs and thus help both North and South; and so on.

The International Development Strategy for the Third Decade exemplified the two types of justification. On the one hand, it pointed out the moral obligation: 'The stark reality confronting mankind today is that close to 850 million people in the developing world are living at the margin of existence'. On the other, it points to mutual interests, arguing that 'in an interdependent world economy, these problems [i.e. slow growth, high inflation and high unemployment in the North, prolonged monetary instability, structural problems and maladjustment] cannot be solved without resolving the particular problems facing the developing countries ... accelerated development of developing countries is of vital importance for the steady growth of the world economy and essential for peace and stability'.

Despite the two justifications, few of the proposed changes have been made. When the *NIEO* (New International Economic Order) was launched it was believed that major changes were possible. Since then aid has remained stagnant, protectionist pressures in the North have accumulated, and there has been no relaxation in restrictions; almost negligible resources were contributed to the Common Fund. A little progress has been made in negotiating a Code of Conduct for MNCs, but it will be on a voluntary basis and few believe it will have much impact. Every assessment that has been made of recent North-South negotiations comes to the same conclusion: 'In recent years, international fora have yielded little or uncertain results', while the world economy has presented an increasingly hostile environment for developing countries.[3] Given this failure, it is clear that the two justifications put forward for the reforms have not been sufficient to produce action. It has been apparent for a long time – since Adam, indeed – that moral reasons are often ineffective by themselves. Recognition of this was behind the appeal to mutual interests, to supplement the moral appeal, which was made in the 1970s. Appeal to interests ought to be more effective since the reason the impact of altruistic appeals on action is limited is that self-interest is the more effective engine of action. Despite this, the appeal to interests also proved ineffective. This can hardly be due to an upsurge of altruism, since if it were, the moral justification would have become operative. Rather it was due to a mistaken identification and analysis of interests. This mistaken identification and analysis of interests is, in my view, at the heart of the failure of past efforts for reform. Correct identification offers the potential for securing change more effectively.

The mutual interests identified in discussion of proposals for reform are at an *aggregate*, *general* and *international* level. But operational interests – that is interests which are sufficiently powerful to produce changes – tend to be *specific* and *national*.

In many of the areas of reform there is an apparent general interest in reform. But there are three reasons why this general interest does not lead to specific political action. First, the gainers are often rather diffuse and poorly organised, in political terms, while the losers are specific, well organised groups. Secondly, the gains may be potential and uncertain, while the losses are immediate and certain. Thirdly, the gains may be unevenly distributed among nations, with some nations suffering a disproportionate share of the losses while others gain disproportionately.

The case for freer trade in manufactures provides an example where each of these reasons apply. There is a strong case that can be made, at a general level, that both North and South would gain if the North allowed free access to their markets to Southern manufacturers. Consumers in the North would gain from the cheaper goods they could buy. Output in the North should increase as resources were more efficiently deployed producing goods in which the North has a comparative advantage. Since in aggregate the South buys more from the North than it sells to it, it is likely that any increase in total imports from the South would be more than offset by extra sales of exports. But this general interest is not reflected in specific and politically operational interests.

In the first place, the gainers from freer trade would be consumers, who generally have little influence over policy because they are poorly organised. In any case, the gains, for each individual consumer, are likely to be quite small and hardly worth defending. In contrast the producers who would lose are normally specific groups of owners, managers and workers who are well organised and present a powerful lobby. Physical capital, in which the owners of the firms involved have invested, will be rendered obsolete, as will the human capital of the workers. The workers may not find alternative occupations – especially where there is high unemployment. They may have to move or to retrain, or both. Hence the general interest of the consumers (which is normally weakly represented) will be powerfully opposed by the particular interest of the producers. While other groups of producer should gain – for example, sellers of machinery to the Third World – their gain is normally not sufficiently certain for them to provide an opposing lobby in favour of free trade. Moreover, since the gains are *potential*, many of those who would gain may not themselves be cognisant of the gains and not in a position to argue for them. (For example, people who would be employed in new export industries.)

Thus even if there were net gains to a particular nation in the North from freer trade, it might oppose it because of the losses of particular powerful groups. In addition, since the North is composed of a number of nations, although there may be net gains for the North as a whole, there may be net losses for particular countries, and these losses may be of decisive significance in decision-making. For example, suppose the UK liberalised its textile imports, this might increase sales of machinery to the South, but the bulk of orders for that machinery might not go to the UK but to such nations as West Germany and Japan. To the extent that decision-making takes place at the national level, the UK will consider the interests of its producers, not those of other Northern nations, and would therefore not approve trade liberalisation. Hence while there is an apparent mutual interest in free trade for North and South, the interest is at a general international level, and not one at the operational level.

Policy-making is thus normally most influenced by pressures from groups that are specific and national. There are occasional exceptions, when some type of general interest is given precedence over particular interests. But in these cases the gains to the general interest need to be very obvious and certain. With the internationalisation of some powerful interest groups (for example, multinational companies, arms manufacturers, large retailers), international interest groups may become critical in determining national action. The internationalisation of decision-making – for example, in the EEC – may also give more weight to international concerns, but even here national interests remain of major significance, and where they seem to be threatened nations normally retain the power to take action of their own. In the past, there have been occasions of major trade liberalisation and of apparently imaginative and generous financial reforms, which might seem to contradict this rather pessimistic diagnosis. But, on closer examination, it invariably turns out that the more grandiose schemes were in the interests of powerful and specific groups.

An example is British trade liberalisation in the nineteenth century, starting with the repeal of the Corn Laws. The intellectual justification for this repeal had been developed by Smith and then Ricardo, but its realisation had to wait until the interests of the manufacturers in cheap food dominated those of agricultural interests in protection, and the shifting power of different interest groups had acquired political expression, through the Reform Act. Free trade in manufactures was clearly in the interests of British manufacturers in the nineteenth century. Protection was introduced in the twentieth century when the British had lost their competitive lead. The next wave of trade liberalisation – after the Second World War – reflected the dominance of the USA politically and economically and the interests of major multinational firms in the free movement of goods and of capital. The Marshall Plan which financed trade and capital liberalisation was in the clear interest of US firms who were thereby provided with markets. In each of these cases, there was a coincidence between particular interests and the 'mutual' interest, which made reforms politically realistic. This coincidence is absent in most elements of the proposals in the IDS, Brandt Reports, etc., as a quick review of some of the proposals makes clear.

Aid provides an example. Apart from some specific commercial and political interests, which do normally produce aid flows, as shown by the heavy receipts of aid (especially military aid) in politically sensitive areas, the case for a greater general flow of aid rests on the argument that the North will benefit both economically and politically from a more prosperous South. It is evident that such gains are diffuse and uncertain – even more so than in the case of freer trade. Hence the 'aid lobby' is not powerful. Multilateral aid directed at poor countries shows least direct connection between aid flows and economic returns, and consequently IDA is the most vulnerable type of aid. Arms control provides another example. The general interest in arms control is very clear. But the groups who gain from selling arms are specific and very powerful, while the gainers from arms control are again diffuse. Moreover, national limitations on arms supplies will not necessarily produce results since other nations may well supply arms if some hold back, so that nations who hold back are guaranteed loss of markets, but may gain nothing.

Commodity price stabilisation is a case where the potential gainers among consumers – within the North – are both uncertain and diffuse, and therefore the proposals are not likely to gain much effective support.

It is not difficult, then, to see why little progress has been made in North-South negotiations. In a few areas, some progress has been recorded, notably in the field of banking and finance and in some specific country negotiations. In each case, change can be seen as the outcome of pressures from powerful interests for whom gains and/or losses are obvious, specific and large. At a general level, the most obvious example is provided by the debt crisis.

It is apparent, in the current debt and banking crisis, that default is not just an option for some countries, but unavoidable unless the debt servicing burden is reduced and new international finance is found. Moreover, it is an option that would hurt some major banks more than individual countries. Apart from the general economic implications of default in major countries, the effects on particular banks (especially in the USA) would be catastrophic. It has been estimated that if Brazilian, Mexican and Korean debts had to be written off the capital and reserves of several major US banks involved in international lending would be wiped out. Since the Mexican crisis of August 1982, the banking crisis has met with substantial response from the international community:

1. The BIS provided large amounts of shortrun bridging finance, as has the US Treasury.
2. The IMF has itself reached agreement with the main countries more rapidly and on terms which are considerably less tough than those offered to less powerful debtors.
3. The Fund has helped to organise continued lending by the private banking community, which recognises that 'It does not appear to me to fly in the fact of reason to suggest that new lending, often with a tinge of doubt attached to it, may on occasions be the best way of protecting the quality of existing lending and ensuring its ultimate soundness' (Peter Cooke, head of banking supervision at the Bank of England, *Financial Times* Conference on World Banking 1983, December 1982).
4. The IMF quota was increased by 47.5 per cent. The measure met considerable opposition in the US Congress because it was recognised as primarily aimed at helping the banks, rather than countries (and it gained support from the US administration for similar reasons).

ALTERNATIVE STRATEGIES

Thus analysis of the changes that have not been achieved – the bulk of those contained in the IDS – and of those that have, provides the same lesson: for effective change there must be support from particular interests; arguments based on the 'general' interest are not sufficient. This lesson needs to be at the forefront in choosing future strategies. At this stage, four alternative strategies may be distinguished.

First, to continue, in a similar way to the past, to identify international reforms that would promote development, and to use every opportunity to put them forward. This strategy may produce some results from time to time, with a particular conjuncture of events in which there is a coincidence between the distribution of gains from change and powerful interests, and it may get further with certain political changes in the North. But in general it seems certain that the changes will be rather minimal; the proposed agenda for reform by bodies such as the Committee for Development Planning, the Brandt Commission and the G77, and the UN Development Decade targets – being continually advocated and never fulfilled – will be taken less and less seriously. Where changes are made, it is likely that they would have occurred without the fanfare of international demands, through the pressure of interests.

A *second* strategy which seems to be being followed in part now (for example, by the non-aligned and the Commonwealth Secretariat Group) is to redefine the agenda for reform to a more modest level, concentrating on a few areas only. This strategy will reduce the gap between aspirations and achievements, mainly by reducing aspirations. It does not seem likely to increase achievements much.

A *third* strategy would be to place less emphasis on the international dimension and more on national policies, with each country trying to maximise its performance through internal efforts, regarding the international environment as 'given'. The most successful countries have in fact followed this strategy very effectively. Japan and South Korea, for example, managed to exploit the existing rules of the game very successfully and made little effort to get them changed.

However, this leaves some countries, e.g. those dependent on a single commodity whose terms of trade fluctuate, in a very difficult position. Moreover, it may be that the external environment is becoming more hostile. However, if negotiations on the international strategy continue to be fruitless, this may be the best strategy to follow.

Focusing on making the best of the prevailing international environment is clearly sensible for particular countries, and would be compatible with simultaneously trying to secure reform of the international system. But in practice it is uncommon for countries to pursue both strategies together. Countries that are most successful within the existing framework rarely make much effort to change it, while countries that are active in pursuit of international reform often neglect domestic changes that would help exploit the existing environment. This fact could be one reason for the comparative failure of North-South negotiations, since the countries with the strongest bargaining position will generally be those which have most been successful economically, while those that are not successful usually have little to bargain with. The debt situation has somewhat changed things, since countries that had been doing very well out of the system and were making few efforts to change it have suddenly become major potential losers, therefore putting their weight behind reform for the first time and strengthening the bargaining position of the South.

The *fourth* strategy is to make use of the concept of operational interest in devising and pursuing international reform. While the reforms identified in the NIEO claims or the Brandt Commission Reports give the broad dimensions in which changes might be sought, specific proposals need to be devised which involve politically operational interests. By bargaining, countries or groups of countries can produce a link between interests and change. The general or mutual interests may thereby be made specific and operational. For example, instead of relying on the general arguments for freer market access, LDCs may link access to their own markets with access for their goods in Northern markets. This type of negotiating strategy has been pursued by a few countries, in some cases with considerable success:

1. A British quota on Indonesian textile exports led the Indonesian Government to cancel orders for textile machinery and aircraft. The British Trade Minister, John Nott said, 'The Indonesians have no right to retaliate in this way ... But they did and it hurts'. The textile quota was raised by 181 per cent. (Quoted by Seers, 1983.)
2. Malaysia boycotted British goods, partly to gain better treatment for her students in Britain. Concessions were made, and the boycott lifted.
3. The Chinese substantially reduced their grain purchases from the USA because of restrictions on textile imports and were threatening to reduce them further. When the USA agreed that it would not impose further restrictions, the Chinese agreed to make up the shortfall in grain purchases.[4]
4. Mrs Gandhi threatened to withhold major contracts from the British unless the British supported the sixth IDA replenishment. The British supported the IDA replenishment.

5. The ASEAN pact countries threatened trade sanctions against Australia unless Australia supported a UN resolution condemning the presence of Vietnamese troops in Kampuchea.
6. Ten countries boycotted Nestlé because of the company's contribution to infant malnutrition in the Third World. After six and a half years, the company agreed to four major changes, involving changed labelling, the distribution of warning literature, the end of expensive gifts to doctors and limiting supplies to hospitals. The boycott was called off, but the boycotting countries agreed to continue to monitor the situation. The boycott was estimated to have cost Nestlé $40m.[5]

Given the repeated failure of the previous negotiating strategy, it seems that there is not much point in continuing on that tack. The lessons, positive and negative, of the past twenty years suggest the two last alternatives would seem to offer most: to concentrate on internal reforms which enable countries to maximise their benefits from the given international environment and to negotiate changes by bargaining, through threats to (or offers of gains to) specific interests in the North. The rest of this chapter will further examine the potential of the last strategy.

An obvious objection to the bargaining approach is that it is liable to introduce all sorts of 'distortions' into international trade and payments. Whereas the International Development Strategy and Brandt Commission approach involves general rules and multilateral negotiations, this approach is likely to lead to specific rules and exemptions, working through bilateral negotiations.

How seriously this objection should be taken depends on what one is comparing with what. To the extent that the present world is an nth best one, riddled with imperfections, and that reform is unlikely, the suggested approach need not make matters worse in this respect, and may even make them better. For example, in reaction to the recent foreign exchange crisis, together with depressed markets for their exports, a number of countries have negotiated barter deals (known as *counter-trade*). Whereas in 1976 an estimated 2 per cent of world trade was counter-trade, in 1982 it was estimated to account for about 30 per cent of world trade.[6] In a multilateral, full employment, free trade world, this would be likely in most circumstances, to reduce welfare. But in the present situation it permits a higher level of trade, output and employment than would otherwise be possible.

A further objection is that the approach could lead to a series of beggar-thy-neighbour actions – a form of escalating economic war between North and South in which ultimately neither side gains. Whether this is so or not depends on the issues at stake, the negotiating stance adopted and the subsequent reactions from each side. The examples given above did not lead to that outcome, but rather an outcome in which most groups could reasonably be argued to have gained. Moreover, while the world may, in some sense, be a net loser,[7] some parties may gain. This would probably be a reasonable assessment of the OPEC action of the 1970s where despite the major losses for many parts of the world, the OPEC countries gained, and would presumably repeat their actions if given the opportunity.

The approach would be likely to enhance the gains of those countries with the strongest bargaining power, and this could be at the expense of the weaker countries. The debt situation provides an example. It is likely that use of the 'debt weapon' will lead to more generous financial treatment of the major debtors (e.g. more financial flows and/or reduced interest rates, and/or some debt write-down). But this may be associated with lesser flows of finance to the poorer but less indebted countries. This need not be the case; the more generous treatment of major debtors could, in principle, also lead to more generous treatment of the poor countries. The actual outcome will depend on whether the major debtor countries have serious concern for the poorer countries, and whether the developed countries wish, or the international agencies are able, to protect their interests.

The more *collective* action that is taken the less the likelihood of a negative outcome. If developing countries can negotiate together then the beggar-thy-neighbour danger will be less, and adverse effects on the poorest countries less likely. Moreover, collective negotiation is likely to be more effective, especially in some areas. For example, OPEC was only able to control the price of oil because the oil producers took joint action; the Andean Pact countries were effective in improving the terms on which they acquired foreign capital without suffering a major reduction in capital inflow, in large part because their action was collective. But collective action is much more difficult to organise than action by individual countries. However, it is clear from these examples that collective action need not involve the whole of the G77, but small sub-groups.

In *devising* the appropriate sub-groups for action, two considerations need to be borne in mind: first, that of the bargaining power of the subgroup, which will vary according to the issue under consideration; and secondly, the political possibility of decisive collective action. It seems that the second consideration would rule out most action at the level of the G77. Smallish regional groupings may best combine the possibility of collective action with negotiating strength. But this will vary from issue to issue. For example, where it is a matter of using producer power the major producers have to be included, which often means countries from all continents. On the other hand, in determining the conditions for tax and other treatment of multinational companies, intra-regional cooperation may be greatly superior to national action, and inter-regional co-operation may not be necessary. In some areas – and especially for large countries – national action can be very effective, as indicated in the examples already quoted.

International analysis of the various options, and subsequently international monitoring, might help in selecting issues and actions which ultimately result in a positive rather than a zero or negative sum game. Any of the three outcomes are possible with a bargaining approach. In contrast, it may be argued, the conventional multilateral approach suggested in the Brandt Commission Reports offers a positive sum game, but since the game is never actually played, this is not a major advantage.

AREAS FOR NEGOTIATION

Once a negotiating strategy is adopted and countries begin to explore the possibilities, a great number are likely to become apparent. But in a preliminary way, the following seem to be obvious potential sources of power offering possibilities of negotiating gains.[8]

1. *Buyer-power*. The Third World as a whole buys substantially more in total than it sells to the North, and the imbalance is particularly great in manufactures. The developed market economies sold $238 billion to developing market economies in 1980 while they bought $66 billion worth of manufactures from them. At times of international recession, when every country is seeking markets, developing countries can threaten to switch their purchases, unless their exports receive reasonable treatment. The threat may be made specific in industrial terms, thus activating specific interests in developed countries. For example, developed market economies export $128 billion of machinery and transport equipment to developing countries. LDCs may pick out this item specifically. For use of buyer-power, the action is likely to be more effective when conducted by single countries or smallish groups of countries in negotiation with particular Northern countries (or groups within the North), so that alternative sources of supply may be assured.

But given the supply potential in many industries of the Comecon countries and the NICs, alternative sources should normally not be a serious problem.

2. *Seller-power*. This is less effective, especially in recession, because of the existence of stocks and of substitutes and the difficulty in controlling all sources of supply. OPEC's success caused over-concentration on this approach, given its limitations.

3. *Contracts*. Large contracts offer potential power because they are related to very specific interests. Thus while any one contract is likely to be very small in relation to the total income of Northern economies, it may be important for particular companies, which in turn may influence Northern government policy. In the case quoted above, Mrs Gandhi was able to relate big contracts to a major aid issue. A country or group of countries may refuse *all* contracts with another country unless certain changes are made; or they may negotiate over a particular contract, either on a general issue, or on the terms of the contract itself. (For example, Thailand recently threatened to withdraw a contract worth $622m. with a British and French consortium because of the strict credit guarantees demanded.)

4. *Investment and technology transfer* by multinational companies. To the extent that multinational firms are earning quasi-rents on their technology sales (which by the nature of the activity they normally are), these may be bargained away by seeking alternative sources of technology. Very often the technology is available in another company in the *same* developing country – and more often in other developing countries. Unitary taxation (or some variant) may ensure proper taxation of MNCs. Unnecessary tax incentives may be removed and codes of conduct may be imposed unilaterally. If these actions are taken on a regional basis, they are less likely to lead to a reduced flow of investment. Where countries already have substantial amounts of foreign investment, control over these assets presents a potential bargaining counter in discussion with the HQ government.

5. *Debtor-power*. Countries that have borrowed heavily from one (or several) banks, especially if these are all based in a single country, may have considerable leverage both over the banks themselves and their country of origin, because of the consequences for the banks and the country of origin if default occurs. Such leverage is likely to be greater the less the *net* flow of finance into the borrowing country (i.e. the smaller new bank lending less repayment of old debt and interest payments). When this net flow becomes negative, as it has in major Latin American countries such as Brazil (and in the Latin American region as

a whole), the leverage becomes very strong. In this situation the borrowing countries are no longer net recipients from the banking system and would actually gain, in terms of foreign exchange, by default.[9]

In one way debtor-power is enhanced by collective action (a borrowers' club), since collectively the debt of several countries will invariably amount to a larger share of any individual bank's lending; but it may also be weakened because the likelihood of forceful collective action may be less. In April 1984, Venezuela, Brazil and Colombia lent $100m to Argentina. This has been interpreted as an example of regional co-operation. But in fact it seems to have been motivated by the desire by these countries to prevent an Argentinian default which might have had serious implications for lending to these countries. It is not an example of the collective use of debtor-power. So far debtor countries appear to have been more effective acting on their own rather than collectively.

However, while there has been no effective *formal* action, informally a number of countries have gained by each others' actions and negotiations. For example, one reporter commented, 'The Philippines ... is likely to benefit from the recent trend towards bigger breaks for troubled debtors' (*Asian Wall Street Journal*, 13 March 1984). There are various areas where countries may gain by being in a similar situation and bargaining on similar matters, without the need for any formal agreement, which is difficult to secure.

Debtor-power may be used (a) to secure a greater flow of resources (private and public); (b) to improve the terms of rescheduling; (c) to secure reduced servicing obligations (for example, lower interest rates); (d) to improve the terms of IMF conditionality; and (e) to put pressure on Northern countries to relax trade restrictions, and take other action which will make it easier for the borrowing countries to repay their debts through greater export earnings.

6. *Political* sensitivity: some countries are – mainly for reasons of geography – in a politically critical position. Countries in such a position may exploit it by making political and military concessions dependent on improvements in aid/finance/trade. There are some parts of the world where this type of political role has brought about considerable flows of aid (for example, South Korea and Taiwan in the 1950s; the Middle East; parts of Central America; Vietnam in the 1960s). Given the virulence of the cold war and other disputes throughout the world, there are a large number of countries which fall into the 'politically sensitive' category and could use this position to exert economic leverage.

Issue linkage

While the negotiating tactic may be concerned with one issue, for example trade, concessions may be sought elsewhere. The concession sought need not be confined to the particular country but could extend to general changes for Third World countries, as those of the NIEO. In the Indian example quoted, the threat against contracts was used to engender support for IDA. In the India case this made sense because of the large share India receives of IDA flows. In other countries such a stance might require an unlikely degree of Third World solidarity. However, if individual countries (or groups of countries) were prepared to negotiate on general Third World issues, it would be sensible for the G77 as a whole to prepare an agreed and co-ordinated agenda, so that countries were making similar demands on each occasion. These demands should not extend to all issues because, as is obvious, the Third World hasn't the power to enforce general and comprehensive demands. Hence priority needs to be given to one or two issues, which would be presented as a negotiating requirement by every Third World country whenever a suitable occasion arose. The problem here is to identify a single issue that is of real relevance to each Third World country – which is of course the reason why the demands of the NIEO were so wide-ranging. Debt relief, reduced interest rates and relaxed conditionality are issues that affect most countries. But even these affect different countries differently. If no single (or few) priority issues can be agreed upon, there could still be gains in groups of countries agreeing on one or two issues, as priorities for bargaining.

Problems of the least developed

The sort of negotiating strategy suggested here would seem to offer most to middle-income countries whose potential power is greatest in most areas. The least developed have small markets; although their debt may be large for them, it is small in relation to the commercial banks' lending. Moreover, their negotiating ability is often weak. The least developed undoubtedly will find less potential in this sort of strategy than other countries. Nonetheless, even for them it would be worth exploring and exploiting the power they have: for example, some of the least developed countries fall into the 'politically sensitive' area. Although their bargaining power is less, the magnitude of their demands is also generally less (for example, the cost of relieving them of some proportion of debt is much less than for some middle-income countries; the potential competitiveness of their exports is also lower). Small and low-income countries have more to gain from taking collective action. For example, any one African country is in a weak position to tax MNCs effectively, but if African countries negotiate together they would be in a much stronger position.

Strengthening the negotiating position

The strength of countries' negotiating position varies according to its circumstances. For example, countries with small markets are in a weak position to exercise buyer-power; countries with little outstanding debt cannot exert debtor-power. Also, the strength of any country's position depends on the possibilities and likelihood of retaliatory action by countries in the North. To some extent these are facts that are determined by history and outside the control of countries in their current actions. But there are ways in which their bargaining power, in the future, may be strengthened by current decisions. These include:

1. *Concentration.* The more concentrated a country's purchases are from a single source (country), the greater the potential loss of the selling country from switching sources. Thus concentration may increase potential buyer-power for any given size of market. Another example lies in debt. The more concentrated the borrowing, the terms of lending institutions and country of origin, the greater the potential debtor-power. But this concentration factor works both ways, also increasing the potential power of Northern countries. Consequently,

2. *Diversification* of selling outlets for a country's exports reduces potential retaliatory action. Brazil provides an example: it has considerable debtor-power arising from heavy past borrowing, the fact that this borrowing was concentrated on a few US banks, and the large *negative* financial flow (large current account surplus) that Brazil has to have at present to meet its debt obligations, which is likely to continue over the next few years at least. These facts put Brazil in a very strong position to exert debtor-power. But its exports are concentrated on a rather few commodities and in the US market (notably for steel and orange juice) so that retaliatory action on trade could be very powerful. This probably accounts for the fact that Brazil has not made much (if any) use of its debtor-power.

3. *Reduced dependence* on the external world: the greater the potential for a country to do without any particular item (for example, capital inflow, technology inflow), the greater the bargaining power. In the past

this has been interpreted as a reason for promoting import-substituting industrialisation – to reduce dependence on imported industrial products, and consequently on export earnings in order to finance them. But in practice it turned out that import-substituting industrialisation led to a new form of dependence that in some ways was greater than the one replaced, since countries that had industrialised in this way became dependent on imports of parts, technology, management, and capital for industrial activity. The countries that have successfully promoted export-oriented manufacturing (South Korea, Taiwan, etc.) turned out to be more independent than countries that had focused almost exclusively on import-substitution. This is because the import-substituting countries remained heavily dependent on traditional exports and on borrowing for essential finance. The export-oriented countries, on the other hand, acquired an ability to exploit the international environment (even when it is unfavourable), and to switch resources, if necessary, to adapt to new conditions, while being less dependent on traditional exports (where a hostile international environment is of greater significance) and, in the case of Taiwan at least, on borrowing for finance. Reduced dependence should not therefore be interpreted in a simple way as necessarily involving a withdrawal from the world economy. Rather it implies a greater ability to withstand external shocks. In some cases, this may be achieved by withdrawal – for example, China and India have been more insulated than many other LDCs against recent shocks. But for small countries especially, it is a matter of the nature of international relationships rather than their extent.

4. *Collective self-reliance*: developing trade, capital and technology links among Southern countries may reduce dependence. Collective self-reliance is often suggested as an alternative to continued North-South negotiations. In fact it need not be an alternative but can be pursued simultaneously with greater collective self-reliance and unity strengthening the South's bargaining position. The need for South-South links and collective self-reliance has long been supported rhetorically by leaders of the South. But in fact few links have been established, especially at the level of the South as a whole. Indeed, as a prospect, collective self-reliance seems as unreal as North-South co-operation. The reasons for the failure to realise South-South self-reliance are similar to those discussed above with respect to North-South relations. While there may be *general* interest in South-South co-operation, these do not operate at the level of particular interests. And, as with North-South relations, it is particular interests that are effective in bringing about action.

Consequently, analysis of how countries of the South might effectively promote collective action requires the same sort of rethinking as in the arena of North-South action, taking into account particular interests of nations and of powerful groups, and exploring how these might be used to bring about effective co-operation. In practice, regional groupings develop where common interests are evident. The financial crisis has acted to create areas of action where common and particular interests meet: this has taken the form of expansion of counter-trade (cited above), and of the early moves towards common markets in both Africa and Latin America. In addition, there have been a series of 'debtor' meetings in Latin America. Analysis of interests suggests that small groupings of countries are more likely to work than large ones; that countries may be able to co-operate effectively on some issues (for example, debt) but not others (for example, trade), and that the relevant groupings may vary according to the issues involved.

CONCLUSIONS

This chapter has analysed reasons for the failure of proposals for changes in North-South relations over the past few decades. The main conclusion from the analysis is that the usual proposals for reform identify mutual interest for reform, but the mutual interests identified are at a very general level, and do not coincide with the interests of particular groups who effectively determine national action. Unless particular interests are identified and incorporated in analysis and proposals, reforms are unlikely to be realised. This conclusion applies to South-South as well as North-South relations. From this perspective, the chapter suggests various areas where the South could make more use of its bargaining power to bring about change; and also actions it might take to enhance this.

It is possible that exploitation of bargaining power to the full, without regard to the consequences for the distribution and efficiency of world resource use, or for retaliatory action, could lead to a situation where every country is ultimately worse off than in the current situation. Consequently, it only makes sense to follow this type of strategy in pursuit of changes that will improve the position of the countries concerned, when these considerations are taken into account. Areas need to be identified that are likely to produce positive sum (preferably) and zero sum (at worst) changes, while excluding negative sum gains. This also applies to the proposals for increasing negotiating strength. For example, reduced dependence is not worth pursuing if it involves a substantial loss in output and income. Increased South-South links seem likely to be an area where there are positive gains, as well as bargaining gains, but this is not invariably the case with every type of additional South-South link. The issues need to be analysed in depth before they can be categorised.

In general, analysis of interests suggests that, both for North--South and South-South relations, small flexible groupings of countries, negotiating on particular issues, are more likely to bring about reform than large global negotiations, of the type that have failed so often in the past.

NOTES

1. This is a revised version of a paper prepared for the Committee on Development Planning for a meeting in December 1983.
2. See Streeten (1976) and (1982).
3. See the reports of the U.N. Committee for Development Planning.
4. *Financial Times*, 13 January 1984. In the latter half of 1984, however, the USA proposed new restrictions on textile imports, seriously affecting China. We have yet to see whether the Chinese will attempt to resume bargaining via grain purchases.
5. *Financial Times*, 27 January 1984.
6. See 'The World of Countertrade', prepared by Business Trend Analysts.
7. There are difficulties in defining gains and losses at a world level because their valuation depends on how one weights gains received by different groups in different countries. Where some lose and some gain, whether there are net gains or losses depends entirely on the weighting system. At a world level the 'compensation principle' makes no sense at all because of the absence of a mechanism to achieve redistribution of income. Even where every group gains (or loses), if relative as well as absolute levels of income matter, how distribution changes – and the value placed on various distributions of income – is relevant to the assessment of the change.
8. Paul Streeten categorised some of these sources of power in 'Dynamics of New Poor Power' (1976).
9. See Stewart (1984) for a more detailed analysis of the debt situation in a bargaining context.

REFERENCES

Lal, D., *The Poverty of Development Economics*, Hobart Paperback, 16, 1983.
Seers, D., *The Political Economy of Nationalism* (Oxford: Oxford University Press, 1983).

Stewart, F., 'The International Debt Situation and North-South Negotiations', paper for the North-South Roundtable on Money and Finance, Vienna,
Streeten, P., 'The Dynamics of New Poor Power', *Resources Policy* 1976.
Streeten, P., Approaches to a New International Economic Order', *World Development*, Vol. 10, No. 2, 1983.

7 Extending Free Trade to Include International Investment: a Welfare-Theoretic Analysis[1]

JAGDISH N. BHAGWATI AND
RICHARD A. BRECHER

The classic gains-from-trade theorem of Samuelson (1939) demonstrates that voluntary trade between agents with given endowments must be mutually advantageous: strictly speaking, it cannot be harmful to any of the agents. This fundamental insight underlies institutions such as the GATT which oversee trade among nations. Recently, the United States has proposed that the GATT be extended to include freedom of private investment flows. This proposal presumes that, if free trade exists initially in goods, the subsequent introduction of free capital mobility *must* also be beneficial to all agents. However, this is simply not true.

Drawing on some of our recent work, the first section below briefly considers why a move to free capital mobility between agents that are already in free trade may harm an agent, and must indeed do so under certain conditions if the other agent benefits. The second section is addressed to explaining this result by reference to the insights obtainable from existing theorems of trade and welfare. In the process, we also show symmetrically that going from no to free trade in goods when agents already have free capital mobility among themselves can also create such conflicting-interest, rather than mutually beneficial, outcomes.

Within the standard ($2 \times 2 \times 2$) model of a two-commodity, two-factor world with two countries, Brecher and Choudhri (1982) have shown that a country's welfare could be diminished by the introduction of unrestricted investment from abroad, when there is already free international trade in goods.[2] As they demonstrated, the country would be immiserised (enriched) if the relative price of its importable is raised (lowered) by the advent of untaxed inflows of foreign capital, assuming no 'trade-pattern reversal' in the sense of this price rising above the autarkic level.[3] Essentially, the proposition reflects the fact that foreign capital earns what it directly contributes, i.e. the value of its marginal product, and hence any resulting, indirect effect on the terms of trade improve or worsen.

But, as Bhagwati (1982) has noted, this result is symmetric for the capital-exporting country, which thus gains (loses) from capital outflows if its terms of trade improve (worsen). Since a terms-of-trade improvement for one country means a deterioration for the other, we immediately reach the startling conclusion that unrestricted international capital mobility in this instance causes the welfare levels of the two trading partners to move in *opposite* directions.

Although such capital mobility is efficient for the world as a whole – whose utility-possibility frontier is thereby shifted outwards – the movement to the new frontier is never in the north-east direction, given the absence of trade-pattern reversal. Thus international flows of capital lead to a dramatically unequal 'distribution of gains between investing and borrowing countries', to use a phrase from Singer's (1950) classic article.

This conclusion, that there is *necessarily* a conflicting-interest outcome from introducing capital mobility among the free-trading partners, is dependent of course on the assumed absence of 'trade-pattern reversal'. It assumes also the continued diversification in production before and after the capital flows, so that the same factor price-ratio corresponds to a given price-ratio for goods in both cases. The conclusion would not be generally valid, therefore, in the specific-factors model where the factor price-ratio corresponding to any goods price-ratio will generally change with the inflow or outflow of capital. However, even in such cases, while necessary conflict of interest between the two free-trading agents does not follow, the possibility of harm to one agent cannot be ruled out altogether.

How does one explain this result, which has immediate consequence for policy questions of considerable importance? There are three ways in which the result can be intuitively understood.

First, recall the theory of immiserising growth, as analysed in Bhagwati (1968), which states that growth in the presence of a distortion may be immiserising. Johnson (1967) showed such immiserisation for a small country with a distorting tariff in place; Bhagwati (1973) noted that this implied immediately that capital inflow into such a country would then be more likely to immiserise the country, since there would not be an added loss-causing factor in view of the earnings of foreign capital; and Brecher and Diaz-Alejandro (1977) showed that the immiserisation of the host country would *necessarily* follow if, in this 2 ×2 ×2 model, the importable commodity was capital-intensive and capital inflows were not large enough to extinguish the country's imports.[4]

By contrast, the Brecher–Choudhri (1982) case, on which the argument here rests, builds on the *other*, early case of immiserising growth: namely, Bhagwati (1958), where growth occurs in a large country with free trade, and therefore with a sub-optimal trade policy. If the source of such growth is the influx of foreign capital, there is (for reasons discussed above) an increased likelihood of immiserisation, which is the *necessary* outcome under the conditions already spelled out.[5]

Second, consider instead the optimal-policy literature, based on the classic work of Kemp (1966) and Jones (1967), which shows that the optimal policy mix for national advantage of a large country in the presence of international capital mobility generally involves duty-cum-subsidy on both trade and capital flows. Capital inflow in the presence of free trade is therefore necessarily in the presence of a sub-optimal policy. Hence, reverting to the logic of our first intuitive explanation, one sees immediately the intuition behind the proposition in this short chapter. In fact, as explained by Brecher and Feenstra (1983), the nationally optimal policy towards foreign investment may be prohibitive when taxes on trade in goods are disallowed. Thus we need not be surprised to find national welfare reduced by the introduction of unrestricted capital mobility when goods trade remains free.

Finally, it is a well-known proposition of international economics that more trade is not necessarily better than less trade from the viewpoint of national welfare. Adding trade in factors, as international capital mobility can be construed, to trade in goods is therefore not necessarily welfare-improving.

All these ways of understanding the results immediately imply the following proposition symmetrically: if we start from a position in which only capital is (perfectly) mobile, the subsequent addition of free trade in goods in the 2 ×2 ×2 model will also lead to necessarily conflicting-

118   *Free Trade and International Investment*

outcome situations and hence to a markedly unequal distribution of world gains, again assuming no trade-pattern reversals in the above sense. This will now be demonstrated.

In figure 7.1, T_2T_1 and $T'_2T'_1$ respectively are the production-possibility frontiers of the home country before and after the inflows of foreign capital have equalised rental rates internationally. By assumption, goods 1 and 2 are produced under constant returns to scale with technology that is relatively intensive in capital and labour respectively. Autarky is at point A, where a community indifference curve touches T_2T_1.

After the capital inflow, the economy cannot be in equilibrium at the autarkic product price-ratio. At this ratio, production would take place at point A', which must lie south-east of A by the Rybczynski Theorem. By the reasoning of Bhagwati and Brecher (1980), however, national income would still be given by the line AB, after payment of foreign profits represented by the length $A'B$ in terms of the second good. (Our analysis would be qualitatively unaffected if foreign profits were given

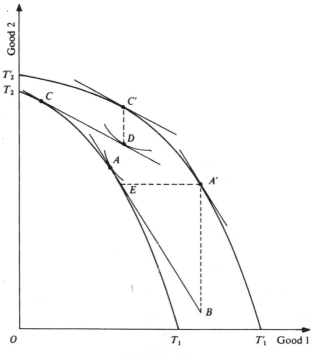

FIGURE 7.1

instead of length EA' in terms of the first good.) Thus consumption would still lie at point A, implying an excess demand (supply) represented by line segment AB in the domestic market for good 2 (1). This market imbalance would lead to a rise in the relative price of the second good in terms of the first, assuming Walrasian stability.

The market-clearing equilibrium will correspond to production at point C' and consumption at point D, with the difference $C'D$ between these two points being absorbed by foreign profits. Thus, after the capital flows but before the trade in goods, the country's relative price of good 2 is above the autarkic level. By similar reasoning, the capital-exporting country will have a relative price of the second commodity below the (foreign) autarkic level, assuming the same factor-intensity ranking as in the home country. (If this ranking were allowed to differ internationally, our principle conclusion below would not be qualitatively changed.) We assume that the product-price ratios now differ between countries, to rule out the uninteresting case where there is no incentive to engage in the commodity trade which is subsequently allowed.

Consequently, when free trade in goods is introduced, the home (foreign) country will lose (gain) if its relative price of commodity 2 decreases, assuming no trade-pattern reversal as defined above. To eliminate the international differences in product prices while preserving equality of world rental rates, the commodity price-ratio of the two countries must move in the same direction, in view of the Stolper–Samuelson Theorem. (We are implicity assuming the world-wide continuation of incomplete specialisation, which is possible under conditions discussed by Brecher and Feenstra, 1983; Chipman, 1971; and Uekawa, 1972.) Thus, once again, one country is immiserised while the other is enriched, given no trade-pattern reversal.

NOTES

1. We have profited from the comments of Robert Feenstra, Peter Neary and especially Lars Svernson at the Yxtahom Conference of the International Economic Association, 2–6 August 1982, where Bhagwati (1982) was presented. Thanks are also due to the National Science Foundation for partial financial support of Bhagwati's research.
2. Also see Grossman (1982) for a welfare analysis of international factor movements in a many-input, many-product model.
3. This result requires incomplete specialisation of production in the initial (pre-inflow) equilibrium. To simplify their exposition, Brecher and Choudhri (1982) assumed further that production with and without the inflow of foreign capital is characterised by diversification (i.e. non-specialisation) in

the relevant range of product-price ratios, thereby avoiding (readily incorporable) complications arising from Bhagwati and Brecher's (1980) analysis when complete specialisation occurs.
4. See also Hamada (1974), Minabe (1974) and Uzawa (1969).
5. It may be thought that such immiserisation would be ruled out if the capital-receiving country continuously maintained an optimal-tariff policy on trade in goods. This would, however, be an incorrect inference from Bhagwati's (1968) proposition that growth in the presence of optimal policies cannot be immiserising. As his analysis does show, an optimal-tariff policy would indeed eliminate immiserising growth if the increment in capital is nationally owned. However, where this increment results from an influx of capital owned by foreigners as in the present instance, there is an additional source of loss from the fact that foreign capital earns its marginal product at domestic prices. We also violate the condition that the foreign offer curve facing the country must be the same before and after the capital augmentation occurs. Grossman (1982) also considers the relationship between immiserising growth for internal expansion and immiserising investment from foreign capital inflows; and he notes that an optimal tariff on goods cannot generally suffice to rule out the latter possibility.

REFERENCES

Bhagwati, Jagdish N., 'Immiserizing Growth: a Geometrical Note', *Review of Economic Studies*, 25, pp. 201-5, June 1958.

Bhagwati, J. N., 'Distortions and Immiserizing Growth: A Generalisation', *Review of Economic Studies*, 35, pp. 481-5, October 1968.

Bhagwati, J. N., 'The Theory of Immiserizing Growth: Further Applications', in Michael B. Connolly and Alexander K. Swoboda (eds) *International Trade and Money* (Toronto: University of Toronto Press, 1973).

Bhagwati, J. N., 'Structural Adjustment and International Factor Mobility: Some Issues', Paper No. 6, International Economics Research Center, Columbia University, *mimeograph*, August 1982.

Bhagwati, J. N., and Richard A. Brecher, 'National Welfare in an Open Economy in the Presence of Foreign-Owned Factors of Production', *Journal of International Economics*, 10, pp. 103-15, February 1980.

Brecher, Richard A. and Ehsan U. Choudhri, 'Immiserizing Investment from Abroad: The Singer-Prebisch Thesis Reconsidered', *Quarterly Journal of Economics*, 97, pp. 181-90, February 1982.

Brecher, R. A. and Carlos F. Diaz-Alejandro, 'Tariffs, Foreign Capital and Immiserizing Growth', *Journal of International Economics*, 7, pp. 317-22, November 1977.

Brecher, R. A. and Robert C. Feenstra, 'International Trade and Capital Mobility between Diversified Economies', *Journal of International Economics*, 14, pp. 321-39, May 1983.

Chipman, John S., 'International Trade with Capital Mobility: A Substitution Theorem', in Jagdish N. Bhagwati *et al.* (eds), *Trade, Balance of Payments and Growth: Papers in International Economics in Honor of Charles P. Kindleberger* (Amsterdam: North-Holland Publishing Company, 1971).

Grossman, Gene M., 'The Gains from International Factor Movements', Princeton University and Tel-Aviv University, mimeograph, November 1982 (revised August 1983); forthcoming in *Journal of International Economics*.

Hamada, Koichi, 'An Economic Analysis of the Duty-Free Zone', *Journal of International Economics*, 4, pp. 225-41, August 1974.

Johnson, Harry G., 'The Possibility of Income Losses from Increased Efficiency or Factor Accumulation in the Presence of Tariffs', *Economic Journal*, 77, pp. 151-4, March 1967.

Jones, Ronald W., 'International Capital Movements and the Theory of Tariffs and Trade', *Quarterly Journal of Economics*, 81, pp. 1-38, February 1967.

Kemp, Murray C., 'The Gain from International Trade and Investment: A Neo-Heckscher-Ohlin Approach', *American Economic Review*, 56, pp. 788-809, September 1966.

Minabe, Nobuo, 'Capital and Technology Movements and Economic Welfare', *American Economic Review*, 64, pp. 1088-100, December 1974.

Samuelson, Paul A., 'The Gains from International Trade', *Canadian Journal of Economics and Political Science*, 5, pp. 195-205, May 1939.

Singer, H.W., 'The Distribution of Gains between Investing and Borrowing Countries', *American Economic Review, Papers and Proceedings*, 40, pp. 473-85, May 1950.

Uekawa, Yasuo, 'On the Existence of Incomplete Specialization in International Trade with Capital Mobility', *Journal of International Economics*, 2, pp. 1-23, February 1972.

Uzawa, H., 'Shihon Jiyuka to Kokumin Keizai (Liberalisation of Foreign Investments and the National Economy)', *Economisuto*, 23, pp. 106-22, December 1969 (in Japan).

8 The Third World and Comparative Advantage in Trade Services[1]

SANJAYA LALL

INTRODUCTION

The role of services in the process of economic growth and structural change has received a great deal of attention in economic literature. By contrast, that of *trade* in services has been a relatively neglected area of theoretical and empirical research. This is puzzling, since what is conventionally defined as 'service' receipts and payments constitutes a significant part of international transactions on the current account.[2] There is perhaps an implicit assumption that theories developed to explain the pattern of trade in physical products can be used without significant amendment to explain that in services. A moment's consideration will show that this assumption may be unfounded. The production of physical commodities is determined by factors and technologies quite different from those which affect the production and sale of services. In view of renewed international interest (in GATT and UNCTAD) in negotiating changes in the structure of regulation governing services trade, it seems apt to consider this question at some length.

This chapter analyses the determinants of comparative advantage in service trade, and how these may affect the emergence of developing countries as exporters of services. It does not break new empirical ground, but concentrates on clarifying the analytical framework within which further empirical research may be undertaken.

DEFINITIONS

'Services' are defined narrowly for present purposes.[3] Following convention, we exclude factor services from the discussion: factor services comprise income from foreign investments, property income[4] and remittances by migrant labour. These payments are governed by quite different factors from those affecting the sale of 'services' in the normal sense, and there are other (quite well developed) branches of economic literature dealing with them. Since we are interested in the *economic* determinants of service trade, moreover, we may also exclude two major sorts of non-factor service trade from the discussion: tourism, which is determined overwhelmingly by natural resource endowments and which does not, in any case, involve the sale of services across national boundaries (i.e. tourists come from abroad to buy services locally); and government services such as diplomatic, military, technical, cultural, and so on, which are not governed by market criteria.

These exclusions leave a fairly heterogeneous collection of transactions that can be counted as service trade which is influenced by economic determinants of comparative advantage. The collection may be grouped into five functional categories:

1. Shipping, transportation and communication services including freight charges, freight insurance and reinsurance, brokerage and data transmission (but excluding port and airport service charges).
2. Financial services, including banking, non-freight insurance and brokerage, accountancy, and various investment-related services.
3. Marketing services, including advertising, wholesaling and retailing.
4. Technological services, including engineering and construction (both civil and industrial), patents, trademarks, consultancy, repairs and similar functions.
5. Commercial services, including franchising, leasing and chartering.

These five kinds of service trade are still too diverse a group to analyse in a short chapter. To facilitate the discussion, therefore, it is proposed to narrow the scope here to two categories of service trade which predominate in international non-factor service transactions. These are items (1) *shipping and transportation* and (4) *technological services* in the above list. Most data compilations on service trade (see, for instance, UNCTAD, 1983) separate shipping and other transportation, but lump technological services under 'other private' services. However, a breakdown of US data for 1980 shows that, of total non-factor service exports of $16.8 billion, $7.9 billion (47 per cent) came from item (1) and $8.5 billion (51 per cent) from item (4). The USA is the world's leading technology exporter, so the significance of the latter category in service trade will certainly be less for other countries. Nevertheless, we may still be justified in concentrating on these two items for the Third World, shipping because of its quantitative importance, and technology because of its growing significance with industrialisation.

Before we consider the determinants of comparative advantage in these two forms of service trade, however, let us review past work on this subject.

EXISTING STUDIES OF COMPARATIVE ADVANTAGE IN SERVICES

Existing studies provide only limited guidance on what determines comparative advantage in services. Dick and Dicke (1979) run various regressions on the determinants of 'revealed comparative advantage' in exports of 'knowledge-intensive' products and services. They define their dependent variables to include both 'knowledge-intensive' goods and services together and each by itself, and seek to test 'whether rich countries have a comparative advantage in supplying services'. They note that the production of services is not necessarily a skill or technology-intensive activity, e.g. tourism or domestic services do not require highly developed human capital resources. However, services that are directly involved in trade 'absorb highly skilled labour – the relatively cheap factor of production in rich countries – distinctly more intensively than average economic activities'. (p. 338).

Dick and Dicke then use four independent variables to 'explain' the OECD's revealed comparative advantage in trade in services: (a) a 'state-of-development' variable, measured by *per capita* income; (b) country-level propensities to spend on science and technology, a measure of availability of productive knowledge; (c) the share of skilled employees in total employment, a skill endowment measure; and (d) a natural resource availability measure. They also introduce market size (to capture scale factors), currency undervaluation and the share of government in total GNP (to capture possible inefficiencies introduced).

None of the regressions on services, using 1973 data for a sample of eighteen OECD countries, proved significant. Contrary to expectations, skill and technological endowments failed to show any significant positive influence (in fact, the signs recorded were negative) on the dependent variable. This led Dick and Dicke to conclude that

> the specialization of OECD countries in the trade of knowledge-intensive services cannot be explained by factor endowment. Other factors are obviously more important. Non-tariff trade barriers,

which are often of a prohibitive nature, seem to play a more important role in the trade of services than in the trade of commodities.

They go on, however, to suggest that

Regardless of trade distortions, it is imaginable that *factor endowments have no significant influence on trade in services.* For one thing, services may not be produced internationally with identical production functions or factor intensities. Production functions or factor intensities can differ due to different degrees of government intervention ... [and] complementarities between traded services and goods may play an important role. Such complementarities seem to exist especially between raw materials and transport services ... It can be assumed that countries with a comparative advantage in the production of raw materials are not only net exporters of raw materials but also of transport services. However, the extremely poor data base precludes rigorous tests of these conjectures and hypotheses. (p. 346, emphasis added).

In his comment on Dick and Dicke's paper, Katouzian (1979) argues that the insignificant results do not necessarily (and should not) lead to a rejection of the underlying hypotheses. Specialisation in the production and export of particular services clearly has depended on relative factor endowments, but Katouzian notes that general factor endowments are a less reliable guide to reality than the 'history, tradition and institution' of each particular service. In other words, in view of the role of technology in trade in commodities, it is the *specificity* of learning (skill and technology generation – the two clearly cannot be separated in the production of services) of each service activity that is crucial to the development of an internationally competitive advantage.

The other study which has tried statistically to 'explain' trade in services is by Sapir and Lutz (1981).[5] They take their dependent variable to be net service trade (exports minus imports) for three types of traded services separately: freight, passenger services, and insurance and reinsurance. Their sample includes developing as well as developed countries (a distinct advantage over the Dick–Dicke study) and comprises, depending on data availability, between 13 and 35 countries. The dependent variable is derived from 1977 IMF data.

Sapir and Lutz seek to test both the neo-factor proportions and neo-technology theories of comparative advantage for services trade, and their independent variables include: capital–labour ratios; three alternative measures of human capital endowment (professional and technical workers in labour force, percentage of total labour force with secondary education, and that with third-level education); technological endowments as measured by national research and development expenditures as a proportion of GDP; and scale economies as reflected in total GDP. The authors also comment on the influence of policy interventions in trade, without attempting to enter these in the quantitative exercises.

The results obtained by Sapir and Lutz are as follows:

(a) *Freight services*: It is hypothesised that shipping is a capital-intensive activity and so also scale-intensive. Thus countries poorly endowed with capital (relative to labour) would tend to be larger net importers of freight services, as would smaller countries. The regression results bear out the capital-intensity effect quite strongly for the sample as a whole (32 countries) as well as for developing countries (20) and developed ones (12) separately. The scale effect appears significant only for the developing countries, presumably because developed countries are such large traders that they all reap existing scale economies.[6]

(b) *Passenger services*: Sapir and Lutz find that physical capital endowment again turns up a significant positive influence on comparative advantage in providing international passenger services. They also use a variable to capture the influence of national airlines (travel credits less debits), which yields the expected positive results. The capital endowments variable is especially significant for the group of (22) developing countries, but insignificant for (9) developed ones.

(c) *Insurance services*: It is expected that human capital and the existence of a well-established financial market will provide a comparative advantage in exporting insurance (and reinsurance) services. The scale factor is also expected to be significant. The results indicate that human capital and scale are indeed positive and significant in (some of) the regression results.

Sapir and Lutz conclude that

> Despite the protectionism from which trade in services suffers, a number of economic factors do, indeed, emerge as determinants of comparative advantage. On the one hand, performance in transportation services (freight and passenger services) appears to be related to capital abundance. For insurance services, performance seems, on the other hand, to hinge upon the availability of human capital. (p. 21)

Sapir and Lutz remark in a footnote (p. 21) that 'human capital also seems to be the main determinant for trade in total private services (including non-merchandise insurance services)'. However, because of the lack of detailed data on this very heterogeneous collection of services, they do not show the results of these regressions in their paper.

Sapir and Lutz take their results to support Balassa's (1981) analysis of the 'stages approach' to comparative advantage. Thus, they suggest that, as Balassa has argued for manufactured goods, 'as developing countries accumulate physical and human capital, they will gain comparative advantage in certain types of services. However, one suspects that industrialized economies will generally retain their prominence in services trade thanks to their technological lead and their abundance of physical and human capital' (p. 21).

Sapir and Lutz conclude from their appreciation of the 'stages' concept that developing countries at the 'upper and of the spectrum can at the same time be net importers of services overall and net exporters of services to other developing economies', a structure of exporting that is already observed in manufactured goods.

The results obtained by Sapir and Lutz are not only more useful and significant than those of Dick and Dicke, but they are also based on a larger sample and sounder methodology. The inclusion of developing countries in the sample clearly makes Sapir and Lutz's analysis much more relevant for this chapter. The consideration of different types of service trade in accordance with their particular characteristics also makes a great deal of sense. The interpretation of Sapir and Lutz is perceptive, and their conclusion on the applicability of Balassa's 'stages approach' seems plausible.

Nevertheless, as the authors themselves admit, both sets of statistical analyses suffer from the paucity of data on relevant variables. They also suffer from an oversimplification of the theories of comparative advantage being tested, and betray a certain insensitivity to such crucial factors as 'history, tradition and institutions', which Katouzian stressed in the development of comparative advantages in services. While they are undoubtedly pioneers in this new and significant area of research therefore, a great deal more analytical and empirical work is needed.

The following section confines itself to the analytical task. Only a major, fresh research effort will be able to come up with the kind of data and methods necessary to conduct a definitive empirical examination of the determinants of trade in services.

DETERMINANTS OF COMPARATIVE ADVANTAGE IN SERVICE TRADE

It was explained in the last section that this chapter would concentrate on the analysis of trade in transportation and technological services. Within transportation, the major element is shipping, and this is used as surrogate for all transportation services: while there are several peculiarities of the shipping sector which affect its fare structure and its nationality (because of 'flags of convenience'), as far as comparative advantage is concerned it is not too unreasonable to regard the underlying factors as similar for sea and other forms of transportation. The following discussion will clarify why this is so. We are, however, aware that a finer degree of discrimination may reveal important differences within the transportation and technology sectors: it is in the interests of obtaining some useful generalisations that we sacrifice refinement.

Both shipping and technology-related services are intermediate services which are intimately linked with the broader process of manufacturing and distribution.[7] The factors which determine comparative advantage in services are very similar to those which determine them in manufactured products: a complex mixture of 'neo' factor-endowments, technology gaps, scale economies, activities of multi-nationals and preference similarities.[8] There are, however, also some differences between them, which are touched on later.. Shipping is an integral part of infrastructural support to the economy, its provision being virtually inseparable from investment in infrastructural capital and its demand being entirely derived from primary and secondary level mining, agricultural and manufacturing activity. Technology-related services are, similary, an integral part of investment activity, mainly in manufacturing and construction industry, and their trade is directly related to trade in investment goods.[9]

What determines particular countries' comparative advantage in the provision of such intermediate, production/commerce-related services? Both shipping and technology-transfer represent activites that are highly intensive in the use of specialised knowledge, skills and a network of international information and procurement networks. Shipping obviously directly requires expensive physical facilities. Technology-transfer *per se* does not require capital goods but is generally associated with the provision of capital goods (there are exceptions, noted later); it is itself a form of 'knowledge transfer' and so must be highly skill- and technology-intensive.

At first sight, therefore, the general thrust of Sapir and Lutz's findings – that comparative advantage in shipping is essentially dependent on physical capital endowments and in 'other services' (dominated by technology-transfer) on skill endowments – seems quite plausible. A moment's reflection shows that such a simple representation of the basis of comparative advantage may be misleading.

Shipping requires not only embodied physical capital but also skills, information and established international financial and commercial contacts. Thus a simple Heckscher – Ohlin type of analysis (in terms, that is, of capital-labour endowments) can be accepted only if this other bundle of requirements was assumed absent. A cursory comparison of leading net exporters of shipping services in 1980[10] – Norway with net shipping earnings of around $4.5 billion, Japan $3.2 billion, and the UK $1.9 billion – with the main net importers in the developed world – the USA with a net shipping deficit of $2.4 billion, Italy $1.9 billion, the Netherlands $1.1 billion and France $0.9 billion – suggests that simple factor endowments have little to do with their revealed comparative advantages. The USA, for instance, is presumably better endowed with physical capital per head than Norway, Japan, or the UK,[11] and yet seems to have a much weaker competitive position (though its trade data are distorted by 'flags of convenience' registration by its carriers in other countries).

A simple comparison of human capital endowments between these countries would also not seem to explain their shipping trade performance. The main reason for this discrepancy – given that shipping evidently requires both physical capital and skills – is the *highly specific nature* of the skills, information and contacts which make for competitiveness in shipping. If all the skills required in the production of shipping services were 'general' skills which any well-educated labour force would have, then overall human capital would serve to explain differences in comparative advantage between countries equally well-endowed with physical capital. Since they are not, and historical circumstances (including government intervention) have shaped the accumulation of specific skills, knowledge and contacts, there are sharp differences in shipping perforamnce between otherwise similar countries. The historical and institutional factors that Katouzian refers to have a dominant influence on comparative advantage because of the *specificity of skills and knowledge*.

For this very reason, it would be wrong to take general skill endowments as the main determinant of comparative advantage in the export of *technology-related services*. Obviously, a minimum skill 'base' has to be present which can generate, assimilate and export technological services. But, given this, actual competitive positions in the international technology market depend on a number of other factors:

1. The experience of the exporting country in a particular technology. This is taken to include its innovativeness in that particular industry; the number and scale of plants already established at home; and the suitability of its technology to the client in question.
2. The availability of manpower that can be spared to take on technology-transfer work abroad.
3. The availability of capital goods, of requisite specifications and at competitive prices in the home country, to provide the embodied element of the service. This may not be essential in every case: for instance, civil construction contractors generally purchase standard capital equipment internationally and simple construction materials locally; certain parts of consultancy work overseas may not involve the purchase of capital goods at all; and engineering contractors generally choose to obtain some specialised equipment from other countries. However, in most cases involving industrial technology-transfer, there would tend to be a strong association between the provision of technological services and that of capital goods. It is important to bear in mind that the 'learning' that underlies internationally saleable technology services could have taken place only if the local capital goods industry were sufficiently advanced to allow local engineering firms or other technology sellers to partake in local investment activity.[12] In turn, these service firms (which very often would be parts or offshoots of capital goods manufacturers) would be most familiar with the equipment made in their home country and best able to communicate their requirements to local manufacturers. For all these reasons, the sale of industrial technology services requires, and is closely associated with, the sale of industrial equipment.[13]
4. The cost of technology services. This is deliberately mentioned last because pure price competition is not a significant element in technology trade. It only becomes relevant when all the technological factors have been accounted for, and when the client has complete confidence in the technological capabilities of the bidder.[14]

We have so far assumed that technology services are being exported between unrelated parties. A great deal of technological trade occurs, in fact, *within* multinational enterprises, and involves the sale of proprietary knowhow and the provision of specialised services from one branch of the enterprise to another. This does not mean, however, that the underlying determinants of country-level comparative advantage would be very different. While the *price* of technology transactions within an MNC could be subject to a substantial degree of arbitrariness, the *source* of the technology would be the country which has the requisite specific skills, knowhow, capital goods and manpower at the right cost. As with independent technology sellers, there would be a strong tendency to source capital equipment from the country of origin, but a very well-established and geographically diversified MNC may well be less prone to this than nationally based engineering or construction companies.

In terms of the sources of comparative advantage, therefore, competitiveness in technological services requires highly specific skills based on previous experience domestically, the existence of a large and diverse capital goods sector and the availability of (competitively priced) manpower. The relative weights of these factors differ from case to case. In the sale of plants involving sophisticated industrial technologies, the specific skill and equipment factors would predominate; in the sale of standard consultancy services, specific skills and their cost would matter; in the sale of simpler civil construction services, the cost and availability of suitable manpower and organisational capability would be the main determinants.

It is important to note that the development of specific technological skills may or may not depend on conventional trade determinants like capital/labour endowments, human capital endowment, overall research and development expenditures or the availability of large markets to exploit scale economies. Clearly there are skills that can be best learnt in an advanced industrial country with all these factors present. There are others that are learnt in countries with low capital-labour endowments, low levels of human capital, small R & D investments and relatively restricted markets. Thus, the fact that India has emerged as one of the leading exporters of technological services in the Third World[15] can be explained by the fact that it has mastered a number of high-skill (but not very innovation-based) technologies to a certain level *below* international frontiers, mainly by production experience and a small input of basic design work. Most of the capital goods involved are not particularly scale-intensive (Amsden, 1980), and the slightly out-of-date nature of the technologies renders them desirable to countries which do not wish to go for very large-scale or highly automated technologies.

To sum up this section, therefore, it would be sensible to argue that the determinants of comparative advantage in services are broadly related to general factor endowments like capital and skills, and to levels of technological activity. This configuration explains the fact that developed countries as a whole are the largest exporters of non-factor services. However, this broad pattern conceals many important variations. The sale of services of any sort requires specific skills, which in turn are based upon particular historical and other circumstances. The specificity of the 'learning' process involved in each service activity, which renders these skills non-transferable across the different categories of services, means that broad factor endowments and innovativeness are not always a reliable guide to comparative advantage. Each case requires separate examination, and the diversity is probably greater than found in trade in industrial products.

In shipping, the main determinant of trading advantage is long experience of trading, backed by considerable investments in shipping facilities. In industrial technology, it is the learning of particular technologies backed by the provision of capital goods. In other technology-related services (like civil construction), it is the availability of skilled manpower at competitive prices. The picture can be made more complex with the addition of more detailed examples, but the broad outlines seem fairly clear. We still have not touched directly on the factors that determine the *comparative advanatage of developing countries* in service trade: this will be the subject of the next section.

TRADE IN SERVICES AND THE COMPARATIVE ADVANTAGE OF DEVELOPING COUNTRIES

An earlier section in this chapter outlined the various determinants of comparative advantage in services. It laid special stress on the significance of the accumulation of *specific* skills and experience in the development of an internationally comptetitive edge in the sale of services. These specific skills have been developed in the past under particular historical circumstances, related to the patterns of industrialisation, trade and government intervention. These circumstances provided advantageous 'learning' conditions to the leaders in industrial development, since these countries provided a large enough demand for new and better services to permit specialisation as well as a supply of educated manpower, the necessary linkages with local manufacturing and infrastructural activity, and the capital necessary to provide the hardware for those which needed it.

This broad constellation of factors may lead one to expect that developing countries cannot develop a comparative advantage in international trade in services. This would be too static and simple a view. The very specificity of the skills that provide comparative advantage in service trade also provides the potential for developing countries to enter into a range of export of fairly complex and high-skill service activities. The specific conditions under which 'learning' takes place in developing countries differs in many respects from conditions in the developed countries: thus in markets of other developing countries, where the application of skills must occur in relatively backward conditions, the *specificity of developing country skills becomes an advantage*.

This is not the only source of potential competitiveness for developing countries. Even in activities where the specificity of learning is not a significant factor, developing countries can gain an edge if they can provide *standardised services at a lower cost* than developed country competitors. This edge will naturally be greater in activities where the fixed capital requirements for market entry are not very large (i.e. scale economies in the provision of the service are not high).

These points are not merely speculative. The area of trade in technology-related services illustrates them quite clearly. Many of the more industrialised developing countries – India, Argentina, Brazil, Mexico, South Korea, and the like – are already established exporters of technological services in various forms (Lall, 1984). In quantitative terms, the largest earner of foreign exchange is the sale of civil construction services: here, South Korea leads the field with some $44 billion worth of contracts won, followed at some distance by India ($6 billion), Brazil ($4 billion) and others. In terms of more complex industrial technologies, India emerges as the largest Third World exporter of industrial turnkey projects and consultancy services, with its enterprises having won some $2.5 billion worth of contracts in Africa, the Middle East and South East Asia. The other NICs also export turnkey industrial projects and consultancy services. In addition, Brazil's Petrobras sells a significant amount of petroleum exploration services overseas; India's computer software exports are booming; many enterprises export technical services of various kinds to other enterprises in the developing world; and there are even some instances of new industrial technologies (e.g. Mexico's HYL process for the direct reduction of steel) being sold on licence internationally.

The skills and knowhow that are being exported by these developing countries are of various types. Following Lall's (1982) classification, we may group them thus:

1. Competitive with technology provided by developing countries: here the technology is slightly adapted to local needs (e.g. trucks are made more rugged, equipment is simpler and less automated, consumer goods are geared to lower-income markets, processes are changed to use different raw materials, and so on), or is identical to that prevalent in the industrialised countries (as with many process industries). Here the competitive edge of the developing countries lies in the adaptations made, or the cheaper cost of skilled manpower, or both.

2. Complementary to technologies provided by developed countries: here firms from developing countries act as sub-contractors or partners of technology sellers from the industrialised countries. In general, the latter provide the very sophisticated components of the technology package, while the former undertake the simpler (but still highly skill-intensive) jobs of detailed engineering, construction supervision, civil construction, commissioning, or training. In fact, given the large labour cost advantage of many developing countries, this complementary type of service export is an obvious means of expansion for their enterprises in sectors where their own technologies are not up to the scales or technological levels prevalent internationally. In some cases it is also a route for expansion when their technologies are up to the mark, but their lack of an established brand-name, or their inability to put together attractive financial packages, puts them at a disadvantage.

3. Non-overlapping with developed country technologies: there are several areas of technological activity that are almost wholly specific to particular developing countries, either because of their special needs (e.g. rural, cottage or handicraft industries in India) or because of their natural resource endowments (e.g. charcoal-based steel manufacture or 'gasohol' in Brazil). These are already emerging as areas of service exports for them.

Lall (1982) also notes that there are limits to the extent to which technology-sellers from the developing countries can go. These limits are set by the 'learning' conditions at home. Thus, very large-scale activities, very expensive or advanced R & D based technologies, very sophisticated consumer goods and very rapidly changing technologies are beyond their capabilities and will continue to be so for some time to come. It is in these areas that the sellers of technological services from the advanced industrial countries will retain a comparative advantage. In more stable, mature technologies, amenable to de-scaling and simplification, with adapted or slightly out-dated products in demand in developing countries, we may expect to see increased market penetration by firms from the developing world.

We concur, therefore, with the general thrust of Sapir and Lutz's (1981) conclusion that there will be a steady progression of developing countries up the ladder (or 'stages') of comparative advantage.[16] The main determinant of this progression will, however, be the specific experience gained at home rather than the general accumulation of physical and human capital, as argued by Sapir and Lutz. The two sets of determinants will obviously concur over a range, but countries like India (with relatively low overall capital and skill endowments per capita) will diverge from the broad trend because of their policies towards local technological development.

By the same token, however, developing countries are unlikely to emerge as major exporters of highly capital-intensive services like shipping. The constraint does not lie in capital requirements *per se*, but in the very large minimum economic size of an internationally viable merchant fleet and the existing network of connections, freight charges and linkages with traders. Nevertheless, a number of developing countries *are* making efforts to build up their shipping capabilities, and some may succeed in the long run as significant exporters of shipping services.

CONCLUSIONS

The dynamics of comparative advantage dictate that developing countries specialise in areas of activity where they are gaining a genuine comparative advantage. This specialisation has to be assisted by government intervention to protect and promote activities where the accumulation of specific skills is feasible. Without active intervention, the development of indigenous service industries may be stunted. With sensible policies, on the other hand, local service enterprises may become internationally competitive. Their entry into world markets will have beneficial linkages with product exports, starting a virtuous circle of cumulative causation whereby skill and commodity exports promote each other.

Any argument for protection must, however, be qualified with the strong proviso that protection must not be pushed to the extent that it creates perpetually inefficient, undynamic and unviable enterprises. The vital role that the service sector plays in overall economic development calls for even greater caution, because its inefficiency can hamper internal growth and external expansion.

Subject to the requirements of sensible protection, therefore, it would be wise to import those services which cannot be produced locally at low costs, and to permit the entry of foreign service firms in those sectors where local production is economical. Both forms of foreign competition must, of course, be closely monitored, and the needs of national development must constantly receive top priority. As structural change proceeds with economic development, and new services arise and existing ones undergo technological progress, the composition of service imports and exports will also change. Exports will occur in activities where local capabilities have mastered the skills involved and local linkages with related activities are well grounded. Imports will occur where technological scale and specific skill factors give foreign producers a decided advantage.

As with all forms of trade, the necessity to import a service is not a 'bad thing', merely a sign of specialisation. What *is* bad is the lack of policies to foster a country's underlying dynamic comparative advantage, or, at the other extreme, an excessive protection of activities in which there is no such advantage.

All this is based on a simplifying assumption: that it is possible to predict, from past experience and current data, where a developing country's comparative advantage will lie in the future. In an area where the underlying theory is vague and the number of possible influences large, prediction is clearly a hazardous task. Moreover, there are many 'non-economic' factors which might intrude to upset the economist's models. This does not mean that there are no 'right' or 'wrong' policies (clearly the enormous differences in achievements by different developing countries pursuing different policies suggest that policies do matter), only that accurate forecasting of the results of detailed policy measures is very difficult. Perhaps the best set of policies is to be extremely flexible and pragmatic and to aim at fostering fully competitive industrial activities. A dynamic and competitive manufacturing base is most likely to lead to a similar service infrastructure, with service exports resulting from timely and judicious policy support.

NOTES

1. I am grateful to Frances Stewart for perceptive comments on an earlier draft.
2. See UNCTAD (1983).
3. See Katouzian (1970) for an illuminating discussion of the definition and evolving nature of services. Some problems of defining trade in services are discussed in UNCTAD (1983).

4. 'Property' income covers only primary property such as real estate. Income from intellectual property, such as royalties, are counted as non-factor income, and so are included in the following analysis.
5. There is an earlier study by these authors (Sapir and Lutz, 1980). However, only the results of the second study are reported here, to prevent repetition.
6. Sapir and Lutz also include a dummy variable for distance from major trading partners and a variable for the composition of trade, measured by the share of manufactures in total imports. The distance variable is insignificant for developing countries, but the manufactures' variable is significant, showing that imports of shipping services are greater the more manufactures are imported as a proportion of all imports.
7. These are what Katouzian (1970) calls 'complementary services'. See his paper for analysis of these services in relation to others (which are less prone to be traded internationally) and a useful set of references.
8. For a review of new trade theories in the context of developing country trade, see Stewart (1983).
9. See Sapir and Lutz (1981), pp. 23–30.
10. See UNCTAD (1983), Table XIII A.
11. Sapir and Lutz (1981) approximate total capital stock by per capita gross fixed investment in 1960–75, and find (Table A.2) that the USA has a lower per capita stock than Norway and Sweden. This is surely a result of the period they chose, and is a misleading indicator of total physical capital stock, since both these countries are relatively late industrialisers.
12. See Lall (1982).
13. The evidence on this is patchy but suggestive: see the papers on technology exports by newly industrialising countries in Lall (ed) 1984.
14. It is important to note here that non-technology related factors may also affect competitiveness – the main ones being the financial package offered and political considerations. These are significant but not germane to the analysis, and are ignored in the text.
15. See my overview of technology exports in Lall (ed.), 1984.
16. The 'stages' approach to comparative advantage is developed fully by Balassa (1981).

REFERENCES

Amsden, A., 'The Industry Characteristics of Intra-Third World Trade in Manufactures', *Economic Development and Cultural Changes*, Vol. 29, pp. 1–19, 1980.

Balassa, B., *The Newly Industrializing Countries in the World Economy* (New York: Pergamon, 1981).

Dick, R. and Dicke, H., 'Patterns of Trade in Knowledge', in H. Giersch (ed.) *International Economic Development and Resource Transfer* (Tübingen: J.C.B. Mohr, 1979).

Katouzian, H., 'The Development of the Service Sector: A New Approach', *Oxford Economic Papers*, Vol. 22, pp. 362–82, 1970.

Katouzian, H., 'Services in International Trade: A Theoretical Interpretation', in H. Giersch (ed.) *International Economic Development and Resource Transfer* (Tübingen: J.C.B. Mohr, 1979).

Lall, S., *Developing Countries as Exporters of Technology* (London: Macmillan, 1982).

Lall, S. (ed.) 'Exports of Technology by Newly Industrialising Countries', special issue of *World Development* Vol.12, No.5–6, 1984.

Sapir, A. and Lutz, E. 'Trade in Non-Factor Services: Past Trends and Current Issues', World Bank Staff Working Paper, No. 410, 1980.

Sapir, A. and Lutz, E., 'Trade in Services: Economic Determinants and Development Related Issues', World Bank Staff Working Paper, No. 480, 1981.

Stewart, F., 'Recent Theories of International Trade: Some Implications for the South', in H. Kierzkowski (ed.), *Monopolistic Competition and International Trade* (Oxford: Oxford University Press, 1983).

UNCTAD, 'Production and Trade in Services, Policies and their Underlying Factors Bearing upon International Services Transactions', Geneva, TD/B/941, 1983.

9 Outward Orientation, Import Instability and African Economic Growth: an Empirical Investigation[1]

G. K. HELLEINER

INTRODUCTION

Beleaguered policy-makers in developing countries have become quite tired of generalised advice. The remedies for macroeconomic malaise or stagnation that are appropriate in one country may be quite unsuited to the problems of another. Today's 'recipe' for stabilisation and development in one country may be disastrous in its effects not only in other countries but also at other times in the same country. 'Norms' and 'averages' for the world, however fascinating to statisticians and development economists, are dubious guides for policy-makers in individual countries. Unhappiness with 'global' prescriptions has rarely been as vociferous as it has become in recent years in the context of the 'conditionality' attached to IMF, World Bank and other official lending. The IMF and the World Bank usually deny that they employ a single 'model' for all their member countries. Whether these institutions, *qua* institutions, do or do not, there can be little doubt that, *within* them, generalised prescriptions abound.

Among the most controversial of these prescriptions relates to the desirable degree of 'outward orientation' or the 'openness' of domestic production. Casual empiricism has been buttressed by a considerable amount of econometric research in support of the proposition that increased exports are frequently conducive to more rapid economic growth. The 'orthodox' advice of the 1970s has accordingly been to encourage exports, to be more 'outward-oriented'. There is much that could be said about the general appropriateness of this advice for developing countries in the 1980s; Paul Streeten has been prominent among those who have questioned it (Streeten, 1982). My purpose in this chapter is a narrower one: to relate the export orientation dispute to the recent circumstances of sub-Saharan Africa.

THE EXTERNAL SECTOR AND AFRICAN GROWTH: ALTERNATIVE APPROACHES

A recent report by the World Bank – the so-called 'Berg Report', named after its principal author – has taken the position that African countries should increase incentives for exporters, reduce barriers to imports, and generally 'liberalize' and 'open up' their economies. The Bank's structural adjustment lending programme unquestionably emphasises, in its conditionality in Africa, the same generalised priority for greater outward orientation and the restructuring of incentives to that end. The role of the external sector is now a controversial basis for generalisations at least in part because the World Bank has made it so.

There are many African governments that have severely discriminated against exports in recent years, and which should be encouraged to seek greater overall balance in their incentive structures. African shares of many individual world markets have declined over the the past decade, and there is no inherent reason for this poor competitive performance. In the mid-1970s there was some positive correlation between export market share maintenance and overall growth performance in African countries (Balassa, 1983). (In the same study, however, there was none between 'import substitution' measures and growth.) One would certainly not want to play down the overall importance of export performance in economies of the African type, even in the dismal circumstances of the early 1980s in which the real prices for such exports as coffee, cocoa, tea, palm oil, groundnuts and some minerals are generally expected to remain depressed.

It must nevertheless be said that the evidence for an association between the degree of export orientation and the rate of economic growth in poor countries (of whatever continent) is extraordinarily weak. None of the recent, much-quoted econometric investigations of interrelationships between exports and growth employ data for very low-income countries. That is because these countries apparently do not behave according to the same patterns and regularities that can be observed for other (better-off) developing countries.

As Michaely reported in his analysis of the 1950–73 relationships between export expansion and economic growth:

> It is interesting to note that the positive association of the economy's growth with the growth of the export share appears to be particularly strong among the more developed countries, and not to exist at all among the least developed ... This seems to indicate that growth is affected by export performance only once countries achieve some minimum level of development. (Michaely, 1977, p. 52)

Heller and Porter's retesting of Michaely's propositions using non-export output instead of total output as the basis for a search for growth-export relationships obtained similar results (1978, p. 192).

Similarly, Tyler rationalised his exclusion of low-income countries from his investigation of similar issues using data for the 1960–77 period (and a different methodology) as follows: 'some basic level of development is necessary for a country to most benefit [sic] from export oriented growth, particularly involving manufactured exports' (1981, p. 124).

The governments of low-income countries in Africa and elsewhere have grounds for caution as they consider policy advice based upon evidence from samples of countries that do not look or behave like theirs.

The most persuasive theoretical case for the observed positive correlation between export expansion and economic growth is that which posits that marginal factor productivities in the export sector exceed those in the non-export sector (Feder, 1983). Plausible explanations for this possibility have to do with externalities, greater utilisation of capacity, the potential for scale economies, the pressure of global competition's effects upon X-efficiency and other such influences. Shifts of resources from the less efficient non-export sector to the more efficient export sector (or indeed expanded export production that does not draw resources away from other activity, but nevertheless throws off externalities) measured by the increased share of national product emanating from the export sector, should, if this analysis is correct, achieve once-and-for-all growth increases. Conversely, reductions in the export share should, on the same assumptions, reduce growth. Less apparent is the rationale for an expectation of *continued*, more rapid growth in countries with higher export shares, or greater 'export orientation', although some authors believe there are grounds for expecting this outcome as well (Krueger, 1981).

Feder's econometric formulation of this hypothesis was as follows:

$$\frac{\dot{Y}}{Y} = \alpha \frac{I}{Y} + \beta \frac{\dot{L}}{L} + \gamma_1 \left[\frac{\dot{X}}{X} \cdot \frac{X}{Y} \right] \qquad [1]$$

where I is gross investment, Y is Gross Domestic Product, L is labour force, and X is exports. The coefficient α is interpreted as the marginal productivity of capital in the non-export sector, and should therefore be positive but lower than that for the economy as a whole (Feder, 1983, pp. 63–4). Unless labour is 'surplus' β should also carry a positive sign. If export activity truly is more productive on the margin than are other activities the sign on γ_1 should be positive as well. If γ_1 is zero, this equation reduces to the conventional neoclassical aggregate production function; that is, there is no special growth significance attached to expanding exports as opposed to non-exports.

A variant on this approach to the openness question, particularly where economies are believed to be constrained by foreign exchange availability and where exports are by no means the sole source of foreign exchange, as may frequently be the case in Africa, one might hypothesise special productivity effects from increased imports. In this version, the postulated 'production function' is:

$$\frac{\dot{Y}}{Y} = \alpha \frac{I}{Y} + \beta \frac{\dot{L}}{L} + \gamma_2 \left[\frac{\dot{M}}{M} \cdot \frac{M}{Y} \right] \qquad [2]$$

where M is imports, and γ_2 is expected to be positive.

These hypotheses concerning the contribution of economic structure, in the openness dimension, to growth are not the only ways in which one might pursue the question of the external sector's influence.

One source of difficulty that is consistently emphasised by policy-makers in low-income African countries is externally created instability. International economists and development economists have long been fascinated by the interrelationships between export instability and economic growth. For some years empirical investigations have been conducted, purporting to demonstrate that these links are positive or negative, tight or loose. The results vary greatly – with the country sample, the time period, and the methodology (Moran, 1983). The earliest major empirical investigation (MacBean, 1966), although limited by serious methodological flaws (Maizels, 1968), seemed to demonstrate that export instability carried no growth costs. It nevertheless received considerable attention – no doubt at least partly because this message was one that was both paradoxical, and therefore appealing to economists, and useful to Northern governments struggling to hold off developing countries' proposals for improved stabilisation mechanisms.

In the welter of subsequent studies and controversy over these issues some of the 'fundamentals' were often neglected (Lim, 1976). In particular, the principal reason for concern with export instability, especially in the poorer countries that enjoyed limited access to international credit, was always its effects upon import volume. The sharp increases in oil prices (and, on occasion, food prices) in the 1970s served to remind many that it was the *purchasing power* of exports, not sheer export earnings, that was of greatest policy interest. As it became evident that some countries could borrow their way through shocks and fluctuations in the purchasing power of their exports, whereas others could not, the salience of import volume stability as a prime policy target also grew. Discontinuities in the flows of intermediate inputs and capital goods, both of which are highly sensitive to fluctuation in overall volume, were clearly damaging to the process of economic growth. So was the diversion of limited governmental management skill to the resolution of balance of payments crises, particularly in low-income countries where the supply of such skill was most limited; but this latter proposition is harder to test. Clearly, 'import instability and its consequences for LDCs deserve more empirical research' (Junginger-Dittel and Reisen, 1979, p. 668).

Even before the 1979-82 shocks, African policy-makers complained about the effects of externally created instability upon their economies. As they saw it, international shocks were more costly to them than any failure on their own part to take full advantage of export opportunities (or probably any other more domestically oriented policy failures). They could take comfort from a recent cross-sectional analysis of African growth experience in the 1970s (prior to the post-1979 crisis) which concluded that 'environmental' variables (terms of trade, instability, etc.) had a greater impact upon growth rates than did 'policy' variables (like the real exchange rate, measures of import adjustment capacity, etc.) (Wheeler, 1984). But that study was itself 'frankly exploratory' (p. 1), and these issues cannot so easily be empirically resolved. Certainly few could quarrel with the *fact* that the 1979 oil price increase and the subsequent severe global recession have dealt a very heavy blow to low-income African countries.

The principal external instability problems faced by African policy-makers can plausibly be taken as those of import volume instability. Cross-sectional study of African and other low-income countries' experience ought to be able to test the proposition that import volume instability is harmful to growth; and to compare this interpretation of the role of the external sector with that of the World Bank and others.

The relationship to be tested then becomes:

$$\frac{\dot{Y}}{Y} = \alpha\frac{I}{Y} + \beta\frac{\dot{L}}{L} + \gamma_3 (IVI) \qquad [3]$$

or

$$\frac{\dot{Y}}{Y} = \alpha\frac{I}{Y} + \beta\frac{\dot{L}}{L} + \gamma_1\frac{\dot{X}}{Y} + \gamma_3 (IVI) \qquad [4]$$

or

$$\frac{\dot{Y}}{Y} = \alpha\frac{I}{Y} + \beta\frac{\dot{L}}{L} + \gamma_2\frac{\dot{M}}{Y} + \gamma_3 (IVI) \qquad [5]$$

where IVI is a measure of the instability of import volume. The coefficient on this variable, γ_3, should carry a negative sign. An alternative looser formulation, where exports are the principal source of foreign exchange and short-term credit is still not readily available, might substitute the income terms of trade (ITT) for IVI.

These alternative equations have been estimated on a cross-sectional basis for a sample of poor countries – those for which data were readily available – and for sub-Saharan African countries, over the period 1960–1979. There are, as usual, major problems with the use of cross-section data to shed light upon the determinants of growth, problems to which Feder and others allude (p. 64 and references cited there). Estimating parameters across a wide sample of countries assumes that the relationships among the variables are the same in all the countries in the sample; in this instance, both production functions and the degree of differentiation between factor productivities in different sectors (export and non-export), together with the response to external instability, have to be assumed everywhere the same.

THE DATA

The low-income and African countries included in this investigation were those for which the data were at hand. The principal binding constraint proved to be the availability of time series on import volume and the purchasing power of exports. Data on these variables for the period 1960-79 had been provided to the author by UNCTAD for another purpose; and, rather than seeking updated series, these were employed in the calculation of the instability indices for the entire 1960-80 period. The only other data source was the *World Development Report*; if countries were not included in its tables, they were excluded from the study.

'Low-income' countries were those so defined by the World Bank in its *World Development Report, 1982*, i.e. those with per capita incomes in 1980 of $410 or less. African countries included in this investigation are those in the 'low-income' category together with those on the lower end of the World Bank's 'middle income' category; only those with per capita incomes of $630 or less in 1980 have been included. (Egypt is regarded as 'non-African' and has also been excluded.)

These definitions and data constraints produced a sample of 24 'low-income' countries and a separate sample of 25 African ones. Of the 24 'low-income' countries, 18 are African. (Data gaps required the dropping of Sierra Leone from both samples in some of the estimation, leaving only 24 African and 23 'low-income' countries.) The sub-Saharan African countries excluded from the African sample because their per capita incomes were above the $630 (1980) cut-off were Cameroon, Congo People's Republic, Nigeria and the Ivory Coast. Excluded because their populations were less than a million, and for which therefore the World Bank did not record the necessary data, are a number of otherwise eligible African countries, e.g. Guinea-Bissau, the Gambia, Cape Verde, Comoros, Equatorial Guinea, Djibouti, Sao Tome and Principe. Swaziland, Botswana, Mauritius and the Seychelles are excluded on grounds of both size and per capita income. The list of countries may be found in the data appendix (Table 9.3).

The investment share of GDP is employed as an approximation to the rate of growth of the capital stock. If one could assume a constant capital-output ratio over time and across countries, the growth of the capital stock – as of national product – would be the investment share times that ratio. Such an assumption would be difficult to defend in its specifics; but it may not be too inaccurate as a rough approximation. In the absence of more comprehensive data, the World Bank's data on 1960 and 1980 investment ratios (*World Development Report, 1982*, pp. 118-19) have simply been averaged to obtain a figure for the 1960-80 period.

The World Bank's *World Development Report* also reports figures for the rate of growth of the labour force by decade (1982, pp. 146-7). The average growth rates for 1960-70 and for 1970-80 have been averaged to obtain the desired overall growth rate for the 1960-80 period.

Export shares of GDP have also been obtained directly from the *World Development Report* (1982, pp. 118–19), and import shares have been calculated from the same source's data on export shares and resource balance (1982, pp. 118–19). (Resource balance is the export share less the import share.)

The instability measures are the coefficients of variation (standard error divided by the mean of the dependent variable) of log-linear time trends of each country's import volume and purchasing power of exports (income terms of trade) over the 1960–79 period. The raw data were supplied by UNCTAD.

REGRESSION RESULTS

The results of the regressions (Table 9.1 and 9.2) show no statistically significant link between the change in export share of GDP and growth. Indeed, the sign on this relationship is consistently negative. These negative results are similar to those previously encountered with countries on the lower end of the per capita income spectrum. Results were no better when the change in export shares was replaced by the change in import shares. Although in some estimated equations the sign was now positive, the relationship with growth was still statistically insignificant.

Neither of the external instability measures is statistically significantly related to growth in the total sample of poor countries, although import volume instability carries the expected negative sign. Instability of the income terms of trade consistently carries a positive sign in these regressions although nowhere it is statistically significant.

In sub-Saharan Africa, however, we have rather a different story. Import volume instability carries a negative sign and this (expected) negative relationship is statistically highly significant. Instability in the income terms of trade also carries a negative sign, and is also statistically significant at somewhat less impressive levels.

As far as external influences are concerned, then, there is no evidence to support the proposition that the degree of export orientation is associated with growth performance either in Africa or in poor countries more generally; and there is support, especially powerful in Africa, for the view that greater import volume instability is associated with slower growth.

The traditional arguments in aggregate production functions (labour and capital) perform quite differently in the two samples of countries.

TABLE 9.1 *Regression results: poor countries' growth, 1960–1980*

Equation	Constant	I/Y	$\Delta L/L$	$\Delta X/Y$	$\Delta M/Y$	IVI	ITT	R^2	F-Statistic
(0)	−1.3768 (.780)	.1904 (2.925)***	.8654 (1.291)*	—	—	—	—	.3156	4.8430
(1)†	−1.4456 (.757)	.1937 (2.747)***	.8745 (1.221)	−.0047 (.188)	—	—	—	.3160	2.9255
(2)†	−1.4493 (.776)	.2007 (2.896)***	.8927 (1.259)	—	−.0154 (.679)	—	—	.3309	3.1323
(3)	−.7452 (.330)	.1707 (2.168)**	.9025 (1.312)*	—	—	−9.189 (.464)	—	.3229	3.1800
(3a)	−1.1701 (.649)	.1711 (2.425)***	.8100 (1.189)	—	—	—	2.9204 (.759)	.3348	3.3553
(4)†	−.6858 (.277)	.1721 (2.049)**	.9051 (1.234)	−.0075 (.291)	—	−10.9376 (.499)	—	.3253	2.1695
(4a)†	−1.2284 (.627)	.1730 (2.239)**	.8232 (1.128)	−.0024 (.094)	—	—	2.8904 (.706)	.3344	2.2606
(5)†	−.5535 (.226)	.1754 (2.117)**	.9283 (1.282)*	—	−.0179 (.761)	−12.4673 (.581)	—	.3432	2.3517
(5a)†	−1.2581 (.659)	.1814 (2.414)***	.8430 (1.169)	—	−.0151 (.658)	—	2.8962 (.721)	.3497	2.4198

NOTES

T-ratios in parentheses. One to three asterisks indicate significance (one-tail) at 10% level, 5% level and 1% level, respectively.
† excludes Sierra Leone.

TABLE 9.2 Regression results: African countries' growth, 1960–1980

Equation	Constant	I/Y	$\frac{\Delta L}{L}$	$\frac{\Delta X}{Y}$	$\frac{\Delta M}{Y}$	IVI	ITI	R^2	F-Statistic
(0)	−1.5184 (.811)	.0130 (.259)	1.9224 (2.092)**	—	—	—	—	.1984	2.7221
(1)†	−1.7465 (.867)	.0188 (.328)	1.9694 (1.942)**	−.0086 (.290)	—	—	—	.2160	1.8368
(2)†	−1.9914 (.969)	.0052 (.095)	2.1400 (2.128)**	—	.0102 (.360)	—	—	.2178	1.8560
(3)	.2305 (.121)	.0179 (.385)	1.9561 (2.304)**	—	—	−41.0858 (2.189)**	—	.3474	3.7256
(3a)	−.7127 (.380)	.0882 (1.307)*	1.4381 (1.533)*	—	—	—	−17.1293 (1.603)*	.2857	2.8001
(4)†	.4922 (.233)	.0372 (.700)	1.7688 (1.892)**	−.0241 (.859)	—	−44.5695 (2.182)**	—	.3731	2.8272
(4a)†	−.8314 (.405)	.0945 (1.250)	1.4269 (1.357)*	−.0111 (.386)	—	—	−16.6922 (1.477)*	.2967	2.0043
(5)†	.2148 (.097)	.0208 (.397)	1.9568 (2.071)**	—	−.0049 (.178)	−41.1602 (1.965)**	—	.3498	2.5560
(5a)†	−1.1119 (.532)	.0777 (1.061)	1.6297 (1.568)*	—	.0102 (.372)	—	−16.4364 (1.457)*	.2963	2.0004

NOTES

T- values are in parentheses. One to three asterisks indicate significance (one-tail) at 10% level, 5% level and 1% level, respectively.
† excludes Sierra Leone.

The growth rate of the labour force fails to meet the 10 per cent significance level in many of the estimated equations for the poor countries; but it always meets this test in the equations for the (labour-scarce) African ones. On the other hand, the investment ratio – proxying the rate of growth of the capital stock – is statistically significant only in the equations for the sample of poor countries. It attains a 10 per cent level of significance in only one of the African equations, and the coefficients attached to it are, in the African case, very low. While the underlying data are highly imperfect, these results do seem to support those who have argued that capital formation in Africa has been singularly unproductive.

CONCLUSIONS

If there is a lesson in the experience of the African countries' interactions with the global economy during the 1960s and 1970s, it would seem to have more to do with the desirability of stabilising import volume than with that of increasing the degree of outward orientation. If the above regressions are to be believed, halving the degree of import instability would add roughly 2 per cent to average growth rates. (The African average ivi is 0.0463.) One way in which more stable import volume can be achieved is through the holding of greater official foreign exchange reserves. The link between reserve holdings and import stability is complex, and not one that would allow easy calculations of the appropriate average increase in reserves; nor is it easy to assess the opportunity cost of the resources held in reserves instead of invested in productive activity. It may well be, however, that African countries have held inadequate reserves by any standards. Certainly, in the 1970s their reserves' share of import value has been well below the norm for other oil-importing developing countries (IMF, 1983, p. 199).

On the face of it, during the 1960s and 1970s the provision of more international liquidity for Africa would have yielded very high returns (no doubt in part because of the unduly illiquid state engendered there by inadequate reserves). Access to short-term credit as required, to stabilise the flow of imports, either from the commercial banks or from official sources – aid donors, the IMF, etc – has unfortunately been very limited in Africa (Helleiner, 1983). Commercial banks have not regarded many African governments as 'creditworthy' At the same time, aid donors have been unwilling or unable significantly to switch their activities between project assistance and balance of payments support in response to changing African needs. The IMF became far more active in Africa in the late 1970s but was still unable to provide more than a small proportion of balance of payments shortfalls.

The post-1979 period dramatically underscored the importance of imports to African growth. As the recession and oil price increase slashed the purchasing power of African exports, inadequate international liquidity meant that African import volumes had to be savagely cut back. The result has been vast underutilisation for capacity, the running down of physical and human capital, and the emergence of a downward spiral in output and an upward spiral of inflation, both of which will be hard to break. The holding of greater reserves, of the size required to reduce excessive import instability over the 1960s and 1970s, would not have significantly protected African countries against external shocks of the dimensions of those of recent years. The world's capacity to supply liquidity to Africa and to other poor areas of the world proved woefully inadequate in the post-1979 episode. The cost in foregone African growth will continue to be registered well into the coming decade.

The evidence, both from the experience of the 1960s and 1970s, and from the post-1979 shock, strongly suggests that African growth would be significantly increased by the provision of increased international liquidity to tide them over temporary balance of payments problems and assist them to stabilise their imports. It is important to recognise that the liquidity needs of African countries are quite distinct from their (universally recognised) need for development finance. Increased development assistance conceivably *could* be employed for the purpose of rebuilding African reserves; but this is only a possibility, and it is not what aid funds have traditionally been intended to provide (besides which most aid donors would probably not approve of such usage of their funds). On the face of it, more liquidity would have been more productive than the provision of increased developmental capital.

Increased provision of 'low-conditionality' finance through the International Monetary Fund seems the most obvious device for meeting this liquidity need. This could be achieved by quota expansion, an expanded compensatory financing facility, resumed and expanded SDR allocations, new facilities to meet unique needs (like the mid-1970s 'oil facility'), or combinations of all of these (Commonwealth Secretariat, 1983). Because of its formula basis and the consequent minimisation of the problems of moral hazard, the compensatory financing facility is probably the most sensible means of supplying low-conditionality finance on which one might seek to build. The African countries thus have a major interest in appropriate international

TABLE 9.3 Data appendix

	(1) Growth rate of GDP[1]	(2) Investment GDP (I/Y)[2]	(3) Growth rate of labour force (L/L)[3]	(4) Growth in export share of GDP (X/Y)	(5) Growth in import share of GDP (M/Y)	(6) Import volume instability (IVI)[4]	(7) Income terms of trade instability (ITT)[4]
\multicolumn{8}{l}{A. Low-income countries}							
Bangladesh	3.8	12	2.3	−2	14	.0697	.0537
Burma	3.7	18	1.3	−12	−7	.0328	.0418
Afghanistan	3.3	15	1.9	7	7	.0506	.0242
India	3.5	20	1.6	0	0	.0289	.0207
Sri Lanka	4.4	25	2.1	−13	4	.0307	.2423
Pakistan	5.7	18	2.2	5	11	.0475	.3528
Chad	0.2	12	1.8	10	31	.0353	.0436
Ethiopia	3.2	11	1.9	6	10	.0309	.0296
Somalia	2.2	13	2.0	2	11	.0315	.0287
Mali	4.1	14.5	2.1	7	14	.0492	.0624
Rwanda	3.4	11	2.5	2	17	.0482	.0675
Upper Volta	3.3	14	1.3	2	18	.0561	.0849
Zaire	1.8	11.5	1.8	−26	−19	.0794	.0577
Malawi	5.6	16	2.4	1	−1	.0296	.0241
Mozambique	0.9	10	1.8	−1	9	.0823	.0909
Sierra Leone	3.0	15[6]	1.7	n.a.	n.a.	.0289	.0418
Tanzania	5.5	18	2.2	−17	2	.0324	.0338
Central African Republic	2.5	15	1.7	6	14	.0475	.0474
Uganda	2.0	7	2.9	−22	−16	.0664	.0452
Benin	3.0	19.5	2.2	16	29	.0269	.0882

TABLE 9.3 (Continued)

	(1) Growth rate of GDP[1]	(2) Investment GDP (I/Y)[2]	(3) Growth rate of labour force (L/L)[3]	(4) Growth in export share of GDP (X/Y)	(5) Growth in import share of GDP (M/Y)	(6) Import volume instability (IVI)[4]	(7) Income terms of trade instability (ITT)[4]
Niger	2.8	21	2.8	16	23	.0528	.0435
Madagascar	1.6	16	1.9	3	9	.0314	.0247
Sudan	2.9	12	2.3	− 6	3	.0434	.0351
Togo	6.0	18.5	2.2	22	27	.0368	.0504
B. Other African countries							
Ghana	1.0	14.5	2.0	−16	−23	.0429	.0286
Kenya	6.0	21	2.8	− 1	− 1	.0341	.0275
Mauritania	1.7[5]	44	2.4	20	17	.0615	.2389
Senegal	2.5	15.5	1.9	− 9	7	.0186	.1180
Angola	−2.2	10.5	1.5	23	15	.0600	.0522
Liberia	3.4	28.5	2.5	14	21	.0553	.0528
Zambia	2.9	24	2.4	−18	3	.0752	.0727

NOTES
1. Average of 1960–70 and 1970–80 growth rates.
2. Average of 1960 and 1980.
3. Average of 1960–70 and 1970–80 growth rates.
4. Calculated for 1960–79, as the coefficient of determination in a loglinear time trend.
5. 1970–1980.
6. 1980.
SOURCES: Columns (1)–(5): *World Development Report, 1982*, pp. 112, 118, 146.
Columns (6) and (7): calculated from UNCTAD data.

monetary reform – reform that ensures a stable, adequate and equitably distributed supply of international liquidity.

NOTE

1. I should like to thank Ismael Hossain for computational assistance.

REFERENCES

Balassa, B., 'Policy Responses to External Shocks in Sub-Saharan African Countries', *Journal of Policy Modelling*, Vol.5, No. 1, March 1983.

Commonwealth Secretariat, *Towards a New Bretton Woods, Challenges For the World Financial and Trading System* (London: Longman, 1983).

Feder, Gershon, 'On Exports and Economic Growth', *Journal of Development Economics*, Vol. 12, Nos. 1/2, February/April 1983.

Helleiner, G. K., 'The IMF and Africa in the 1980s', *Princeton Essays in International Finance*, No. 152, July 1983.

Heller, Peter S. and Porter, Richard C., 'Exports and Growth: an Empirical Reinvestigation', *Journal of Development Economics*, Vol. 5, No. 2, June 1978.

IMF, *World Economic Outlook* (Washington, DC: IMF, 1983).

Junginger-Dittel, Klaus O. and Reisen, Helmut, 'Import Instability and LDCs' Response', *Weltwirtschaftliches Archiv*, Band 115, Heft 4, 1979.

Krueger, Anne, 'Export-Led Industrial Growth Reconsidered', in Wontack Hong and Lawrence B. Krause (eds), *Trade and Growth of the Advanced Developing Countries in the Pacific Basin* (Seoul: Korea Development Institute, 1981).

Lim, David, 'Export Instability and Economic Growth: a Return to Fundamentals', *Oxford Bulletin of Economics and Statistics*, Vol. 38, No. 4, November 1976.

MacBean, Alasdair I., *Export Instability and Economic Development* (London: Allen & Unwin, 1966).

Maizels, A., Review of MacBean book, *American Economic Review*, Vol. 58, June 1968, pp. 575–80.

Michaely, Michael, 'Exports and Growth: An Empirical Investigation', *Journal of Development Economics*, Vol. 4, No. 1, March 1977.

Moran, Christian, 'Export Fluctuations and Economic Growth: an Empirical Analysis', *Journal of Development Economics*, Vol. 12, Nos. 1/2, February/April 1983.

Streeten, Paul, 'Outward-Looking Industrialization and Trade Strategies', paper presented to North-South Roundtable, Oiso, Japan, 1982.

Tyler, William G., 'Growth and Export Expansion in Developing Countries: Some Empirical Evidence', *Journal of Development Economics*, Vol. 9, No. 1, August 1981.

Wheeler, David, 'Sources of Stagnation in Sub-Saharan Africa', *World Development*, Vol. 12, No. 1, January 1984.

World Bank, *Accelerated Development in Sub-Saharan Africa, Agenda for Action* (Washington, DC: World Bank, 1981).

World Bank, *World Development Report, 1982*.

10 The Early 1980s in Latin America: The 1930s One More Time?

CARLOS F. DIAZ-ALEJANDRO

INTRODUCTION

The reader need not be held in suspense. No, the differences between the early 1980s and the early 1930s in Latin America are more significant than their similarities. But the question is pertinent, and the comparison could cast light on both historical episodes, while deepening understanding of the cyclical behaviour of peripheral, semi-industrialised economies, and about their interaction with the international economy.

Depressions have proven to be more interesting than booms to students of Latin America: the early 1890s, the crisis of 1920–1 and the 1930s have received more attention than booms before and after. Scholarly morbidity is not the only explanation for this apparent bias for gloom: negative external shocks arising from the international economy have long been viewed in Latin America as leading both to short-term economic and political autonomy, with net welfare consequences of crises being moot.

The story of the 1930s in at least the larger or more autonomous Latin American countries has been particularly influential in generating a sanguine attitude towards external shocks. By the 1970s it could be argued that economies and public sectors that weathered remarkably well the shocks of the 1930s were even better prepared, fifty years and much industrialisation later, to handle whatever the international economy threw at them in the 1980s.

That optimism was flawed. Available evidence indicates that while the severity of the quantifiable external shock has been milder during the early 1980s than during the early 1930s, the performance of at least several major Latin American economies has been weaker in the recent period. In Argentina, Brazil and Chile, per capita gross domestic product and industrial output are doing worse in the early 1980s than in the early 1930s (see Diaz-Alejandro, 1983, pp. 8–9; Naciones Unidas, 1983b, Table 2). While data do not always allow precise comparisons, Mexico and Venezuela appear to do better during the most recent depressive episode, for obvious reasons. Colombian performance during both crises is relatively strong. While several Latin American countries recovered earlier and faster than the United States during the early 1930s, the opposite has occurred during the early 1980s in all countries.

The rest of this chapter is organised as follows: *similarities* between the two historical episodes will be discussed first, including parallels in their preceding conditions. Salient *contrasts* will then be analysed, both regarding the structures of the Latin American economies and their links with the international economy. Conclusions and caveats will close the chapter.

SIMILARITIES

Similarities between the 1980s and the 1930s may be found in the booms that preceded them; in the nature of the external shocks; and in some aspects of the domestic response.

Both the late 1920s and the late 1970s witnessed significant capital inflows into the major Latin American economies. External terms of trade and demand for exports were reasonably good, with precise conditions for each country depending on the commodity lottery. As during other 'good times' in the history of these economies, there was a tendency for international reserves to grow and for nominal exchange rates to lag behind the difference between domestic and external inflation. As during the late 1920s, when most Latin American countries sought fixed nominal exchange rates (in the context of the gold standard), during the late 1970s and very early 1980s some countries moved either to fix nominal exchange rates, or to fix their rate of change ahead of time. The combination of external circumstances and domestic policy in both episodes led to real exchange rates that were overvalued relative to the historical norm. It is likely that this phenomenon could also be found during other boom periods in Latin American economic history. It also appears that capital inflows during both the 1920s and the 1970s generated significant expansions in public expenditures, either in the form of public works (during the 1920s), or in investments by public enterprises (during the 1970s).

The deterioration in the commodity terms of trade during the early 1980s has approached, for some countries, the magnitude of the collapse of the early 1930s. Table 10.1 compares three-year averages, presenting percentage changes between the indicated triennia. Brazil, Colombia and Chile show the closest three-year declines during the two historical episodes; for Brazil the recent decline is steeper if 1975–7 is taken as the base for comparison. For large oil exporters, such as Mexico and Venezuela, the story is quite different, while the deterioration in the terms of trade of Argentina and Peru during the early 1980s looks mild compared with those of the early 1930s. The recent period is both more heterogeneous and less catastrophic regarding the Latin American merchandise terms of trade than the earlier episode. The longer-term importance of oil and of good or bad luck with other major commodities are highlighted in the last column of Table 10.1, comparing the early 1980s with the early 1970s, before the first oil shock.

During both the early 1930s and the early 1980s, ex-post real interest rates soared. In the earlier historical episode nominal interest rates both in London and New York remained around their historical norm, while dollar and sterling price levels declined sharply. In the early 1980s the decline in the rate of international inflation has been steeper than that in nominal interest rates. Both episodes witnessed an increase in interest due to foreigner creditors expressed as a share of exports.

Even as real interest rates soared, capital inflows declined sharply during both crises. Those inflows weakened as early as 1929, much

TABLE 10.1 *Percentage changes in commodity terms of trade: the early 1930s compared with the early 1980s*

	1928–29–30 to 1931–2–3	1978–79–80 to 1981–2–3	1975–6–7 to 1981–2–3	1971–2–3 to 1981–2–3
Argentina	−29	−2	−9	−34
Brazil	−32	−31	−42	−45
Colombia	−24	−22	−19	+9
Chile	−38	−28	−32	−53
Mexico	−33	+19	+44	+65
Peru	−30*	−12	−6	+11
Venezuela	−21	+21	+47	+281

*Refers to percentage change between 1929–30 and 1932–3.

SOURCE: Basic data obtained from Naciones Unidas 1976, 1983a, and 1983b.

before there were hints of possible irregularities in debt service. During the early 1980s, serious declines in the voluntary capital inflow awaited the Malvinas/Falklands war. More or less contemporaneous decreases in terms of trade and capital inflows, of course, have been a feature of peripheral cycles since the nineteenth century.

A severe cut in the volume of imports, from cyclical peak to trough, is shared by both historical experiences. The orders of magnitude are similar for some countries, such as Argentina and Mexico, as may be seen in Table 10.2. The same table, however, shows that the import cut of the early 1980s in most cases has not reached the brutality of the early 1930s. Colombia and Peru even show average import volumes for 1982–3 which exceed those of 1979–80–81.

Exchange rate devaluations were a crucial element in the adjustment of early 1930s. Abandonment of gold standard parities came early in some countries, while others waited until they were forced into devaluation by lack of reserves. Steep nominal depreciations far outdistanced the differential between local and international price level changes, so that when 1930–4 is compared with 1925–9, one obtains significant devaluations in the *real* exchange rate, particularly that applied to imports (the early 1930s witnessed the establishment of multiple exchange rates). Average real import exchange rates rose between 1925–9 and 1930–4 by between 32 per cent (Mexico) and 86 per cent (Chile), with Argentina, Brazil, Colombia, Peru and Uruguay depreciating within that range (see Diaz-Alejandro, 1982, p. 339, Table 20.4).

TABLE 10.2 *Percentage changes in average annual import values: the early 1930s compared with the early 1980s*

	Average for 1928–29–30 to average for 1931–2	Average for 1979–80–81 to average for 1982–3
Argentina	−43	−42
Brazil	−56	−23
Colombia	−55	+18
Chile	−64	−40
Mexico	−50	−40
Peru	−50*	+2
Venezuela	−58	−22

*Compares average for 1929–30 to average for 1931–2.

SOURCES: As in Table 10.1.

The timing of the large nominal devaluations of the early 1980s has also been spread out, and their impact on *real* exchange rates has also varied from country to country. But the turn-round in real exchange rates from the trend and levels of the late 1970s and very early 1980s has been remarkable, as may be seen in Table 10.3. The cases of Argentina, Chile and Mexico show the clearest pattern of an appreciating trend followed by abrupt real depreciations. Other countries show weaker or less clear trends, but by 1982 or 1983 most of them registered real exchange rates significantly higher than those for 1976-80.

Both the early 1930s and the early 1980s show that real exchange rates are, sooner or later, sensitive changes in external terms of trade and changes in capital flows, contrary to mindless interpretations of the purchasing power parity doctrine which became fashionable during the late 1977 s in some South American countries. As noted earlier, one may conjecture that the combination during booms of favourable terms of trade, capital inflows and real exchange rates below long-term averages is likely to be found in Latin American business cycles since at least last century, and similarly for the opposite phenomena once the boom collapses.

As during the 1930s, large devaluations were accompanied by either the tightening or the introduction of exchange controls, even in countries such as Mexico with a tradition of free convertibility, and even where Central Bank officials were on record as opposing them. After the devaluations there was probably some redundancy in exchange control

TABLE 10.3 *Indices of real exchange rates (1980 = 100)*

	1976-7-8	1979-80	1981	1982
Argentina	209	113	129	305
Brazil	77	91	95	98
Chile	110	107	92	116
Colombia	112	100	100	100
Mexico	117	105	92	138
Peru	94	105	92	98
Venezuela	108	104	95	92
South Korea	101	95	102	108

SOURCE: Basic data obtained from International Monetary Fund, 1984, Nominal exchange rates refer to period average implicit rates, line '*rf.*' Those rates were adjusted by inflation in the United States and in the home country, as measured by consumer prices, line 64.

mechanisms, but public officials burned by capital account shocks and sudden capital flights preferred to keep them around, at least as stand-by policy tools.

An induced increase in public sector deficits during 'bad times' is another cyclical regularity common to the early 1980s and early 1930s. In contrast with the early 1930s, however, one cannot find during the early 1980s examples of *autonomous* increases in the budget deficit comparable to those documented for Brazil, involving the coffee valorisation scheme. We now turn to this and other salient contrasts between the two depressive episodes in Latin America.

CONTRASTS

Major contrasts between the 1980s and the 1930s may be found in several characteristics of the Latin American balance of payments, in domestic policies and economic conditions, and in features of the international political economy impinging upon Latin American countries.

Export sectors by the late 1970s were smaller relative to Gross Domestic Product and more diversified than in the late 1920s. Together with more diversified domestic productive structures and larger public sectors, the smaller and more diversified export sectors were supposed to make Latin American economies less vulnerable to external shocks. Diversification refers both to products and to markets: by the late 1970s Brazilian exports, for example, included a large variety of primary and manufactured products, shipped all over the world. The expansion of intra-Latin American trade was noteworthy during the 1960s and 1970s. In contrast with the 1920s, national ownerships of traditional export activities, even in their marketing aspects, was the rule rather than the exception. For countries such as Argentina, Brazil and Chile, these structural changes in their export sectors seem to make their disappointing early 1980s performance the more puzzling.

Viewed from the import side, some of these changes offer clues for explaining the contrasts in performance. The ratio of imports to home production was indeed larger in the late 1920s than in the late 1970s; imports also included then many items than were competitive rather than complementary to domestic production. Import restrictions during late 1920s were milder in most Latin American countries than during the later 1970s. There was ample room for import substitution when relative prices changed in the early 1930s, as a result of real devaluations and tighter import restrictions. The Brazilian import bill of the early 1980s is not so easily dented, as after many years of extreme protectionism it is made up mostly by close complements to domestic production, which are not as easily substitutable as the textiles, cement and pharmaceutical imports of the late 1920s. Indeed, during the early 1980s, the Latin American imports that have proven to be more easily substitutable, or postponable, have been imports from other Latin American countries: intra-Latin American trade has shrunk more than trade with the rest of the world.

Changes in the characteristics of links with international capital markets are more noteworthy than those observed in merchandise trade. During the late 1920s, foreign capital represented a larger share of the Latin American capital stock than during the late 1970s; in the earlier years there was substantial direct foreign investment in export and export-related activities, and the foreign debt was in the form of long-term bonds. Profits and profit-remittances of direct foreign investment in the export sector tended to fluctuate with the terms of trade; bonds, however, represented interest and amortisation claims on foreign exchange earnings which were fixed in nominal terms. The external debt accumulated by the late 1970s was in large proportion owed to a few hundred banks, rather than to thousand of bondholders, although bank debt also carried claims on foreign exchange fixed in nominal terms.

Has bank debt made Latin American countries more vulnerable to external shocks than bond debt? Ex-ante the answer appeared moot. Lending banks, being closer to the monetary systems of industrialised countries, seemed more vulnerable to pressures from debtors, as in the celebrated Keynesian remark. The consequence of disappointed widows, orphans and other scattered Northern bondholders could be said to have been less threating to Northern financial structures than bankruptcies of their major banks induced by Latin American defaults. By the late 1970s, gunboat and dollar diplomacy appeared irrevocably gone.

As noted earlier, during both the very early 1930s and 1980s service charges on the external debt rose dramatically as a percentage of Latin American exports. Serious irregularities on debt servicing began to appear during 1931, and by most 1934 countries had unilaterally suspended regular amortisation and debt payments, while profit remittances lagged and were in many cases controlled by exchange authorities. As of May 1984, interest payments on the Latin American debt had remained current; during the early 1980s there have been sporadic scares but no major defaults. Extraordinary efforts have been made by major countries to maintain punctual interest payments, and to reschedule principal. As bank debt involves shorter maturities than bond debt, the rescheduling process has involved more frequent and frantic negotiations than those carried out with representatives of foreign bondholders during the 1930s.

The burden of adjusting to unexpected shocks was borne to a large extent by foreign direct investors and bondholders in the early 1930s; during the early 1980s a much larger share of that burden has been borne by Latin American countries, with most lenders paying a small price for the mistaken forecasts of the later 1970s. In combination with other circumstances, resulting from mistaken domestic policies, military incompetence became obvious, even in the military field, encouraging democratisation openings. Democratisation under delicate economic and social circumstances appears to have resulted in a cautious attitude towards policy experimentation in the economic areas.

The most significant contrast between the early 1930s and the early 1980s is found in what may be broadly defined as the international political economy, which probably explains several other contrasts already noted. The early 1930s provided clear signals that an international economic order based on the gold standard, free trade and British hegemony, stretching back to the end of the Napoleonic wars, was irrevocably finished. The celebrated sanctity of international contracts was also shaken quite early during the 1930s when Germany suspended reparations and Britain and France stopped servicing First World War loans from the United States. Industrialised nations turned inward, and the London world economic conference was a clear failure. 'The end of *laissez-faire*' was proclaimed by academics, politicians and newspapers. Liberal and democratic ideologies were in retreat, pressured by apparently vigorous fascists and bolsheviks. Economic recovery in industrial countries, often proclaimed to be around the corner, came late and slowly; major economies remained dead in the water. Banking systems, especially in the United States, underwent massive bankruptcies, and financial and business leaders were targets of ridicule and investigations.

The early 1980s present a very different picture. Post-Second World-War international institutions have resisted the crisis, and in some cases have been strengthened, like the International Monetary Fund. The General Agreement on Tariffs and Trade has been buffeted and eroded by protectionist pressures echoing those of the early 1930s, but on the whole protectionist excesses comparable to those of the earlier episode have been avoided. The international banking and financial systems have had several scares, but no major collapses have occurred. The volume of international trade has stagnated, but it has not declined sharply. The volume of Latin American exports, as a result, has done better this time around. Since early 1983 the United States economy has experienced a cyclical upswing, which by early 1984 appeared to have spread to Europe. In both Britain and the United States the early 1980s witnessed an upsurge of neo-*laissez-faire* ideology, which met with approval from the electorate of those countries, to the surprise of many observers. The United States re-established vigorous claims to international hegemony, often in an alarming style. Sharp alternatives to democratic neo-liberalism, represented by heirs to the fascists and bolsheviks of the early 1930s, had lost much of their glitter by the early 1980s. In the Mediterranean world, always of interest to Latin America, a prudent social-democratic trend was visible.

The structure of incentives and penalties presented to Latin American policy-makers by the international political economy of the early 1980s is clearly very different from that of the early 1930s. The expected benefits of maintaining external economic links are greater, while the costs of a sharp cut-off loom larger. This time around the Centre holds, is watchful, and is in a mean mood. There is no visible Kindlebergian hegemonic crisis to provide latitude in policy-making. More countries today are in the tricky external situation of the Argentina of the 1930s, a situation which led Argentina to maintain punctual debt servicing. A recovering Centre with intact financial institutions, in contrast with the early 1930s, also provides a magnet for savers in the periphery, limiting policy room in the exchange and monetary fields.

CAVEATS AND CONCLUSIONS

Data availability, plus the sheer weight of their populations and economies, have biased this chapter towards discussion of the large and medium Latin American countries, neglecting Caribbean, Central America and other smaller economies in the region. Heterogeneity in economic and political circumstances among these nations seems greater than during the 1930s. In Central America, external shocks have interacted with convulsed domestic political conditions to produce an economic depression which is probably deeper than that of the early 1930s. On the other hand, the centrally planned Cuban economy of the early 1980s appears more stable than that of the early 1930s, at least as measured by sugar output. Smaller Caribbean islands, which import oil and export sugar to the world market, may have suffered during the early 1980s terms of trade declines as large as those of the 1930s.

Another topic not explored in this paper is the extent to which domestic policies, both during the late 1970s boom and the subsequent recession, dampened the cycle and contributed to a higher growth trend. One may suggest, however, that prudent restraints on external borrowing, avoidance of gross overvaluation and domestic financial excesses, plus absence of runaway inflation during the late 1970s have helped Colombia to weather the early 1980s better than others.

Travellers to South America around 1932 would report that in cities like Sao Paulo textile mills were working three shifts per day, and that the prevailing mood contrasted with the gloom found in North America. During 1984 economic optimism has returned to New York and Washington DC, but not to Buenos Aires and Brasilia. Increasingly, the most optimistic projections for Latin American countries involve reaching by 1990 the per capita incomes reached in 1980, accepting a decade of zero growth and, in constrast with the 1930s, little structural change. Projections rest delicately on how much foreign exchange will be left, after debt servicing, to raise import volumes above the extraordinarily depressed levels of the early 1980s. Events which could upset even modest recovery scenarios are much too easily imagined.

It can be argued that the 1980s conservative political and economic programmes within major industrialised countries have been surprisingly successful in meeting their objectives. The conservative restoration has extended to the international political economy, in which the mood of the late 1970s has been altered, in favour of a rejuvenated old order. While the depression of the early 1930s had a liberating impact on major Latin American countries, that of the early 1980s has had a chastising, disciplining effect. Much of what has occurred so far is compatible with rational behaviour of dominant economic and political forces at the Centre, maximising their economic advantage and political power. But these forces could be misled by *hubris* into pushing their advantage too far. The structure of carrots and sticks which the international economy offers Latin American countries *circa* 1984 stills favours maintaining existing external links and playing by the dominant rules of the game, but just barely. Delays in economic recovery or humiliating demands on Latin American policy-makers could again make unilateral moratoria and all import-substitution projects look good. A situation where interest on the Latin American external debt amply exceeds new net lending (the 1983 figures were $39 billion and $22 billion, respectively) cannot be expected to last very long (see Inter-American Development Bank, 1984, p. 19).

It is tempting to conclude that the 1980s are more like the 1890s than like the 1930s in Latin America. But it is more accurate to conclude that while all booms are prosperous in a similar fashion each depression paints the details of its misery in a different way.

REFERENCES

Diaz-Alejandro, Carlos F., 'Latin America in Depression, 1929-39', Chapter 20 in Mark Gersovitz *et al.* (eds.) *The Theory and Experience of Economic Development; Essays in Honor of Sir W. Arthur Lewis* (London: Allen & Unwin, 1982), pp. 334–55.

Diaz-Alejandro, Carlos F., 'Stories of the 1930s for the 1980s', Chapter 1 in Pedro Aspe Armella *et al.* (eds), *Financial Policies and the World Capital Market: The Problem of Latin American Countries* (Chicago: University of Chicago Press, 1983), pp. 5–35.

Inter-American Development Bank, *External Debt and Economic Development in Latin America; Background and Prospects* (Washington, DC, January, 1984).

International Monetary Fund, *International Financial Statistics*, February 1984.

Naciones Unidas, *America Latina: Relacion de Precios del Intercambio* (Santiago de Chile, 1976).

Naciones Unidas, *Estudio Economico de America Latina, 1982* (Santiago de Chile, 1983a).

Naciones Unidas, *Balance Preliminar de la Economia Latino-Americana durante 1983* (Santiago de Chile, 1983b).

11 Communal Land Tenure Systems and their Role in Rural Development[1]

KEITH GRIFFIN

Dispassionate analysis of land tenure systems and their role in rural development has been hampered by ideological conflict. Political rhetoric in North America and Western Europe reflecting a general hostility towards the Soviet Union has helped to create a widely held view that communal tenure systems invariably result in stagnation of production, inefficiency of resource allocation and coercion of the peasantry. Where they survive, communal systems are thought to do so partly because of large imports of food from the West and partly because of the existence of a tiny private sector which somehow manages to flourish despite attempts by governments to suppress it.

These claims may of course be true, and we shall want to examine them below. Before doing so, however, it is important to recognise that there are many different kinds of communal land tenure systems and a great deal of experience has been gained in the operation of these systems from all over the globe. In twelve countries, accounting for nearly a third of the world's population, collective agriculture in one form or another can be said to be dominant. These twelve countries include the world's largest (China) and two of the smallest (Albania and Mongolia), one country which has had over fifty years of experience in running a collective system (the USSR) and one which has had less than half that time (Cuba). The full list of the twelve, ranked in descending order by size of population, is as follows: China,[2] the USSR,[3] Vietnam,[4] Romania, North Korea,[5] East Germany, Czechoslovakia, Hungary, Cuba,[6] Bulgaria, Albania and Mongolia.

In addition, there are many other countries which have a small collective sector in agriculture or where experiments have been tried or where it is government policy to encourage the development of a communal land system. These countries include Poland and Yugoslavia in Europe, Israel and Algeria in the Mediterranean basin,[7] Kampuchea and Laos in Asia, Mexico[8] and Nicaragua in Latin America, and Tanzania,[9] Mozambique[10] and Ethiopia in Africa. We exclude from consideration countries where traditional forms of communal tenure continue to exist, as for example in parts of western and southern Africa, since these fall outside our purview. Even so, it is clear that interest in communal land tenure systems is widespread and possibly increasing.

This does not imply, of course, that the adoption of a communal tenure system is open to any country regardless of its political system. One must beware of the fallacy of eclecticism[11] in this as in other areas of social and economic policy. Regime types evidently must be taken into account whenever one analyses a land tenure system or land reform,[12] including of course a communal land system. All that we hope to have established at this point is that communal systems deserve careful study by scholars and should not be dismissed by economists and other specialists in development as unworthy of attention.

THE GROWTH OF PRODUCTION

Data on the average annual percentage rate of growth of agricultural output are presented in Table 11.1. The table contains data not only on the twelve countries where communal agriculture predominates but also on countries (or groups of countries) where individual tenure systems predominate. As indicated in the notes to the table, the period covered by the data is not the same in each country and hence caution must be exercised when drawing conclusions. Our objectives, however, are modest, and the data certainly are good enough to test many commonly voiced propositions, for instance that 'collective farming has proved to be the surest way of reducing agricultural production in many countries'[13].

Let us begin by considering the data for the twelve countries which practise some form of collective agriculture. As can be seen, their growth performance varies widely. At one extreme is North Korea, where the rate of growth since the middle of the 1960s has been 5.1 per cent a year, while at the other extreme is Mongolia, where the rate of growth has been only 1.3 per cent. The unweighted average rate of growth of the twelve countries is 2.7 per cent a year. This compares with an annual rate of growth during 1960–81 of 1.5 per cent a year in what the

TABLE 11.1 *The growth of agricultural production (per cent per annum)*

Countries with communal tenure systems		Countries with individual tenure systems	
USSR	1.7	USA	1.1
East Germany	1.7	West Germany	1.4
Czechoslovakia	2.3	Belgium	0.1
Hungary	3.1	France	1.1
Bulgaria	1.4	Netherlands	3.4
Romania	3.7	United Kingdom	1.9
Albania	2.9	Italy	2.0
China	4.6	India	1.9
North Korea	5.1	South Korea	3.7
Vietnam	3.2	Other low-income countries	2.5
Cuba	2.1	Middle-income countries	3.2
Mongolia	1.3		

NOTES
The periods covered are the following:

Romania and Hungary, 1960–81; China, 1950–81; all other countries with communal tenure systems, 1966–81; countries with individual tenure systems, 1960–80.

The category 'other low-income countries' includes countries with a per capita GNP of US$ 410 or less (in 1981 prices) other than China and India.

SOURCES: FAO, *Production Yearbook*; IBRD, *World Development Report 1983*; and official Chinese sources.

World Bank calls the industrial market economies and 2.5 per cent in the 'other low-income countries', i.e. in low-income countries other than India and China. Thus by international standards, agricultural growth rates in countries that have adopted communal land tenure systems appear to be high. Far from suffering from stagnation, our twelve countries have done relatively well.

This impression is confirmed when one compares similar countries or groups of countries, in one of which communal systems are the dominant form of land tenure while in the other individual tenure systems dominate. The countries selected for comparison are listed on the right-hand side of Table 11.1.

The general pattern that emerges is fairly clear. Agriculture in China grew much faster than in India (4.6 versus 1.9 per cent); half again as fast in the Soviet Union as in the United States (1.7 versus 1.1 per cent); and half again as fast in our six Eastern European countries as in the six major Western European countries of France, the UK, West Germany, Italy, Netherlands and Belgium (2.5 versus 1.7 per cent a year). Indeed, not even South Korea, one of the four 'baby tigers' of the developing world, which enjoyed an agricultural growth rate of 3.7 per cent a year, could match North Korea's rate of 5.1 per cent.[14]

Within our group of twelve countries, the seven low- and middle-income countries grew significantly faster than the others. That is, the average rate of growth of agricultural production in Vietnam, China, Mongolia, Albania, North Korea, Cuba and Romania was 3.2 per cent a year, whereas it was only 2 per cent a year in Bulgaria, Hungary, the USSR, Czechoslovakia and East Germany. Evidently it cannot be claimed that communal land tenure systems are appropriate only in more advanced economies practising mechanised farming. If anything, the evidence suggests that the poorer the country, the better the growth performance is likely to be of its communal tenure system. In fact the rank correlation between per capita income and the rate of growth of agriculture in our twelve countries is -0.38.

On the whole, the larger countries appear at first glance to have done better than the smaller. That is, China, Vietnam, Romania and North Korea enjoyed noticeably faster rates of growth of agriculture than did Cuba, Bulgaria and Mongolia. There are exceptions, of course: the Soviet Union, a large country, grew relatively slowly while Albania, a small country, grew slightly faster than average. The general tendency, however, is evident from the fact that when growth rates are weighted by size of population the average annual rate of growth rises from 2.8 to 4.0 per cent. China, however, with its huge population, obviously makes a big difference to the outcome of the calculation, and if one excludes China (thereby giving the Soviet Union a huge weight) the weighted average growth rate becomes less than the unweighted average (2.2 versus 2.6 per cent). It seems safe to conclude, therefore, that there seems to be no systematic tendency for large countries to enjoy faster growth than small.

THE GROWTH OF OUTPUT PER HEAD

Of course, the growth of production is only half the story; the other half is the growth of population. If one focuses not on the rate of expansion of production unadjusted for population increase, but on the growth of output per head, the superiority of our twelve countries with communal land tenure systems becomes even more apparent. The reason for this is that in most cases the rate of demographic expansion in our sample countries is slower than in similar countries where individual tenure predominates (see Table 11.2).

Thus in China during 1960–81 the population expanded by 1.9 per cent a year whereas in India it grew by 2.2 per cent; in consequence per capita agricultural production rose in China while in India it tended to fall by about 0.3 per cent a year. Similarly, the population growth rate in the Soviet Union is about 0.1 per cent per annum less than in the United States and as a result per capita agricultural output per head has been rising slowly but steadily in the Soviet Union and (a fact not widely known) but falling about 0.1 per cent a year in the United States (because of government policies to restrict output).

In our six Eastern European countries the population is growing marginally faster than in the six Western European countries with which we previously compared them, namely, 0.9 versus 0.6 per cent a year.[15] Even so, agricultural production per head is growing about 45 per cent faster in Eastern Europe (1.6 as compared to 1.1 per cent a year).

The population of North Korea is growing much faster than that of South Korea, namely 2.8 compared to 2.1 per cent a year. Nonetheless,

TABLE 11.2 *Population growth rates, 1960–81 (per cent per annum)*

Countries with communal tenure systems		Countries with individual tenure systems	
USSR	1.1	USA	1.2
East Germany	−0.1	West Germany	0.5
Czechoslovakia	0.6	Belgium	0.4
Hungary	0.4	France	0.8
Bulgaria	0.7	Netherlands	1.1
Romania	0.9	United Kingdom	0.3
Albania	2.7	Italy	0.5
China	1.9	India	2.2
North Korea	2.8	South Korea	2.1
Vietnam	3.0	Other low-income countries	2.6
Cuba	1.6	Middle-income countries	2.5
Mongolia	3.0		

NOTES
The figure for West Germany refers to 1960–70. The category 'other low-income countries' includes countries with a per capita GNP of US$ 410 or less (in 1981 prices) other than China and India.

SOURCES: IBRD, *World Development Report 1983*.

agricultural output per head appears to have grown much faster in the North than in the South (2.3 versus 1.6 per cent a year). Vietnam can perhaps best be compared with the average of the World Bank's 'low-income countries other than China and India'. If one does this it transpires that the population growth rate in Vietnam exceeds the average of other low-income countries (3.0 versus 2.6 per cent a year), but whereas output per head has increased by 0.2 per cent per year in Vietnam, it has fallen by 0.1 per cent on average in the other low-income countries.

Cuba and Mongolia are 'middle-income countries' and can be compared with them. The population growth rate in the middle-income countries is, on average, 2.5 per cent. This is faster than the rate in Cuba (1.6 per cent) but slower than the rate in Mongolia (3.0 per cent). Agricultural production per head, however, has increased by 0.7 per cent per annum in the middle-income countries and this is faster than in Cuba (0.5 per cent) or Mongolia (where output per head has fallen sharply by 1.6 per cent a year).

In summary, during the period 1960–81, agricultural output per head fell by about 0.3 per cent a year in India and 0.1 per cent a year in the 'other low-income countries'. It rose by about 0.7 per cent a year in the 'middle-income countries' and by 0.6 per cent a year in the nineteen industrial market economy countries. We cannot give an exactly comparable figure for our twelve countries with communal land tenure systems, but it is clear that on average they performed far better than any of the above. For example, for what it is worth, an unweighted average of our data suggests that agricultural output per head in the twelve countries increased about 1.2 per cent a year during a broadly comparable period.

No importance should be attached to any of the specific figures we have presented – the data are too crude for that – but there can be little doubt that whether measured in terms of the growth of production or in terms of the growth of output per head, agricultural performance in countries where communal tenure systems dominate has in general been significantly better than in countries where individual tenure systems dominate.

THE GROWTH OF LABOUR PRODUCTIVITY IN AGRICULTURE

Another possible indicator of performance is changes over time in the productivity of labour in the agricultural sector. Unfortunately, how-

TABLE 11.3 *The growth of the agricultural labour force and labour productivity (per cent per annum)*

	(1) Total labour force, 1960–80	(2) Percentage of labour force in agriculture 1960	(2) Percentage of labour force in agriculture 1980	(3) Agricultural labour force, 1960–80	(4) Labour productivity in agriculture
Countries with communal tenure systems					
USSR	1.0	42	14	−2.4	4.1
East Germany	0.2	18	10	−1.9	3.6
Czechoslovakia	0.9	26	11	−2.1	4.4
Hungary	0.5	37	21	−2.2	5.3
Bulgaria	0.5	56	37	−1.2	2.6
Romania	0.8	67	29	−2.0	5.3
Albania	2.5	71	61	1.7	1.2
China	1.9*	n.a.	69	n.a.	2.7**
North Korea	2.6	62	49	1.1	4.0
Vietnam	1.9*	79†	71	n.a.	1.3**
Cuba	1.4	39	23	−1.0	3.1
Mongolia	2.3	70	55	1.0	0.3

TABLE 11.3 (Continued)

	(1) Total labour force, 1960–80	(2) Percentage of labour force in agriculture 1960	(2) Percentage of labour force in agriculture 1980	(3) Agricultural labour force, 1960–80	(4) Labour productivity in agriculture
Countries with individual tenure systems					
USA	1.7	7	2	−2.3	3.4
West Germany	0.5	14	4	−2.7	4.1
Belgium	0.5	8	3	−2.5	2.6
France	0.9	22	8	−2.4	3.6
Netherlands	1.5	11	6	−1.2	4.6
United Kingdom	0.5	4	2	−2.1	4.0
Italy	0.3	31	11	−2.4	4.4
India	1.6	74	69	1.3	0.6
South Korea	2.9	66	34	−0.4	4.1
Other low income countries	2.1	82	73	1.5	1.0
Middle income countries	2.2	62	45	0.6	2.6

NOTES
* This figure refers to 1970–80.
** Estimate obtained by subtracting the rate of growth of the total labour force from the rate of growth of agricultural output, and hence understates the rate of growth of labour productivity in agriculture.
† This figure refers to North Vietnam only.

SOURCES: Col. (1): *IBRD, World Development Report* 1982; col. (2): *IBRD World Development Report* 1983; and for North Vietnam, 1960, 'Report of the Central Census Commission Concerning the Result of the Census in the Whole North', *Nhan Dan*, 2 November 1960, p. 3; col. (3): inferred from cols (1) and (2); col. (4): Table 11.1 minus col. (3).

ever, we do not have direct measurements of labour productivity; the estimates of trends presented in Table 11.3 should be regarded as rough approximations only.

In the Soviet Union and Eastern Europe other than Albania the agricultural labour force actually declined during the period 1960 to 1980. A similar phenomenon occurred in the United States and Western Europe. As a result, in both groups of countries the productivity of labour in the agricultural sector increased more rapidly than total output in the sector. The rise in labour productivity was broadly comparable in both sets of countries and was quite impressive. Hence there is nothing in these data to suggest that the performance of countries with communal tenure systems is inferior to those with individual tenure systems.

The same general conclusion is true of the underdeveloped countries. The productivity of the agricultural labour force in China grew much faster than in India, even if one uses an upward biased estimate of the rate of growth of the agricultural labour force in China and hence produces a downward biased estimate of the rate of growth of labour productivity in Chinese agriculture (see the notes to Table 11.3). North and South Korea performed equally well; Vietnam did better (again, even with a downward biased estimate of the growth of labour productivity) than the average of the 'other low-income countries', while Mongolia performed noticeably less well; Cuba out-performed the average of the 'middle-income countries' by a significant margin. Thus the record of the Third World countries with communal tenure systems does not compare unfavourably with the record of the other Third World countries, and in the case of China, North Korea and Cuba, labour productivity in the agricultural sector has increased much faster than in the typical underdeveloped country with an individual tenure system.

INTERNATIONAL TRADE IN AGRICULTURAL PRODUCTS

Despite the relatively good growth performance, it has often been claimed that the weakness of communal tenure systems can be seen by examining the figures on international trade. Some have gone so far as to argue that 'countries that were once food exporters tend to become food importers'.[16] That is, it is widely believed that countries which practise some form of collective agriculture have been forced to rely on massive imports of agricultural products to feed their population and satisfy domestic demand. This claim is not as simple as it seems and raises two issues, one of interpretation and another of fact.

First, it is doubtful whether a country's balance of trade in agricultural products can tell us anything useful about the effects of the country's land tenure system. For example, a trade surplus might reflect nothing more than planners' preferences, as embodied perhaps in a compulsory delivery scheme, rather than the virtues of a communal tenure system. Alternatively, a trade deficit in agricultural products could reflect a demand pattern with a high propensity to consume food, perhaps because socialist countries tend to have a more equal distribution of income and tend to place more emphasis on the satisfaction of basic needs. Conversely, a country may be a net exporter of foodstuffs while its population starves (as in nineteenth-century Ireland during the famine) or at times when the nutritional needs of a large section of the population are unmet (as in India today) or during periods when the per capita availability of food is declining (as in several African countries). Of course, a negative balance of trade in agricultural products could be due to unsatisfactory performance of the agricultural sector, but it could equally well be a reflection of the fact that the country in question has a comparative advantage in non-agricultural activities such as manufacturing. No one would be so foolish as to claim that the UK trade deficit in food is evidence of inefficiency in British agriculture, yet such claims often are made when it comes to countries where communal tenure systems dominate.[17] In general, the products a country exports and imports are far more likely to reflect its resource endowment and level of development than the strength or weakness of its land tenure system.

Second, even if one does not accept the point about comparative advantage, it simply is not correct to claim that countries with communal tenure systems must rely heavily on imports of agricultural products. This can readily be seen by inspecting the data in Table 11.4. The data refer to our twelve sample countries for the years 1981 and 1982 and cover all international trade in agriculture, fishing and forestry products.

The first thing to note about Table 11.4 is that six out of the twelve countries had a positive balance of trade in agricultural products in 1981 and in 1982. These six countries were Hungary, Bulgaria, Romania, Albania, Cuba and Mongolia. Thus they covered three continents (Europe, Asia and Latin America) and included both poor countries and rich. Since these countries were net exporters of foodstuffs, the criticism of food import dependence clearly cannot be applied to them. This

TABLE 11.4 *Balance of international trade in agricultural, fishery and forestry products, 1981 and 1982 (millions of US dollars)*

	1981	1982
USSR	−16,292.2	−14,585.0
East Germany	−1,934.1	−2,010.9
Czechoslovakia	−1,173.5	−1,060.5
Hungary	870.6	1,160.4
Bulgaria	312.0	682.5
Romania	199.2	513.1
Albania	14.0	15.4
China	−4,261.6	−4,420.0
North Korea	−117.8	−76.6
Vietnam	−207.6	−20.2
Cuba	3,155.0	2,564.4
Mongolia	97.4	96.6

SOURCE: *FAO, Trade Yearbook 1982*, Vol. 36, 1983. The figures for China are estimates made by FAO. It may be of interest to some to note that of the nine countries previously compared with the twelve above, five had a trade deficit in agricultural products (West Germany, Belgium, the UK, Italy and South Korea) and four a surplus (USA, France, Netherlands and India).

leaves us with the six countries that are net importers of agricultural products.

The next thing to note about the table is that two-thirds of the countries with a negative trade balance in agriculture are highly industrialised. In Czechoslovakia, 75 per cent of net material product originates in industry; in East Germany 70 per cent; and in the Soviet Union 62 per cent.[18] One cannot be so precise for North Korea, but it is well-known that prior to partition agriculture predominated in the southern part of the country while industry was located largely in the north. One estimate suggests that already by 1970 industry accounted for 74 per cent of North Korea's national product.[19] In each of these four countries, therefore, it is hardly surprising that there are net imports of agricultural products. The composition of aggregate output strongly suggests that these countries should have a comparative advantage in the export of manufactured goods and consequently should import foodstuffs and some raw materials. If this view is accepted, it follows that nothing can be inferred from the trade figures about the performance of their communal tenure system.

176   *Communal Land Tenure Systems*

Vietnam, one of the remaining two countries with a negative balance of trade in agricultural products, obviously is a special case. Its economy has been so badly disrupted by war and that it is impossible to tell whether the present trading pattern will persist or not. Vietnam certainly was once a net exporter of rice and it may well become so again – the tendency for gross imports of agricultural products gradually to decline is encouraging – but for the time being the picture remains unclear. All one can say is that the latest figures (for 1982) are encouraging.

Finally, there is China. In general, foreign trade turnover accounts for only about 10 per cent of China's GNP. The country is basically self-sufficient in food, fuel and manufactured consumer goods. Until 1976 the country had an export surplus in agricultural, fishery and forestry products, but since then the balance of trade in those products has become negative. The major reason for this is the abrupt change in the composition of China's exports that occurred between 1970 and 1975, when China first became a significant supplier of petroleum. (A similar transformation occurred in Nigeria in roughly the same period.) A subsidiary reason may be a rise in the volume of food imports and fall in food exports in response to government measures to raise the real incomes and consumption of both peasants and workers.

In 1970 fuels accounted for only 1 per cent of China's exports; by 1975 they accounted for 14 per cent, and the proportion continued to rise steadily so that by 1980 they accounted for 22 per cent. That is to say, between 1970 and 1980 the share of fuels in China's total exports increased by 21 percentage points. The opposite occurred with regard to exports of food and raw materials other than fuel. In 1970 these products (SITC O, 1 and 2) accounted for 48 per cent of China's total exports, whereas by 1980 they accounted for only 27 per cent, a fall of exactly 21 percentage points. In other words, during the decade of the 1970s China reduced substantially its dependence on exports of food and raw materials other than fuel.

Turning to imports, it is noteworthy that something broadly similar has been happening here as well. There has been a gradual tendency for the share of foodstuffs in total imports to fall and for the share of machinery to rise. Thus between 1970 and 1980 imports of machinery (SITC 7) rose from 15 to 28 per cent of the total, while imports of food (SITC 0 and 1) decline from 19 to 14 per cent of the total. That is, during the decade of the 1970s China actually reduced her dependence on imported food (while increasing her dependence on imported machinery).

Thus the data for China in Table 11.4 are misleading. The negative trade balance in agricultural, fishery and forestry products is due to a change in the country's comparative advantage as reflected in a changed composition of both exports and imports; it has nothing to do with an alleged inability of the country to feed itself. Indeed, net international trade in food represents a tiny fraction of China's total trade[20] and, more important, of domestic food consumption.

RESOURCE UTILISATION AND ALLOCATIVE EFFICIENCY

A general criticism made of communal land tenure systems is that they tend to be inefficient. Some writers seem to believe that communal tenure is an inherently inefficient way of organising rural development and that collective agriculture must inevitably result in a waste of resources. This, however, is clearly wrong. As the respected American agricultural economist D. Gale Johnson has stated, 'It now seems quite evident that any form of land tenure can be made efficient'.[21] Indeed, as he says, 'in terms of efficiency, it makes little difference whether the land is owned by the state (all of the people), by the members of collective farms or by private persons, either as landlords or operators'.[22] Recent research has clearly demonstrated that there can be no *a priori* presumption that one form of tenure system is more efficient than all others.

This being so, the issue comes down to the actual practice of collective agriculture in the countries that have adopted this system. The evaluation of historical experience, however, is never as conclusive as the results of an exercise in theory, and hence judgement inescapably influences one's assessment. This judgement, moreover, is based not only on what one knows about the behaviour of a particular system over time but also on how it compares with other systems, in our case with individual tenure systems. There can be little doubt that there is considerable inefficiency in countries that have adopted individual tenure systems. In Western Europe and North America, farming is heavily subsidised, an excessive amount of resources has been allocated to agriculture, and despite attempts by governments to restrain output through acreage controls there are large production surpluses combined with relatively high food prices for consumers. In Third World countries with individual land tenure systems the problems are rather different. In many cases the internal terms of trade have been turned deliberately against agriculture.[23] Within the agricultural sector, factor markets function far from perfectly,[24] access to government provided services such as technical assistance is very uneven,[25] and as a result there often are large differences in productivity across farm sizes.[26]

There are analogous problems in the countries that have communal land systems. Farm prices have often been kept low in order to provide cheap food for the urban population. Decision-making is sometimes highly centralised – as in the USSR, East Germany, Czechoslovakia and Bulgaria – and this has introduced unnecessary rigidity into the sector. Frequently, communal systems have been built on the assumption that there are economies of large scale in agriculture and that efficiency can be increased through mechanised operations on large fields.[27] The Russian system in particular appears to have been built on this assumption, yet there is little empirical evidence to support it.

More generally, it is widely believed that there are economic advantages in conducting field operations collectively, i.e. ploughing, sowing, weeding and harvesting. The system used in Tanzania's ujamaa villages, for instance, to the extent that it is not derived entirely from ideological preferences, seems implicitly to be based on this belief, yet there is no evidence that peasants tend to resist this variant of collective cultivation. Be that as it may, in countries where emphasis is placed on large-scale collective farming there is a problem about the composition of output. The reason for this is that some crops lend themselves more readily to this method of production than others. Wheat and cotton growing, sheep and cattle ranching, tea and coffee plantations are examples of activities that can be undertaken efficiently on a large scale. More difficult, given the existing known technology and the resource endowments of most poor countries, are such things as rice cultivation, pig raising, horticulture and the management of soft-fruit orchards.

This problem of the appropriate scale of production can be overcome by creating an institutional hierarchy within the collective system whereby those activities that benefit from economies of scale are undertaken at the collective (or commune) level and those which are best done on a small scale are assigned to individual households or to groups of households (e.g. in China until recently, to production teams). It is misleading to think of communal systems as necessarily being institutionally homogeneous. In fact in most systems the household economy and its private sector form an integral part of the communal land tenure system.[28] The private sector should not be regarded as a residual vestige of an earlier individual tenure system which perhaps is tolerated only reluctantly, but as an essential component of an efficient communal system. The private sector is largely complementary to the collective sector: it absorbs labour that could not otherwise be employed; it occupies a relatively small amount of land to grow products that are of great value and which require great care; it engages in small-scale livestock and poultry raising; and it produces handicrafts and other articles using labour-intensive methods of production.

A well-organised communal system, with a flexibly designed institutional hierarchy, should in principle be more efficient than the individual tenure systems one actually encounters in most Third World countries. One particular advantage of a communal system is that it can ensure that resources are fully utilised, that is, that every scrap of land is cultivated, that irrigation water is allocated efficiently, and above all that labour is fully employed. Of course, not all communal systems have achieved this ideal in practice, but the potential is there and at least one country has had some success in translating this potential advantage into concrete reality.[29]

One characteristic of all communal land tenure systems is that they are intensive in their use of management skills. Collective farming, narrowly defined, requires skilled management because important decisions have to be made about the allocation of labour among various tasks, the optimal timing of agricultural operations and the appropriate use of heterogeneous pieces of land. Decentralising decision-making to the level at which economies of scale are exhausted will obviously help, but even if this is done a scarcity of good managers is likely to be a problem.

If decentralisation takes the form of dividing the communally owned land between a private and a collective sector, as it does in the great majority of communal systems, a further problem is raised about the optimal allocation of labour between the private plot or field and the collective field. It is commonly observed that a disproportionate amount of agricultural labour is devoted to the private sector and too little to the collective sector, with the result that yields are much higher in the private sector than in the collective sector while the productivity of labour is much higher in the collective sector than in the private. The phenomenon is analogous to one noted earlier in countries with individual tenure systems, namely a tendency for there to be large differences in productivity of land and labour across farm sizes. This source of allocative inefficiency is not easy to eliminate, although the introduction of the 'production responsibility system' in China and other economic reforms can be regarded as an attempt to do so.

A related managerial problem of communal systems is labour incentives in the collective sector. The task is to devise a set of work incentives to ensure that everyone contributes the right quantity and quality of effort. This is a problem which of course is common to any organisation larger than the single person enterprise – and is known in the economics literature as the 'free rider' issue – but it is especially important in communal systems because members cannot normally be fired for poor performance. No general solution to this problem has been found in either capitalist or socialist enterprises: both rely on a changing blend of monetary rewards, non-material incentives and commands, and both never seem to achieve more than a partial success. If the individual tenure systems have sharper material incentives, this may be because they are more tolerant of inequality and unemployment. If the communal tenure systems are more successful in eliminating extreme forms or poverty, this may be because they are more willing to use commands and restrict so-called bourgeois freedoms.

Yet another, and very important, managerial problem arises from the fact that by their very nature communal systems are multi-purpose development institutions. They often combine (a) the functions of local government, e.g. local policing and the administration of justice; (b) the provision of social services, and in particular health and elementary education services; (c) the development of industry and other non-agricultural rural activities, with (d) responsibility for ensuring a high rate of saving and capital accumulation and an efficient pattern of investment. These numerous and very different tasks undoubtedly place severe demands on the limited supplies of managerial ability. At the same time, it is likely that any alternative system designed to achieve the same results would be at least as demanding of managerial skills as are communal systems. For example, a rural development strategy based on small peasant farms and individual land tenure will be highly intensive in its use of management skills; moreover, because these skills will have to be supplied by the government rather than by the commune or collective, they are likely to be much more costly. Hence in the majority of cases the true alternative to the communal system is likely to be not less management but less development.

TENURE SYSTEMS AND COMPREHENSIVE DEVELOPMENT

This, of course, is the ultimate test. Do communal land tenure systems possess advantages that individual tenure systems lack when it comes to promoting all-round economic, social and political development in rural areas? Alas, there is no unambiguous answer to this question since objectives vary from one country to another and any particular objective can almost always be achieved in more than one way. Nevertheless, communal systems are characterised by a set of features which makes them attractive to those concerned with combining sustained growth of output, the alleviation of poverty, the provision of basic needs and the creation of an egalitarian society. The adoption of a communal land tenure system does not guarantee that any of these objectives will be attained, but it does make their attainment somewhat easier.

First, as we have seen, it is possible within a collective system to ensure that labour is fully employed. In much of the Third World seasonal unemployment is common, and it is widely believed that much labour is 'surplus' to the needs of production. In countries with communal tenure systems, in contrast, labour tends to be largely a fixed cost – its marginal cost to the collective certainly is low, if not zero – and consequently it 'pays' the collective to employ labour even on projects which have a low rate of return. As a result, output is higher and poverty lower than would otherwise be the case.

Second, the distribution of income in rural areas tends to be more equal in countries where communal systems predominate than in countries where individual tenure is the rule. The reason for this is that in communal systems there is little or no income from property – there is only income from labour – and hence a major source of inequality no longer exists. The combination of a higher level of output and a more equitable distribution of income can make an enormous difference in reducing the extent of malnutrition and acute poverty in a low-income country. Furthermore communal tenure systems have an advantage over small-scale, egalitarian, individual peasant farming systems in that they are more likely to be successful in preventing inequalities from reappearing once the land reform has been completed. That is, communal tenure systems not only create equality, they also tend to perpetuate it.[30]

Third, communal systems contain a high potential for capital accumulation. In the early stages of rural development a high level of investment can most easily be achieved by mobilising labour with low opportunity costs for capital construction projects. In this case investment is 'financed' not by reducing current consumption, but by reducing leisure. In the later stages of development investment can be financed by allocating a portion of collective income to a collective accumulation fund. Given a measure of collective self-discipline, the annual flow of funds into investment can rapidly become a significant proportion of total collective income. In fact it is this feature of communal systems that accounts for the relatively rapid rates of growth they have enjoyed.

In Hebei province, China, for example, the rate of savings and investment on the communes rose very rapidly during the period 1962–

78. At the beginning of the period collective accumulation accounted for only 7 per cent of net collective income, the rest being distributed to commune members for consumption. By the end of the period, however, the rate of accumulation had increased nearly three times, to about 19 per cent of net collective income, and accumulation per capita had risen from 3.3 yuan to 18 yuan (see Table 11.5).

Some governments, however, give high priority to urban development and particularly to promoting the expansion of heavy industry. Where this occurs, they are able through compulsory delivery schemes to extract a marketable surplus of food from the collectives to feed the urban population. Some analysts regard this as an important advantage of collective agriculture, and it certainly was important historically in the Soviet Union, but it obscures an even more important advantage of a communal system, namely that it provides a framework for industrialising the countryside and thereby diversifying the rural economy. In contrast to most Third World countries, where the level of rural industrialisation is low and its geographical distribution is very uneven, manufacturing activities are widely spread in countries where communal systems dominate, and income from manufacturing and construction often accounts for a substantial part of the total income of many rural households. This is a fourth advantage of communal systems which is of considerable significance.

In the majority of Third World countries the public administration is highly centralised and bureaucratic, expensive in relation to available resources and ill-suited to reaching those in poverty, particularly the poor who inhabit the rural areas.[31] As a result there are few social services available in the countryside and such services as exist tend to be

TABLE 11.5 *Capital accumulation in Hebei province, 1962–78*

	Collective accumulation as a percentage of net collective income	*Collective accumulation per capita (yuan)*
1962	7	3.3
1965	12	7.0
1970	14	9.9
1973	18	13.6
1977	21	15.4
1978	19	18.0

SOURCES: M. S. Marshall, Jr., *Institutional Transportation and Economic Growth in Rural China*, Oxford D. Phil. thesis, 1982, Table 7.10, p. 257.

concentrated in the relatively more prosperous regions and to be monopolised by the better-off households in those regions. Some of these tendencies can be counteracted by devolving responsibility for the provision of basic services to the local community, encouraging a high degree of participation by local people in the organisation and running of social services and by constructing strong linkages between the grass roots organisations and higher levels of administration. It is one of the virtues of a communal system that it provides an institutional framework in which this can be done.

This fifth feature helps to explain why countries that have adopted communal tenure systems seem to have done so much better than most other countries in meeting the basic needs of their population and distributing public services in an equitable way. Communal systems are well designed to assist in the administration of health and nutrition programmes, to deliver potable water and basic sanitation facilities, to promote family planning programmes, to provide primary and secondary education, and to assist those in need in their old age.

The data in Table 11.6 illustrate this, although in each case they refer to the nation as a whole and not just to the rural population. Even so, they suggest that in practice the seven underdeveloped countries in our sample of twelve have a superior record to the average Third World country in reducing the infant mortality rate, providing basic health services (as measured by population per nursing person), ensuring basic literacy, providing a secondary education, and enabling people to enjoy a long life. These are advantages which deserve careful consideration when assessing the role of communal land tenure systems in promoting rural development.

Finally, communal systems provide an institutional framework for local participation in political affairs. The average peasant family living on a Chinese commune, for example, has a much bigger voice in local affairs than does the typical landless labourer, tenant or small peasant farmer in, say, Pakistan or Bangladesh. Indeed, in most Third World countries the mass of the rural population is oppressed by local landlords and their allies in government and they have no effective political influence at the local level. They might or might not have a vote in national elections, depending on whether the government is a dictatorship (as in the Philippines) or a democracy (as in India), but their power to alter matters which most directly impinge upon their daily lives is negligible.

The macro-political regimes in countries where communal land tenure systems predominate are authoritarian and are no more desirable to a

TABLE 11.6 Health, education and life expectancy

Country	Infant mortality rate (aged 0–1) 1981	Population per nursing person 1980	Adult literacy (percentage) 1980	Secondary school enrolment (percentage of age group) 1980	Life expectancy at birth (years) 1981
Vietnam	97	2930	87	48	63
China	71	1890	69	34	67
Mongolia	53	240	95**	89	64
Albania	48†	310	n.a.	63	70
North Korea	33	n.a.	n.a.	n.a.	66
Cuba	19	360	95	71	73
Romania	29	270	98	75	71
Low-income countries	99	4668	52	29	58
Middle-income countries	81	1769	65	39	60

NOTES
* Countries are ranked by level of GNP per capita. The 'low-income countries' include Vietnam and China, while the 'middle-income' countries include the other five in our list.
** The data refer to 1960.
† The data refer to 1980.

SOURCE: IBRD, *World Development Report* 1983.

liberal than authoritarian regimes in countries where individual tenure systems prevail. From the point of view of the rural population, however, the former have been successful in greatly reducing 'the day-to-day repression of "normal" society'[32] and in virtually eliminating the overt violence directed against the peasantry that is a commonplace elsewhere in the Third World.

There is little truth in the proposition that peasants invariably oppose communal systems and must be coerced into accepting them. There was, of course, coercion in the Soviet Union in the 1930s at the time of collectivisation, and it is from that period that communal systems have been associated in the West with rural terror and violence. The objective of the Soviet government, however, was not to promote rural development but to squeeze wage goods out of the countryside to supply the cities and to finance a huge defence expenditure programme. The peasants predictably resisted fiercely. In Eastern Europe conditions were very different, and the Russian example was not followed. For a start, the tempo of collectivisation was slower; indeed it was a fairly gradual process, lasting several years or even a decade. In Hungary, for example, collectivisation began in 1949 and, because of peasant resistance, was not completed until 1962. Furthermore, in Eastern Europe there was less pressure from the central government to collectivise, and in Poland and Yugoslavia most of the co-operatives were dissolved because of resistance from the peasantry. In Hungary collectivisation came to a halt between 1953 and 1955, and 500 collectives were actually disbanded. Landowners throughout Eastern Europe were of course dispossessed, but there was no significant 'liquidation of kulaks' and in fact the majority of the landowners were subsequently employed in the collective sector. The landless joined the collectives voluntarily, although many of the more prosperous peasants did not. Today, however, there is little evidence that the rural population of Eastern Europe is hostile to communal land tenure systems, although there is abundant evidence that they (and their urban fellow citizens) are hostile towards their Russian overlords.

In Cuba the land reforms of 1959 and 1963 were very popular, and there 'seems to have been no move among the agricultural labour force for dividing the land of the estates into separate, small units'.[33] The North Korean land reform of 1946, which created small peasant holdings, was carried out with popular support and mass participation and has been described as the fastest and most peaceful land reform of any post-revolutionary society in Asia or Europe.[34] Collectivisation was carried out between 1953 and 1958, i.e. not until after the Korean War, and was a response to the problems caused by the devastation and heavy loss of life (particularly among adult males) that occurred during the war. Indeed, 'the war had anyway caused a kind of co-operative agriculture to be introduced',[35] and it was not difficult to obtain the consent of the peasantry to build on this foundation. Finally, in China the commune system was created by a government which came to power as a result of a peasant revolution. The major objective of the system in China has always been rural betterment, and it would be very difficult to argue that the commune system as it has evolved in that vast country does not enjoy the support of the great majority of the rural population.[36] The present shift towards assigning responsibility to households for cultivating collectively owned land should not be interpreted as a rejection of communal land tenure systems in general.

Thus the claim that communal tenure systems are always resisted by the peasantry and hence always entail massive coercion will not stand up to even cursory examination. It is true, of course, that the agrarian reforms leading to the establishment of communal systems have been no less violent than other types of land reform, and the losers naturally have resisted whenever they could, but it would be wrong to argue that landless workers and small peasants, who were the intended beneficiaries of the reforms, have resisted communal systems where they would have welcomed an individual tenure system. Indeed, in countries where they are well established it appears that communal systems are accepted largely without question and are recognised as having contributed to rural development. Increasingly this is recognised in other countries, too, and many governments in the Third World have responded by attempting to create islands of communal production in a sea of individual tenure. Alas, however, historical experience does not augur well for the success of these attempts.

More often than not in such cases the communal sector is starved of resources, denied credit and technical assistance, and confined to inhospitable terrain. It is subjected to continuous political harassment by the defenders of individual tenure and given little chance to develop within a favourable environment. Either its growth is nipped in the bud or it is forced to endure a lingering and painful death. Examples of the latter include the collective *ejido* in Mexico and of the former the *asentamiento* in Chile. On occasion a communal system has been implanted in part of the agricultural sector and has brought measurable gains to its members. Where this has occurred there is a danger that the members of the collective will become a new vested interest and will try to prevent other sections of the rural population from acquiring the benefits of membership. This happened, for instance, on the workers' self-managed farms (*unités d'autogestion*) in Algeria, and on the *asentamientos* in Chile until they were destroyed in General Pinochet's counter-revolution.

Thus the problem small communal systems face is how to avoid becoming either an endangered species or a privileged minority. Few countries have solved this problem. In most instances, but certainly not in all, peaceful coexistence is unlikely to be viable in the long run, and a choice will have to be made between a communal or individual tenure system. It would be idle to pretend that such a choice is straightforward or that one system is clearly superior to the other. In principle both systems are capable of achieving the same results. Guatemala, for example, has achieved a rapid rate of growth of agricultural output; Brazil has enjoyed a high rate of growth of agricultural income per head; Taiwan has been remarkably successful in industrialising the countryside and diversifying sources of income in rural areas; Sri Lanka has an enviable record in delivering social services in rural areas and ensuring that the basic needs of its people are satisfied; and after the land reform, South Korea appears to have achieved an equitable distribution of income in the countryside. These are all countries where individual land tenure dominates.

Communal systems have two things working in their favour, however, which make them an attractive instrument for rural development. First, the system brings together many desirable features under a single institutional framework. This makes it possible, once the system is established and functioning properly, to combine sustained rapid growth of agricultural production, rural industrialisation, rising per capita consumption, a high rate of investment, an equal distribution of income, the provision of essential social services and a high degree of participation in local affairs. It is the combination of all these things, rather than marked superiority in achieving any one particular objective, that makes communal systems worth considering seriously.

Secondly, the performance of communal systems in attaining each of the objectives mentioned above is better than the average performance in countries where individual tenure systems prevail. It is not the case that communal systems perform better in some respects and worse in others: they perform better in all respects. Thus there is no need to sacrifice one goal to achieve another. Of course, the performance of the communal system in a particular country may be inferior to the average performance of countries where individual tenure systems dominate. Similarly, the performance of the individual tenure system in a particular country may be superior to the average performance of countries where communal systems dominate. In general, however, communal systems have done better than individual tenure systems. Hence, in terms of probabilities of success, the communal land tenure system is the better vehicle for promoting rural development.

Critics of this view could argue that the achievements cited should be attributed not to communal land tenure systems narrowly defined but to a comprehensive set of socialist agricultural policies of which communal tenure forms only a part. Rapid accumulation, for example, may be due to a system of centrally planned savings, and this may require communal tenure as a precondition, but a high rate of investment does not spring from communal tenure automatically. Similarly, the achievements in health, education and welfare may reflect not sectoral but national social and economic prioities, and communal structures may simply be a vehicle for implementing these policies. While this argument is true as far as it goes, it stops short of the central point, which is that it is misleading to separate communal systems from their wider context. Policies necessarily are interrelated, and when examining a set of policies and institutions the question is whether or not they are coherent and reinforce one another. The evidence that we have assembled in this chapter suggests that in countries in which communal systems are dominant, institutional arrangements and government policies in practice have tended to be coherent. The result has been a considerable improvement in the well-being of the rural population.

NOTES

1. I am grateful to Andrea Boltho, A. K. Ghose, Ken Post, Louis Putterman and Frances Stewart for helpful comments on an earlier draft of this chapter.
2. The commune system in China is undergoing rapid change. For a recent analysis see Keith Griffin (ed.) *Institutional Reform and Economic Development in the Chinese Countryside* (London: Macmillan, 1984).
3. Much of the controversy surrounding Soviet agriculture originated during the period of collectivisation during the early 1930s. A good discussion is contained in Alec Nove, *An Economic History of the USSR* (London: Allen Lane, 1969), Ch.7. For an analysis of the role of collective farming in the development of an economically backward part of the Soviet Union see Azizur Rahman Khan and Dharam Ghai, *Collective Agriculture and Rural Development in Soviet Central Asia* (London: Macmillan, 1979).
4. Very little is known about collective agriculture in Vietnam. See, however, Nguyen Huu Dong, 'Collective and Family Agriculture in Socialist Economies', IDS *Bulletin*, Vol. 13, No. 4, September 1982.

5. The best study is Joseph Sang-hoon Chung, *The North Korean Economy: Structure and Development* (Stanford: Hoover Institution Press, 1974).
6. See Arthur MacEwan, 'Cuban Agriculture and Development: Contradictions and Progress', in Dharam Ghai, *et al.* (eds) *Agrarian Systems and Rural Development* (London: Macmillan, 1979).
7. For a discussion of the attempt in Algeria to establish workers' self-managed farms see Keith Griffin, *Land Concentration and Rural Poverty*, (London: Macmillan, 2nd edition, 1981), Ch. 1. On Israel see Haim Barkai, *Growth Patterns of the Kibbutz Economy* (Amsterdam: North Holland Publishing Co., 1977) and Yehuda Don, 'Dynamics of Development in the Israeli Kibbutz', in Peter Dorner (ed.), *Co-operative and Commune: Group Farming in the Economic Development of Agriculture* (Madison: University of Wisconsin Press, 1977).
8. There is a large literature on the Mexican *ejido*. One excellent study that is often overlooked, however, is Cynthia Hewitt de Alcantara, *Modernizing Mexican Agriculture: Socioeconomic Implications of Technological Change 1940–1970* (Geneva: UNRISD, 1976), Ch. V.
9. See Dharam Ghai and Reginald Herbold Green, 'Ujamaa and Villagisation in Tanzania', in Dharam Ghai *et al.* (eds), *op. cit.*
10. See R. K. Srivastava and I. Livingstone, 'Growth and Distribution: The Case of Mozambique', in Dharam Ghai and Samir Radwan (eds), *Agrarian Policies and Rural Poverty in Africa* (Geneva: International Labour Office, 1983).
11. Keith Griffin, *The Political Economy of Agrarian Change*, (London: Macmillan, 2nd edition, 1979), Ch. 8. The phrase was coined originally by Marshall Wolfe.
12. For an excellent example of how this should be done see Alain de Janvry, *The Agrarian Question and Reformism in Latin America* (Johns Hopkins University Press, 1981). An early attempt at a comparative analysis is Jack Dunman, *Agriculture: Capitalist and Socialist* (London: Lawrence & Wishart, 1975); see especially the chapters on the GDR (Ch. 4), Poland (Ch. 5), Hungary (Ch. 6) and Yugoslavia (Ch. 7). Z. Kozlowski argues that agricultural growth in Eastern Europe has been relatively slow given the very rapid rate of growth of industry, and this has resulted in a chronic disequilibrium between supply and demand for foodstuffs. See his 'Agriculture in the Economic Growth of the East European Socialist Countries', in Lloyd Reynolds, (ed.), *Agriculture in Development Theory* (Yale University Press, 1975).
13. Doreen Warriner, *Land Reform in Principle and Practice* (Oxford: Oxford University Press, 1969), p. 67.
14. The other three 'baby tigers' are Hong Kong, Singapore and Taiwan.
15. These are unweighted averages and the figure for Eastern Europe is strongly influenced by Albania, where the population is growing about 2.7 per cent a year.
16. Lloyd G. Reynolds, *Image and Reality in Economic Development* (Yale University Press, 1977), p. 400.
17. Conversely, few people claim that Poland's deficit in agricultural trade indicates the weakness of individual tenure systems. Yet of the seven largest

importers of cereals, five are countries with individual tenure systems (Japan, Italy, Poland, the UK and Brazil) and two are countries with communal tenure systems (USSR and China).
18. See IBRD, *World Development Report 1982*. The figures in the text refer to 1980.
19. Jon Halliday, 'The North Korean Model: Gaps and Questions', *World Development*, September/October 1981, p. 894.
20. The value of food (SITC O,1) as a percentage of total exports and imports was as follows:

	exports	imports
1966	31	27
1970	29	19
1975	30	12
1980	18	14

21. D. Gale Johnson, 'Agriculture in the Centrally Planned Economies', *American Journal of Agricultural Economics*, December 1982, p. 845.
22. *Ibid.* There is a large literature on the theory of collective enterprise. For recent contributions see Louis Putterman, 'Voluntary Collectivization: A Model of Producers' Institutional Choice', *Journal of Comparative Economics*, Vol. 4, June 1980, and Louis Putterman, 'On Optimality of Collective Institutional Choice', *Journal of Comparative Economics*, Vol. 5, December 1981.
23. See, for example, Michael Lipton, *Why Poor People Stay Poor: Urban Bias in World Development* (London: Temple Smith, 1977) and I.M.D. Little, *Economic Development: Theory, Policy and International Relations*, (New York: Basic Books, 1982), pp. 160–1. Recently, however, it has been argued that relative food prices have increased and this has led to the further impoverishment of landless labourers and small peasants who are net buyers of food grains. See the paper by myself and A. K. Ghose reprinted in my *Land Concentration and Rural Poverty*, Ch. 8.
24. Keith Griffin, *The Political Economy of Agrarian Change*.
25. See, for example, the special issue of *Development and Change*, Vol. VI, No. 2, 1975.
26. R. Albert Berry and William R. Cline, *Agrarian Structure and Productivity in Developing Countries* (Johns Hopkins University Press, 1979).
27. Michael Ellman, 'Agricultural Productivity Under Socialism', *World Development*, September/October 1981. Even if one agrees that given the factor proportions prevailing in most Third World countries, the economies of scale in crop cultivation are limited, a communal system may be able to exploit economies of scale in marketing output, purchasing material inputs, acquiring technical knowledge and, as we shall argue below, managing rural development. In addition, large units may be able to spread risks by diversifying output, assuming the collective is large enough to contain a variety of soil types and growing conditions.
28. See Keith Griffin (ed.), *Institutional Reform and Economic Development in the Chinese Countryside*, Ch. 2.
29. See Keith Griffin, *International Inequality and National Poverty*, (London: Macmillan, 1978), Ch. 9 on 'Efficiency, Equality and Accumulation in

Rural China: Notes on the Chinese System of Incentives', and Thomas G. Rawski, *Economic Growth and Employment in China* (Oxford: Oxford University Press, 1979), Ch. 4.
30. Louis Putterman, 'A Modified Collective Agriculture in Rural Growth-with-Equity: Reconsidering the private, Unimodal Solution', *World Development*, February 1983.
31. See Keith Griffin and Jeffrey James, *The Transition to Egalitarian Development* (London: Macmillan, 1981), Ch. 5; Norman T. Uphoff and Milton J. Esman, *Local Organization for Rural Development: Analysis of Asian Experience* (Cornell University, Rural Development Committee, 1974).
32. Barrington Moore, Jr., *Social Origins of Dictatorship and Democracy: Lord and Peasant in the Making of the Modern World* (London: Allen Lane, 1967), p. 505. Professor Ken Post of the Institute of Social Studies in The Hague has suggested to me that one advantage of collective systems is that the peasantry sometimes can use them to protect themselves against the state.
33. Arthur MacEwan, *Cuban Agriculture and Development*, p. 333.
34. Jon Halliday, 'The North Korean Model', p. 890.
35. *Ibid.* p. 893. It is ironical that the first agrarian reform in North Korea was a Jeffersonian redistributive reform carried out during the Russian occupation, whereas the second reform consisted of socialist collectivisation and was carried out in response to the suffering inflicted by the Americans during the Korean War.
36. This does not imply that every reform in post-liberation rural China has enjoyed the support of the peasantry or that every reform has led to rural betterment. The Great Leap Forward and the accompanying disasters and starvation are examples of what can happen when things go wrong. It does not follow, however, that such errors are intrinsic to communal tenure systems or that events would have been less disastrous if no attempt had been made to introduce communal land reforms.

12 World Food Security: National and International Measures for Stabilisation of Supplies

NURUL ISLAM

The objective of world food security in a wider sense and a broader perspective is to assure all people, at all times, the physical and economic access to the basic food they need. Sustained physical availability, the stability of adequate food supplies, and command over purchasing power to secure access to food are all necessary components of food security at the level of individuals, households and nations. Measures are needed at national, regional and global levels, not only to expand food supplies through increasing production, especially in low-income, food-deficit countries, but also to maximise the stability of supplies in the face of production fluctuations and to secure access to food supplies on the part of all, especially the poor people and poor nations.

The three components of food security listed above are not unrelated, even though the attainment of one does not assure the achievement of the other. Higher levels of production do not bring in their train greater stability in year-to-year production; in fact higher yield may be associated – and in many cases *is* associated – with a greater variability of yield. No doubt at a higher level of food availability or consumption an individual or a nation can withstand the effects of shortfalls in food supplies or food consumption without much distress or deterioration in nutritional status, as compared to a situation where the average level of consumption is near the minimum nutritional requirements. At the same time, at a higher level of income and food consumption, an individual or a nation has greater capability and resources to build up stocks to face possible shortfalls in production.

Adequate and stable supplies for a nation do not necessarily ensure that every individual, especially the rural and urban poor, rural landless or urban jobless, would have access to food; they may have neither the resources to produce, nor employment and income to be able to purchase, food. Significant inequalities in consumption levels coexist with high levels of aggregate food supplies, both within and between nations. Moreover, year-to-year stability of food supplies either at national or household levels does not imply that they are adequate to meet the minimum nutritional requirements. In the long run, food supplies should be adequate not only to meet the minimum nutritional requirements of all, but also to meet the effective demand for food from a growing population with rising income levels.

This chapter concentrates on one aspect of the broader concept of food security, namely the problems and possibilities of achieving the optimum stability of supplies in the face of fluctuations in domestic food production, as well as in supplies and prices in world trade. The discussion is limited to the analysis of cereals only. Of the three components of world food security, this is an area where there are still many unsettled questions and continuing controversy – some real, some imaginary, as well as some minor and some important – as to the sources and consequences of instability, and as to the feasibility and cost-effectiveness of those measures suggested to reduce instability or offset its effects both at world level and at the level of individual countries.

NATURE, MAGNITUDE AND SOURCES OF INSTABILITY

The evidence indicates that variability of cereal production, measured in terms of average percentage variation from trend, increased during the 1970s compared to the 1960s. The world average variability in yield of cereals per hectare has increased by more than 50 per cent (from 2.26 to 3.36 per cent), whereas variability in production increased by 30 per cent (from 2.57 to 3.22 per cent). The extent of variability in developed countries is higher than in developing countries, both in respect of yield as well as of total production: the largest increase in yield variability is in the USA, from 3.19 to 10.38 per cent, whereas the average for all developed countries increased from 2.43 to 5.65 per cent.

Throughout the last two decades variability in yield and in production in the USA and the USSR was higher than the average variability in developed countries as a whole. During the 1970s the highest variability in yield occurred in the USSR (15.89 per cent), with the USA following (10.38 per cent). During the 1970s the variability in yield (3.36 per cent) and in production (2.29 per cent) in another large cereal-producing and importing country compare with 2.38 per cent and 3.46 per cent respectively for the developing countries as a whole.

The fluctuations in world trade are considerably greater than that in domestic production because only a small proportion of world cereal production is traded. Except for major exporters like the USA, Australia and Canada, the percentage of output that is internationally traded is small.

Moreover, since world trade is dominated by a few exporters, it is the degree of fluctuation in their domestic production that is mainly relevant in determining variations in world supplies. The percentage variation in yield is generally greater in exporting countries, most of whom depend on rain-fed agriculture. For example, percentage variability in yield during the 1970s was 7 per cent in the EEC, 8.64 per cent in Canada, 18.43 per cent in Australia and 10.38 per cent in the USA, as against the average for the world of 3.36 per cent and for the developed countries of 5.65 per cent.

Among the big importers in the world market are the USSR and China. The high degree of yield variability in these countries causes corresponding variation in their import demand, given the increasing tendency on their part to protect domestic consumption from the impact of fluctuations in production. The year-to-year changes in the Soviet cereal imports in absolute amounts as well as a percentage of world trade have been considerable. During the 1970s Soviet imports sometimes increased in one year by 13–20 per cent, and in the next year fell by 11–15 per cent. As a percentage of world trade Soviet imports have varied from 18 per cent in one year to 4 per cent in the next (1972–3 and 1973–4), again decreased from 18 per cent in 1975–6 to 7 per cent in 1976–7, and again from 12 per cent in 1977–8 to 9 per cent in 1978–9. In 1981–2 the percentage rose to 21 per cent. The cereal imports of China, during the 1970s, in some cases rose from one year to the next by as much as 170 per cent (from 1976–7 to 1977–8 or fell by 60 per cent between two years (as from 1974–5 to 1975–6).[1]

What is important from the point of view of the impact of variations in imports on the stability of world trade is not only the percentage variation from year to year in countries' imports, but also the relative importance of these imports in world cereal trade. The larger the volume of imports, the greater is the impact on world trade of a percentage change in countries' imports. The proportion of Soviet cereal imports in world trade averaged between 15 and 21 per cent during the early 1970s, and that of China varied between 14 and 16 per cent during the same period.

There are various factors that contribute to production variability, some of which have become more important in recent years. Yield variations are often equated with the weather, but can also result from input shortages, the use of marginal land, crop disease and poor husbandry. Climatologists have various notions about long-term climatic change, but seen to have no way of predicting weather fluctuations from season to season. What weather does do is to give a skewed yield distribution, with a few sharp yield decreases and many average or slightly above average years. This unevenness is perhaps more important than yield variance *per se*. Other causes of yield variation are more tractable. The spread of high-yield variety of seeds has often been associated with a reduction in the genetic heterogeneity of seeds and hence increased the risk of simultaneous and similar fluctuations in output in different fields/regions in a country. Input shortages, including the timeliness of input supplies and variations in their price, can be as serious as bad weather. Similarly, the control of pest and diseases rests as much on the organisation of pest control measures on scientific skills. The expansion of crop production to land only marginally suited to its production can magnify the weather-related and other causes of yield variations.

Scientific advance seems to be moving us in two directions – to control variations in yield through disease and pest control and appropriate seed varieties, and to increase variations by contributing to greater genetic homogeneity and by breeding out resistance to disease found in indigenous species as a result of the search for higher yields through new varieties. A choice based on better information on·both average levels and variability of yields has to be made between two considerations: to preserve the genetic heterogeneity of crops, or to expend additional resources to control pests and diseases.

The instability of the area under crops, which also contributes to variability in output, seems less well studied. Farmers, owing either to the attraction of other crops or to the general lack of profitability from farming can at times sharply reduce supply. Where producer-oriented price support systems exist, such fluctuations are rare.

INTERRELATED INSTABILITY IN CEREALS AND FEED SECTORS

Instability in perennial crops and in livestock products can be just as troublesome as yield changes in annual crops. These cycles arise from an inevitable feature of the production process in which investment implies, at least in aggregate, a temporary fall in production. Disease problems also often have an effect lasting for more than one year. This suggests that government policies need to be particularly sensitive in such areas. Governments can create investment cycles by their own action if they encourage the planting of perennials or the building up of livestock herds at certain times which then lead to overproduction later in the cycle. Developing country livestock is usually based on short-cycle enterprises such as poultry and pigs, and the use of imported feed will tend to instability generated by the uneven availability of local crops. International feed prices could, however, have significant repercussions of emerging livestock industries and food crop shortages if they in turn generate the occasional slaughtering of the breeding herd, which could destabilise the livestock markets and, in principle, the feedgrain markets.

Is the spread of livestock enterprises based on the utilisation of cereals a positive or negative influence on the stability of food supplies? The answer seems to depend on (a) the source of the instability and (b) the reactions of governments to price changes. If the source of instability is in foodgrain (or other staple crop) production, then the availability of a parallel feedgrain marketing system can be an advantage. Even if the type of grain is not directly appropriate for switching to human use it should be easier to effect a substitution if the buying, storage and transportation systems for feed products is in place. Moreover, the livestock herd itself can be run down at times of food shortages, although at a fairly high cost in terms of instability in the supply of livestock products. A policy to preserve stability in the livestock sector will tend to reduce its effectiveness as a food reserve: a policy of deliberately using the livestock sector as a food security device will place a heavy burden on a small industry and possibly hamper the development of a profitable integrated agricultural system. If the source of instability is from the feedgrain sector, then there is the opposite dilemma: whether to allow the foodgrain sector to help stabilise the livestock activity. Some degree of instability in the market for food crops might then be attributable to the existence of livestock sector. Whether positive factors outweigh the negative depends to a large extent on policy reactions.

Instability arising from outside the agricultural sector has received considerable attention in recent years. In the halcyon days of macro-stability, when the three macro-prices – inflation, interest rates and exchange rates – were, at the least, fairly predictable, agriculture could largely ignore monetary matters. Nowadays, inflation can turn remunerative prices into heavy taxes, interest rates can make debt repayment a major cost and stifle new investment, and exchange rates can create or destroy foreign markets almost overnight. The problems are essentially short-term: they are the instability of these variables and the uncertainty they create.

PRICE INSTABILITY

The problem of price instability is of broad concern to all trading countries. The fluctuation in the world price of cereals, which is the most important traded food item in world trade, has been aggravated in recent years. World market prices were relatively stable during the 1950s and upto the mid-1960s. The situation changed in the 1970s when prices became highly volatile. Aside from the crisis year of 1973–4, this variability is significant in other years as well. During the 1970s wheat prices varied more than eight times as much as during the 1960s; the price variability of rice exports more than doubled. The coefficient of variation in export prices (in real terms) of wheat was 3.6 per cent during the 1960s and 30.0 per cent during the 1970s, whereas that of rice (in real terms) was 17.5 per cent during the 1960s and 39.0 per cent during the 1970s.[2] Between 1950 and 1971 the largest year-to-year percentage change in US prices of commercial wheat was 16 per cent between August 1977 and April 1979 the US export price of wheat increased by 80 per cent; during the calendar year 1980, corn export prices increased by 50 per cent, primarily in response to reduced crop in the USA and low yields in the USSR.

The sources of increased variability in the prices of cereals are many and various. The major reasons for stability in cereal prices during the 1950s and 1960s were the support policies of the USA and Canada and concomitant carry-over stocks held by them; the stocks were held either directly by the government or under its control. By the early 1970s, the major grain exporters were no longer willing to carry large stocks: they made major efforts to control surpluses by output/acreage reduction programmes. Wheat and feedgrain stocks held by major exporters in 1961–2 were 14.4 per cent of world production, compared to 9.6 per cent in 1970–1 and 8.6 per cent in 1972–3.

Individual countries, both developed and developing – the former more successfully than the latter – adopt policies to shelter their economies from the direct effects of international market instability through border mechanisms which neutralise world price movements or through state trading or direct interventions in domestic cereal/food markets which have the same effect. National policies are directed towards stabilising domestic prices and domestic consumption levels by varying net trade. This shifts the impact of variability in production on to international markets, which are left free to the play of market forces.

During the late 1960s and 1970s an increasing proportion of the world's production and consumption occurred in nations which pursued internal price stability through managed trade. This was true of the EEC and a few developing countries like India. It was also true of centrally planned economies, whose share in world net imports of cereals increased from 8 per cent in the early 1970s to 30 per cent in the early 1980s. In the Soviet Union, for example, in the earlier periods, substantial shortfalls in supply were tolerated; in the later periods, serious efforts were made to reduce or eliminate them. There is no reason to expect that policy-induced international price instability will decrease during the 1980s. If anything, it is likely to increase.

This has at least three disadvantages. First, a volatile world price is a much less reliable indicator of efficient resource allocation. This matters a great deal in a period when developing countries are deciding on incentive levels for domestic agriculture. Secondly, the allocation of burdens and benefits is arbitrary, leading to further tensions in the trade system. If a country is unsuccessful in its insulation policy, it will suffer unduly, especially if it is unable to finance the losses from selling high-priced imports on to a stable domestic market. Thirdly, it will destabilise other related markets where domestic insulation is not so complete – in particular the livestock sector.

The problem, then, is to get the right balance between domestic market stability and world market stability. To try for the latter alone is likely to be costly and impracticable.

SOURCES OF CONSUMPTION INSTABILITY IN DEVELOPING COUNTRIES

Food security at national levels can be achieved only if a degree of stability in consumption levels is attained. Obviously, a complete stabilisation of consumption levels is not feasible; adjustment in consumption levels at times of shortfalls in production or supplies up to a limit is expected. The lower the average level of consumption, the lower is the limit to further squeeze on consumption. Moreover, the consumption levels of the poorest need to be protected at times of shortages.

The year-to-year variability in food/cereal consumption in individual developing countries is quite high. Levels of variability of 10 per cent or more are observed in six out of twenty-four countries. The coefficient of variation ranges from a low of 3 per cent to as high as 20-30 per cent.

At the level of individual developing countries the sources of instability in food supplies and prices are twofold: fluctuations in domestic food production and in import prices. Variability in consumption of cereals is highly correlated with changes in domestic production. Consumption may vary with changes in disposable income. Individual countries try to offset variations in domestic production by imports of foodgrains, but do not necessarily succeed in completely offsetting variations in domestic production and in stabilising consumption. Foreign exchange for imports of cereals may not be available to enable an offsetting purchase of imports. Moreover, even if foreign exchange for food imports is available, the volume of imports depends on the price of imports — a rise in import price cuts down the volume of imports. In many countries, the food import bill (including cereals and other staples) constitutes a high proportion of foreign exchange earnings, especially in years of low exchange earnings and high food prices, rising to as high as 40-50 per cent of foreign exchange earnings in exceptional cases. Also, marketing and distribution facilities, including port facilities, may not be flexible enough to handle large year-to-year variations in cereal imports.

Import bills pf developing countries are therefore dependent on (a) fluctuations in domestic production, and (b) variability in import price. During the 1960s, when prices were stable, variability of import volume was more important than that of prices in determining the variability of import volume was more important than that of prices in determining the variability of import bills. In contrast, during the 1970s, in ten out of a smaple of eighteen countries, price changes explained more than 60 per cent of the variability in import bills.[3]

NATIONAL MEASURES FOR STABILISING SUPPLIES

National measures to enhance the stability of food supplies in the face of fluctuations in food availability are needed mainly in three spheres. The first set of measures is directed towards reducing the degree of fluctuations in output. An extension of irrigation facilities, wherever physically feasible and economically justifiable, would help to offset the uncertainty, irregularity and inadequacy in the amount of rainfall; it would also help extend multiple cropping and expand the land area under cultivation, thus both reducing seasonal fluctuations and spreading the risks of year-to-year fluctuations. In the same category are measures designed to ensure a smooth flow of purchased inputs such as fertilisers, improved seeds and pesticides at the right time and in appropriate quantity. Also important are continued research efforts to reduce variability to yield from new varieties of plants, while striving to improve their average yield and to reduce the impact of pests and diseases while efforts are made to develop pest- and disease-resistant varieties of seeds.

The second category of domestic measures relates to the strengthening of the state of national preparedness to meet efficiently and readily the impact of food shortages so that distress and suffering can be mitigated. Foremost in this category is the improvement of physical infrastructure for the marketing and distribution of food, including the improvement and expansion of logistic and transportation facilities, including storage facilities. Many developing countries do indeed suffer from serious logistic and transportation bottlenecks in ensuring the quick delivery of both imported and domestic food supplies. It is necessary to improve national preparedness to meet food shortages in various ways: by establishing or strengthening national monitoring and early warning systems for basic food supplies; by establishing, if necessary, special units of government arrangements to deal with disasters and food emergencies; by compiling a manual of food relief activities and tasks to be undertaken and procedures to be adopted in the event of food shortages. It is important to monitor transportation and logistic factors regularly.

The third category of national measures relates to the food stock or reserve policies in food-deficit, low-income countries. An individual country can hold food reserves or foreign exchange in order to secure access to food supplies at times of shortages.

Holding stocks is more expensive than holding foreign exchange. For one thing there are investment costs in storage capacity as well as in its maintenance and operation. Secondly, food stocks are subject to wastage and spoilage, whereas foreign currency held in banks is not. But there are a number of advantages in holding food reserves as against foreign exchange. First, it is not always possible to get physical access to imports, if a country has command over foreign exchange. Recent experience indicates that embargoes or export restraint can be applied which prevent access to supplies. It is undoubtedly true that embargoes can, at a cost, be circumvented either by obtaining supplies from alternative sources or from re-export through third countries; but this involves extra search or transaction costs on the part of a country cut off from its traditional and familiar sources of food supplies. Secondly, while physical availability at times of world shortages may not be a serious problem, even though a small importing country usually has to pay higher prices under these conditions, it may still face the problem of shortage of shipping space. When the amounts to be transported are small when there is an extraordinary demand for shipping services for all importers, and when the country happens not to be located on the traditional or convenient international shipping routes, this problem may become acute. For such cereals as rice or white maize the markets are then at the world level, and transactions generally take a much longer time. Domestic stocks in these cases are essential to meet shortfalls in supplies. This is especially true if the size of a country's import demand is large in relation to the total volume of international trade.

Thirdly, even when supplies are available and shipping can be arranged, the kind of food supplies available may not correspond to the consumption patterns of the country. A country which habitually consumes maize may, for instance, have to import wheat, Traditional crops consumed by some developing countries, such as sorghum, millet or roots and tubers, are not commodities that are heavily traded on the world market.

Under all these circumstances, the advantages of holding food reserves cannot be ignored. Domestic food reserves can consist primarily of domestically produced traditional crops. For countries that have attained a high degree of self-sufficiency, and in good years generate export surpluses with deficits in bad years, domestic stockholding offers a way of taking excess output off the market at times of surplus and using the stocks for meeting deficit in bad years. It is difficult for a country which generates occasional surpluses to enter the world market easily without incurring significant marketing costs and without avoiding price concessions. In good years the domestic market-clearing prices may be above the f.o.b. price and in bad years its domestic price will be below the c.i.f. price. If this is the case then domestic storage capacity would be a viable alternative, particularly if the gap between the low and high prices is wide enough to cover the storage cost.

The most important reason why a minimum amount of domestic food reserves is needed for food security purposes is the time lag in obtaining supplies from abroad. Pipeline or working stocks of traders or households are not likely to be enough to meet food security needs during the time that elapses before imports are physically available for domestic distribution. Most countries consider the expense of holding minimum food reserves to tide over this gap as a necessary and essential cost of relieving human suffering and possible starvation.

Obviously, delays in obtaining supplies vary from country to country, depending not only on location, i.e. whether a country is land-locked or borders on the sea, or is near the traditional international shipping routes, but also on its skill, knowledge and expertise in operating in world markets, including arrangements for shipping and transportation. The difficulties of obtaining supplies are aggravated at a time when domestic shortfalls in production in a developing country coincide with shortfalls in major consuming/producing areas. Major importing countries like India and China already have large stocks partly for meeting the needs of their public food distribution systems and partly for purposes of price stabilisation in the domestic market. A part of this stock is also used for meeting shortfalls in domestic production. The establishment of minimum food security stocks in the sense explained above does not constitute an alternative to trade or a reliance on imports as a means of meeting domestic shortages but is a necessary supplement to it.

Many developing importing countries do not have adequate skill and expertise in operating in the world cereal markets, in terms of buying the right quantity at the right time in order to obtain the most advantageous terms of purchase. There is a need for assistance to developing countries to augment their skill and expertise. Also, many countries do not have adequate infrastructure for holding and operating pipeline or working stocks to carry surpluses from harvest seasons or surplus areas to lean seasons or deficit areas within the country to even out seasonal variations in supply as well as across the various regions in the country.

In addition, there is a need for training in management and the operation of pipeline stocks, to be held by private traders or public agents, depending on the nature of the food market of a country, storage capacity and distribution facilities. There is a need for public investment or financial assistance to stimulate private investment in these latter.

INTERNATIONAL MEASURES FOR FOOD SECURITY

Among the international measures to meet shortfalls in food production or to dampen the rise in prices, an important measure that has been discussed in various forums in the post-Second World War period, especially since the World Food Conference in 1974, is the proposal for international food reserves. Various formulations of the proposals for international reserves in the context of world food security have been debated.

It is recognised that stocks are essential for imparting stability to prices in the face of fluctuations in production. If world cereal production and the availability of cereals in world trade out of current output levels fluctuate as described above, then stocks must be held by some countries or by all – stocks that will be 'adequate' and 'available' to act as a buffer to promote market stability. In other words, stocks need to be accumulated at times of low prices and released when prices go up. What level of stocks is to be considered adequate? The level of world stocks of cereals that is to be considered adequate for the purpose of market stability would depend on the price range within which stability is sought, apart from the level of world production and trade in cereals. This criterion for judging adequacy of stocks is different from what is relevant to the concept of food security, i.e. meeting the minimum consumption requirements (at around the level of average consumption of the recent past years) and times of production shortfalls.

WORLD FOOD SECURITY RESERVES

The discussion on world food reserves, their level and adequacy has often been marred by a lack of clear distinction between working or pipeline stocks on the one hand, and reserve stocks on the other. Carry-over stocks at the beginning of a year consist of supplies from harvests of previous seasons (or from imports) which are available at the beginning of the new crop season. They comprise both working stocks and reserve stocks. Working stocks are stocks required to assure a smooth and uninterrupted flow of supplies from the farmer, or point of imports, to the final consumer. Working stocks comprise stocks held by farmers, processors and merchants, including the quantities in transit or afloat, as well as those held by governments for sale through public distribution systems and for intra-seasonal supply and price stabilisation. Reserve stocks are in excess of working stocks, and include stocks which can be drawn on to meet unexpected deficits in supplies due to crop shortfalls, emergency food shortages and other contingencies.

An attempt has been made by FAO in the past to estimate the level of world stocks of cereals that would be adequate to meet shortfalls in world food production. The objective behind the estimate was to measure the level of reserve stocks needed to maintain the long-term trend in consumption and to cover the world for one year's unexpected and unplannable events such as crop failures due to low yields in various regions. The methodology followed was as follows.

For the exporting countries, an estimate was made of total cereal production and available exports in a bad crop year. In order to establish available exports, an estimate was made of the trend value of domestic output in exporting countries.[4] The trend value of production (based on the utilisation of the full production area) is subsequently adjusted downwards by assuming that yields per hectare would be reduced by specified amounts related to either the two standard deviations from trend or to the lowest actual yield level that was achieved in the past, when droughts or plant diseases affected the cereal crop production. In the rice-importing countries, the same assumption was made to derive net imports in a bad year. For imports of wheat and coarse grains, in the absence of data, it was assumed that their net imports would increase by two standard deviations from the trend. The excess of the 'adjusted' import requirements in a bad year over the adjusted estimate of what is available in the exporting countries for exports and stocks in the bad year determines the amount by which carry-over stocks at the onset of the bad crop year need to be drawn down in order to meet the shortfall in world production. Expressed as a percentage of the previous years' annual consumption, this works out at 5–6 per cent. It is to be noted that between the mid-1950s and early 1970s the amount of absolute maximum single-year shortfall in world cereal production works out at approximately 5–6 per cent of 1973–4 world consumption.

An analysis of historical data on stocks for several years for each of the three crops was undertaken with a view to identifying stock levels in those years when the price situation was more or less equilibrated, i.e. when stocks did not include any 'surplus' element beyond 'working' and 'reserve' stocks. The stocks at the end of the year 1973–4, when there was an extremely tight supply and demand situation and high prices, were assumed to be all working stocks, which exclude any reserves for unforeseen shortages. Deducting the 1973–4 stocks as working stocks, the size of food security stocks was calculated for normal years. It was estimated that the figures shown in Table 12.1 are the normal ratios of working stocks and reserve stocks for different crops, for exporters and importers separately.

The calculation of minimum safe levels of food reserves, including both working and reserve stocks, for the world as a whole and for all cereals, implies first that stocks, irrespective of where they are located, are available to all countries at times of production shortfalls to meet

TABLE 12.1 *Safe level of stocks as percentage of total disappearance on annual consumption*

	Wheat Exporters	Wheat Importers	Combined	Coarse grains Exporters	Coarse grains Importers	Combined	Rice Exporters/Importers (combined)
Total	50	16	(26)	22	10	(15)	15.1
Reserve	(33)	(2)	(9.5)	(8)	(1)	(3.7)	(4.7)

SOURCE: *Approaches to World Food Security* (Rome: FAO 1983), p. 34. Exporters' stocks are as a percentage of total exporters' disappearance; importers' stocks are a percentage of domestic consumption, and combined stocks are a percentage of total world annual consumption.

shortages; and secondly, that different cereals are completely substitutable for each other. Looked at from the point of an individual country, e.g. a food-deficit, low-income country, required stocks would be very different, as an individual country has a choice between holding stocks and acquiring supplies through imports. As shown in Table 12.1, what are adequate stocks for importers is different from what is adequate from the point of view of exporters if exporters are to be a reliable and dependable source of supplies for the importers. Moreover, the safe level of stocks was considered to be adequate to meet one year of worst shortfall, and not two consecutive years of bad harvests.

The FAO Secretariat's estimate of the minimum safe level of cereal stocks, set at 17–18 per cent of annual consumption (12 per cent of annual consumption is considered a working stock, whereas 5–6 per cent is considered adequate as food security reserves), is used by policymakers/analysts in general for evaluating the adequacy of world stocks from year to year, in the absence of any other available yardstick. The year-to-year variation in world cereal stocks in absolute amounts and as a percentage of annual consumption, including their distribution amongst various groups of countries, are shown in Tables 12.2 and 12.3.

The relevant question is whether the separate and independent interests of exporters and importers would result in a size of world stocks that would meet the worst shortfalls in production experienced in recent years. The question has been mooted whether it is necessary, either from the point of view of relieving human distress or from the point of view of cost-effectiveness, to hold stocks which take care of the worst food crisis. In other words should consumption be maintained at the *trend* level, except in the poorest countries where accommodation through shortfall

TABLE 12.2 *World carry-over stocks as percentage of total utilisation (million tons)*

	Wheat	Coarse Grains	Rice (milled)
1960–61	34.8	25.1	9.8*
1966–67	29.4	14.6	6.0
1971–72	23.5	14.2	7.1
1976–77	26.2	11.3	7.6
1978–79	23.8	12.2	10.9
1979–80	18.3	12.3	9.0
1980–81	17.1	11.2	8.3
1981–82	19.5	15.4	7.6
1982–83	21.1	19.3	5.6
1983–84	23.6	14.1	5.1

NOTE
* 1961–2.

SOURCE: The World Food Institute, *World Food Trade and US Agriculture* 1960–82 (Iowa State University, August 1983) (3rd annual edition).

TABLE 12.3 *Share of different countries in world cereal stocks*

	Total world cereal stocks (% of annual cereal consumption)	North America	Others	EEC	Japan	USSR	Developing countries
1972	18	44.2	26.9	6.5	2.5	9.7	28.8
1973	14	37.2	32.4	7.6	2.3	13.4	30.3
1974	15	25.6	38.8	8.3	2.5	20.0	35.5
1975	14	23.1	38.6	11.0	2.0	15.1	38.4
1976	14	26.2	27.7	7.7	3.1	6.9	46.2
1977	18	32.7	27.3	6.0	2.9	9.8	40.1
1978	17	39.2	22.0	5.8	3.7	4.2	38.8
1979	19	34.6	30.0	6.5	3.6	11.0	35.4
1980	18	36.2	25.0	6.2	4.2	6.3	38.7
1981	16	32.5	25.4	6.8	3.8	6.1	42.0
1982	19	43.4	21.0	5.3	2.7	5.1	35.6

SOURCE: FAO, *Food Outlook* 1982, *Statistical Supplement*, March 1983, p. 21.

in consumption would have both serious and long-term adverse consequences for health and undernutrition? Should not a certain level of fall in consumption, let us say 6.5–10 per cent below trend, be allowed in most countries of the world, provided efforts are undertaken internally by different countries to maintain at the minimum level food consumption of the poorest and vulnerable groups during a disaster?

As has been explained above, it is not enough that world stocks are at the safe minimum level; what is equally important is how the stocks are distributed around the world in the exporting and consuming countries. If stocks are concentrated, as they often are in developed exporting countries, there is no assurance that at times of food shortages they are easily accessible to the food-deficit, importing countries. Apart from the logistical problem and the bottlenecks in transportation, distribution and marketing, there is the question of bans or embargoes on exporters for various reasons, including the desire to avoid a price rise in the exporting countries themselves. Furthermore, even if the physical availability is not a problem, the price may rise beyond the purchasing capacity of low-income food-deficit countries.

INTERNATIONAL GRAINS NEGOTIATIONS

International negotiations over the six years, 1973–9, have centred on a system of internationally co-ordinated buffer stocks, designed primarily to stabilise prices within a given range. It was expected that, at the same time, this would ensure that stocks so held would also be able to meet shortfalls in world cereal production. The market will have to bear a part of the shortfall through rising prices. The stocks under international agreement were expected to help iron out extreme fluctuation, as happened in 1972–3.

How are the benefits of price stabilisation distributed among producers and consumers, between exporting and importing countries? During a period of price rises, the food import bill of deficit countries goes up, while exporters increase their profits. With price stabilisation, importers gain and exporters lose. The net balance sheet of gains and losses for producers and consumers would depend on the assumptions about elasticity of demand and supplies, as well as the behaviour pattern of countries in which production fluctuates strongly (such as the USSR) because of climate and other factors; the latter usually enter and leave the market unpredictably from year to year.[5] Various analyses of the costs and profitability of buffer stocks show that in most cases such buffer stocks are expected to lose money over time, especially if price bands are narrow. This is expected; a buffer stock would protect consumers against unknown events, for example a crop failure every five years or more. Private traders do not, and are unlikely to, hedge against major crop failures because of private risk aversion and storage costs. There are no profits to be earned in constantly investing in importable prospects. The market is not likely to be stabilised in extreme situations by private traders. The behaviour of the public and private stocks in the USA during the 1960s and early 1970s shows that when public stocks decline private stocks increase, but the latter increases proportionately much less, and therefore do not offset the decline in the former. When public stocks were generally depleted to negligible amounts in 1975, for example, the amount of private stocks were not comparable to public stocks held in earlier years, and would have been inadequate to meet any serious shortfall in production.[6]

Why is private stockholding in exporting and importing countries not enough to stabilise world prices? Apart from working or pipeline stocks, the private trader or stockholder will hold excess stocks or reserve stocks only if he finds it profitable. It is worthwhile for a private speculator to hold stocks if the expected future price is greater than the current market price plus carrying or storage costs. He does not hold stocks to stabilise prices within a predetermined range. Unless the predetermined price range by accident happens to be equal to the current and anticipated market price, as seen from the point of view of the speculators, it is unlikely that the size of these two sets of stocks would be the same.

Public stockholding has usually been discussed in the context of stabilising price within a predetermined range. The lower the range of prices, the higher is the size of stocks, and vice-versa. Public stockholding to some extent does substitute for private stocks. Apart from stabilising prices, public stocks may be held to raise prices above the competitive level. This would result in a growing accumulation of stocks, which would eventually be disposed of in the long run, with the result that stocks as a means of raising prices over the long-run competitive level are only a short-term measure. The public authority need not hold all the desired stocks itself; it could provide a subsidy to the private traders or producers to hold stocks on behalf of the public sector, above the levels at which the private traders would otherwise hold for speculative purposes.

The considerations that weigh with the public authorities to take concerted action at an international level to stabilise prices are many and various. First, a greater stability of world cereal prices would help the heavily import-dependent poor countries and save the increase in import costs at times of rising prices. The greater the food import bill, and the greater proportion of export earnings, constituted by the food import bill, the higher would be the saving in import costs from not having to pay higher prices, for poor, food-deficit countries at times of shortfall in world production and high prices.

Secondly, considerable instability of world prices may stimulate national action to follow protectionist policies in order to achieve a higher level of food self-sufficiency and to reduce the level of import dependence, thus resulting in a pattern of world food production which is not compatible with comparative cost considerations and results in misallocation of resources.

Thirdly, instability in world supplies and prices would persuade individual countries to insulate domestic production and consumption from the impact of variations in world prices, by varying net trade with a view to stabilising domestic prices. The result would be an intensification of instability in world markets, which in a vicious cycle of action and reaction would lead to attempts at further insulation of domestic markets. This is more true of the developed importing countries, which can afford the costs of domestic support price policies to insulate the domestic market.

Fourthly, faced with high instability of world supplies and prices, national governments in the developing countries that want to embark upon a policy of stabilising the food consumption of the poor and vulnerable groups would find such measures too costly and may abandon such poverty-alleviating and equity-promoting measures.

The wider the range within which prices are to be stabilised, the smaller is the amount of publicly held stocks and the smaller is the degree of substitution of private stocks by public stocks. The abundant stocks that were held by the USA and Canada in the 1950s and 1960s for domestic reasons of supporting producers' incomes in their own farm economies, held price fluctuation within a very narrow range.

From the late 1960s and in the 1970s the USA and Canada were following different policy measures for stabilising farmers' income, such as acreage control programmes and deficiency payments or direct income transfers to farmers; the acquisition of stocks with a view to raising or stabilising farmers' income was no longer the principal consideration of stockholding policy in North America. The downward pressure on prices resulting from an upward swing in production to the extent that it was not offset by acreage reduction in exporting countries, was partly met through stock-building in the importing countries. In the 1970s importers were increasingly building up stocks.

It must be noted that stocks that would be needed to stabilise prices within a range narrower than that which would result in the absence of public intervention, would not pay for themselves. The costs of holding stabilisation stocks need to be subsidised. This is what happened to stockholding by the USA and Canada in the 1960s; during the 1970s the public authorities subsidised both publicly held and farmer-owned reserves in the USA. Because there were large grain reserves in the 1960s, prices were held within a very narrow range. During the 1970s publicly held stocks in the USA were smaller. Moreover, there is no obligation on the part of the US public authorities to sell when market prices rise above support prices; it is permissive, not obligatory. Market prices could, in theory, be given a much greater role in rationing supplies.

The present system of stocks in various countries, both developed and developing, results from domestic policy objectives. There is no consensus as to how high these stocks should be; they were not adequate to prevent prices falling below costs of production in many countries, as in 1982–3, or rising to exorbitant levels with dire consequences for the poorer importing countries, as in 1972–3.

BREAKDOWN OF NEGOTIATIONS

The protracted negotiations for an International Wheat Agreement, which broke down in 1974, were designed to create a framework of international action to promote stability in supplies and prices and to provide some measure of food security for the low-income, food-deficit countries.

It was always understood that the publicly held stocks under the auspices of an international agreement would not be a *net* addition to world cereal stocks, since they were likely either partly to replace private stocks or public stocks of individual nations held prior to the international agreement. They were supposed to operate under a set of internationally agreed rules for their acquisition and release, with specific trigger prices, so that divergent actions would not be taken by countries. Even though the strictly enforced trigger prices were not agreed upon, there is still a need for a greater degree of harmonisation of stock targets and policies than exists at present. Individual countries first need to formulate their own national stock policies and targets and let it be widely understood and known; secondly, they need to harmonise so that at times of shortages some countries need not start building stocks and thus aggravate shortages, or vice-versa. There needs to be a harmonisation of policies in respect of the release or acquisition of stocks; there should be a much greater exchange of information and knowledge of each other's behaviour in the grain market. Speculators in the world grain market, who have accentuated physical scarcity in the past, will have to contend with the fact that there are publicly held stocks that would intervene to reduce the extreme fluctuation in prices.

The negotiations for an international grain agreement broke down because there was no consensus between the exporters and importers, or between developed and developing countries, in respect of the major economic provisions of such an agreement.

First, there was no agreement between major exporters, i.e. North America on the one hand, and the EEC on the other, on the size of the buffer stocks, with the USA arguing for a larger and the EEC for a smaller reserve.

Secondly, there was no agreement on the trigger prices, i.e. ceiling and floor prices, at which buffer stocks would intervene in the market. The exporters were arguing for higher ceiling prices on the grounds that they are essential for offsetting the low profits or losses they incur at times of good harvests and low prices.

Thirdly, there was the question of whether the size of stocks that were discussed, i.e. between 30 and 60 million tons, was consistent with the range of prices within which stability was to be sought. The EEC was seen to be arguing for a narrower price range and a smaller reserve, implying, according to the USA, that somehow exporters would in any case be obliged to hold stocks outside the agreement, which would contribute to the stability of the market.

Fourthly, in any case, there was no clear understanding as to how internationally co-ordinated reserves would relate to the rest of the stocks held by individual countries outside the agreement for domestic price stabilisation or for meeting domestic shortages.

Fifthly, there was no agreement on how the stockholding obligation would be shared among the exporters and importers, among the developed and devloping countries. In many other commodity agreements, stocks are held by the exporters rather than by importers and exporters, and are in some cases partly financed by levies on exports. In this agreement, every signatory, importer or exporter as the case may be, was to undertake the obligations to hold stocks at their own expense.

Sixthly, while there was a recognition of the fact that developing countries suffered from a lack of resources, both to build storage capacity and hold stocks, there was no agreement as to how and to what extent developing countries were to be assisted in either building up food security infrastructure or in purchasing or procuring food reserves. The developing countries argued that if they were to hold reserves as part of their obligations under the International Grains Agreement, the latter should provide for financial and technical assistance to enable them to fulfil their obligation. The developed countries, on the other hand, argued that they should seek ways of fulfilling the obligations by seeking assistance from the external resources presently available to them for development purposes, rather than creating additional financial facilities.

Seventhly, developing countries argued that they should have an assured and preferential access to supplies at times of food shortages in view of their limited capacity to buy in the open market at times of shortages and high prices. This was not acceptable to the others.

The foregoing analysis reveals the complexity of issues underlying the negotiation of an international agreement, especially if market stability and achievement of food security, i.e. meeting the urgent import requirements of food-deficit, low-income countries at times of food shortages, are mixed together in one package.

The search for an international agreement was more or less abandoned in the face of the unwillingness of the most important exporter, the USA, to enter into any such negotiations, and in view of its clear position that national stocks for the purposes of stability and food security should be left entirely to national decisions, without any international co-ordination, and that all countries should be encouraged to build up stocks in the light of their own requirements and capabilities.

ALTERNATIVE MEASURES FOR PROMOTING WORLD FOOD SECURITY

What alternative measures are available to promote world food security, especially to meet the requirements of low-income, food-deficit countries? In the absence of an international agreement on grains to promote market stability in supplies and prices, price fluctuations are likely to be greater. The impact of high prices on the low-income, food-deficit countries can be moderated if international assistance is available to finance the extra cost of food imports. The recently (1981) established IMF cereal financing facility, which covers the extra cost of cereal imports in a particular year – over the average cost of cereal imports in the past five years – is a step in the right direction. It covers the extra cost of cereal imports, not only due to a rise in import price but also due to a shortfall in domestic production. The new facility is an expansion of the pre-existing IMF compensatory financing for export shortfalls. In so far as a rise in export earnings accompanies a rise in cereal import costs, access to finance for the extra cost of cereal imports is reduced by the extent of increase in average export earnings over the past five years. The terms of finance are not concessional; it is a 3–5 year loan, and not for a long period. To date only a few countries have taken advantage of the facility, partly because world cereal prices have been depressed in the last two or three years due to large surplus, and partly because heavy drawings on the compensatory financing for shortfalls in exports have not left scope for any additional drawings for cereal imports, which are permissible under the IMF quota limitations.

An expansion of the facility in terms of more liberalised terms of access and wider coverage of commodities, in order to include imports of sugar and edible oils, for example, in addition to cereals, has been urged by the developing countries. Under the facility, the shortfall in net export crops is calculated as (a) trend exports *minus* actual exports, *plus* (b) actual import costs *minus* trend cereal import costs. The total amount of credit is constrained to 100 per cent of a country's quota for each of the two components (loss of export earnings and excess cost of cereal imports) and 125 per cent of the quota for the combined total.

Another source of stability of food supplies available to food-deficit countries is the Food Aid Convention, re-negotiated in 1980, under which food-aid donors undertake to provide, irrespective of fluctuations in their domestic production and in the availability of export surplus for commercial sales, a minimum food aid of 7.6 million tons a year, primarily to the low-income, food-deficit countries.

The total food-aid flows in recent years, both bilateral and multilateral, are at about 9 million tons, which falls short of the minimum target laid down by the World Food Conference in 1974. Recent estimates of food aid requirements put the figure at 20 million tons by 1985, indicating that requirements exceed actual aid flows by a wide margin.

While the overall flow of food aid up to a certain amount, i.e. 7.6 million tons, has been stabilised, the actual flow above this level fluctuates according to the available export surplus and the multiplicity of policy considerations governing food aid. Under this present agreement, there is no provision for an expansion of food aid when food shortages, scarcities and high prices occur in the world market. Moreover, the year-to-year flow of food aid to individual food-deficit countries is not necessarily related to the fluctuations in the domestic food production of the recipient countries, nor is it related to the fluctuations in world prices of food to help relieve the import burden of the food-deficit countries which rely on commercial purchases, in addition to food aid, for meeting their food requirements. A system of food aid could conceivably be devised by an international agreement under which food aid would be distributed among recipient countries from year to year, in such a manner as to stabilise the food consumption within a certain range, let us say 5 per cent, of their trend value of consumption. In order to make such a scheme feasible, its coverage may have to be restricted to the very low-income, food-deficit countries and should be limited to compensating shortfalls in trend value of production only to 95 per cent or so. This scheme must leave a part of food aid, the inter-country and inter-temporal allocation of which would be predominantly governed by political/strategic considerations.

Developing countries are concerned that at times of food shortages and high prices in the world market they may be crowded out of the world market. Hence proposals have been put forward for long-term sales and purchase agreements between developing countries on the one hand, and the major exporters on the other, so that they are assured of minimum supplies at times of shortages, while undertaking to buy a minimum quantity from the exporters during periods of low prices. This is the nature of trade agreements for the purchase of wheat that have been concluded by the Soviet Union and China with some exporters such as the USA, Canada and Argentina. Usually, such agreements do not specify prices, which are left to the market forces, but specify the quantities that will be traded. Hence they do not protect the importing countries from the impact of high prices unless such purchases are combined with price concessions or subsidised export credit or blended credit, as has been done in a few cases.

An alternative proposal to ensure that developing countries would have access to supplies – in a way, preferential access – at times of shortages, is for the developed exporting countries to set aside funds/stocks of cerals to meet the urgent import requirements of the food-deficit countries, especially the low-income countries among them. In recent years, a few countries have done so, foremost among them being the USA, which has set up an International Emergency Food Reserve of 4 million tons, intended specifically to meet its obligations for food aid under the Food Aid Convention, as well as to meet food emergencies in developing countries caused by crop failures or man-made disasters. Where food allocations are made in financial terms and food aid obligations in quantitative terms, financial allocations may or may not be adequate to secure the required quantity of cereals, depending on the market price prevailing at the time of purchase. The food reserves built up by the developed, exporting countries protect food aid disbursements from being eroded by a rise in food prices. So far none of these reserves are intended to meet the demands of commercial purchases by the low-income, food-deficit countries. It is worth examining, first, whether many more developed countries should not set up such reserves and, secondly, whether the scope of such reserves could not be extended to cover commercial purchases by low-income countries as well. The concept of such unilateral reserves to be held by developed countries for meeting the food needs of low-income, food-deficit countries was incorporated in the International Undertaking on World Food Security, endorsed by the World Food Conference in 1974.

This unilateral action, taken separately by individual countries, does not require any international agreement, and is hence easier to implement otherwise. Each country could do it within the context of national systems and procedures; no uniformity is required, at least to start the system. As experience accumulates with this type of reserve, and as several countries adopt it, it may be appropriate to learn from experience, to improve upon it, and to explore the possibility of systematising it under an international framework or umbrella of some sort.

The search for world food security, in the narrow or restricted sense of stabilising supplies with a view to stabilizing prices and consumption, within socially acceptable limits and consistent with the improvement of producers' incentives, raises complex and difficult issues. They encompass both domestic food policy and international co-operation in trade and development, for the promotion of stability, growth and equity.

NOTES

1. The World Food Institute, *World Food Trade and US Agriculture 1960 – 62* (Iowa State University, August 1983), pp.34-5.
2. B. Huddleston, Gale Johnson, S. Reutlinger and A. Valdés, 'Financial Arrangements for Food Security', October 1981, Research Report (IFPRI).
3. B. Huddleston *et al.*, 'Financial Arrangements for Food Security'.
4. The year for which trend values were established was 1974 – 5 on the basis of historical data from 1955 – 6 to 1972 – 3.
5. If demand is non-linear in the sense that prices rise more when supplies are short, then they fall when supplies increase in equal quantity (the demand curve is linked, the upper section being less elastic than the lower section) and if importers only respond partially this year to price changes (reducing price elasticity of import demand) and if production response to price changes takes place only with a time lag of one year, for example, a price stabilisation policy is more likely to benefit the consumer rather than the producers/exporters.

6. A. Sarris, P. Abbot and L. Taylor, 'Grain Reserves, Emergency Relief and Food Aid', in W.R. Cline (ed.), *Policy Alternatives in a New International Economic Order* 1978 (Washington DC: Overseas Development Council, 1978).

13 Bureaucratic, Engineering and Economic Men: Decision-Making for Technology in Tanzania's State-Owned Enterprises [1]

JEFFREY JAMES

INTRODUCTION

In a recent speech the President of Tanzania observed that 'Working towards the goal of 'people-oriented development' means ... allowing our national objectives to determine what type of technology we adopt or adapt from the North'.[2] Because Tanzania, following the Arusha Declaration of 1967, has relied extensively upon public enterprise, and since the government has had the chance to influence directly the technology chosen by these enterprises, one might reasonably expect to find in the latter a fairly close reflection of national objectives. Yet what evidence is available suggests that this has not occurred: on the contrary, the degree of coincidence in manufacturing parastatals appears to be remarkably slight.

Clark's study of socialist development and public investment in Tanzania between 1964 and 1973, for example, found that

> The failure of the post-Arusha companies to distinguish themselves significantly and favourably from the pre-Arusha companies points to one of the most important conclusions which can be made about the performance of the manufacturing parastatals, indeed about all parastatals. *There has been as yet no developmental innovation on the part of parastatals to make themselves more consistent with the Tanzanian ideology.*[3]

More recently, Perkins has studied technology choice by Tanzanian parastatals in ten manufacturing industries. She concludes that, 'In general the observed pattern of technological choice... only reflects to a limited degree Tanzania's articulated development goals.'[4] In particular, the technology choices of parastatals were found to be large-scale and capital-intensive, often technically inefficient compared to other techniques in the same industries. These choices have therefore 'failed to promote the achievement of major national development objectives, such as employment creation, economic self-reliance, decentralisation of development, rapid growth of output, conservation of scarce development capital and efficient allocation of resources.'[5]

Both Clark and Perkins observed, moreover, a distinct tendency for parastatals, when faced with a choice between products, to opt for the much more sophisticated alternative.

Although there is no shortage of attempts to explain these findings, most existing explanations offer only a limited degree of insight into the problem because they fail to analyse adequately the process by which technology decisions are *actually* made in public enterprises. In this chapter, it is contended that these decisions can only be properly understood when they are viewed as the outcome of a clearly defined sequence of behaviours in the firm. More specifically, it is argued that the choice of technology in Tanzania's public enterprises is a very highly staged or sequential process, and that at each stage there are systematic biases that operate to impede the selection of technologies that accord with the country's development goals. Evidence for this view is drawn from a series of case studies of decisions in a range of manufacturing industries.

The first part of the chapter sets out the conceptual framework of analysis. Following a description of the research method, the results of the field-work are then presented.

A CONCEPTUAL FRAMEWORK

According to Gillis, the traditional view in economics is that managers of public enterprises are 'cosmic maximisers'. That is, they are 'motivated solely by a desire to maximise a clearly defined measure of social welfare, as defined by the parent government, under conditions of perfect information on all shadow prices, externalities and risk.'[6] This idealised model, we should note, embodies not only the basic behavioural assumptions of traditional neoclassical micro-theory, but it also contains a particular and extreme view of the political/economic relationship between the public enterprise and the agencies of its parent government.

It is apparent even from the brief description of the Tanzanian problem presented above that this idealised model will not do. For in that country, what has to be explained is precisely why the technological behaviour of public enterprises *diverges* so sharply from what appear to be many of the most important objectives of the government. Consequently, an alternative theoretical framework is required which, on the one hand, posits alternative behavioural assumptions at the level of the firm and which, on the other hand, contains an alternative and more realistic model of the relationship between the firm and the agencies of government. It needs to be stressed that both of these modifications are necessary for an alternative framework, for even if public enterprises do seek to pursue goals different from those that have been articulated by government, it becomes necessary to explain the relationship between the two that *enables* them to do so. We shall begin with the behavioural alternatives to the simple neoclassical model.

Behavioural alternatives to the neoclassical model

In the context of firms in developing countries, three main alternatives to the neoclassical model have been proposed, namely Leibenstein's X-efficiency theory, Williams' 'bureaucratic man' hypothesis, and the notion of 'engineering man' associated with Wells and Pickett.

X-efficiency theory. The central focus of X-efficiency theory is the possibility of the non-minimisation of costs (i.e. X-inefficiency) within the firm (a possibility that does not arise in the neoclassical theory).[7] Whether X-inefficiency occurs and the extent to which it occurs depends principally upon two factors, namely the degree to which effort is a variable in the firm and the amount of 'pressure' that operates on this variable.

That effort is to some degree variable, follows from the fact that job contracts in the firm are rarely fully specified. In consequence, all individuals have *some* scope for individual interpretations of their jobs. With the notion that there is some degree of discretion available with respect to effort in the firm, comes the possibility that without sufficient pressure, the effort will not be used most effectively. What, then, determines the degree of pressure and hence the extent of X-inefficiency?

Leibenstein distinguishes between pressure from the 'bottom' and pressure from the 'top'.[8] The former refers essentially to the degree of competition faced by the firm. At the one extreme, the perfectly competitive environment 'puts tremendous pressure on any individual firm'. At the opposite extreme is the monopolistic environment which 'puts much less pressure on the owners of the firm or on the managers'. By pressure from the top is meant the pressure for performance from the firm's owners or owners' representatives. Total pressure will be equal to whichever is the higher of these two sources.

One further aspect of X-efficiency theory should be noted. It is the question of the extent to which an effective 'cybernetic entity' operates within the firm. That is, is there any kind of feedback mechanism between costs per unit and effort which operates to increase effort when costs are judged to be too high? In general, 'How well such a feedback mechanism works will depend on three aspects of the system: (1) the appropriateness of the observed results, (2) the effectiveness of the transmission to the effort source, and (3) the responsiveness of the effort source'.[9] The important point is that we should consider not only the impact of pressure, through effort, on the choice and use of technology, but also any reverse casuality between them.

The engineering man hypothesis. In seeking to explain data collected from a sample of private and publicly owned firms in Indonesia, Wells formulated the hypothesis that

> the managers' choice of technology appears to be influenced by two objective functions, which, in low-wage countries, are generally conflicting. The first objective, that of the 'economic-man', is to minimise costs. This leads to a relatively labour-intensive production process. On the other hand, the objective of the 'engineering man' tends to lead toward more sophisticated, automated technology.[10]

Engineering man has among his main objectives (a) a desire to manage machines rather than workers, (b) a desire to produce the highest possible product quality, and (c) a preference for using sophisticated machinery that appeals to his sense of 'aesthetics'.

As in the case of X-efficiency theory (where the degree of competition is a fundamental determinant of effort and hence costs), the degree of competition is crucial in determining the degree to which costs are allowed to rise beyond minimum levels, i.e. the degree to which the preferences of engineering man dominate those of economic man. In competitive conditions one may expect a greater degree of attention to cost minimisation and a smaller role for engineering man than under monopoly or oligopoly, where the converse is more likely to be true.

While, as noted above, the influence of product quality does form part of the engineering man hypothesis, the relationship between product choice and technology is not dealt with in any detail by Wells. In Stewart's approach, in contrast, this issue finds its most elaborate and sophisticated expression.[11] Using a Lancasterian characteristics approach to conceptualise product quality, she shows that the relationship between products and techniques has to be understood in the dynamic/ historical context of the industrialised countries. Since almost all new products and techniques are developed in and for these societies, it follows that they are likely to be closely associated with average incomes and other socio-economic features of these societies. In this dynamic scheme, products acquire an increasingly high proportion of 'high-income' characteristics over time, and, partly as a result, the techniques required to produce them become increasingly capital-intensive and large-scale. What evolves, consequently, is a very close inter-temporal relationship between products (defined as bundles of characteristics) and the nature of production technology. The closeness of this relationship, which derives, as we have said, mainly from historical factors, means that once the product is chosen by the firm and is closely specified in terms of its characteristics, the range of alternative technologies is frequently very narrow. However, to the extent that the same human needs can be met by products embodying characteristics in different proportions, the range of available technologies can be substantially widened.

The bureaucratic man hypothesis. Among the behavioural alternatives to the simple neoclassical model that we have so far considered, only the bureaucratic man hypothesis was specifically formulated to explain the choice of technology in Tanzanian public enterprises. Partly for this reason, it is also the least well-known of the three alternatives (and we shall therefore elaborate the model somewhat more fully).

The point of departure of this approach, which has been proposed by Williams, is the connection between the economic environment and managerial goals.[12] In the environment in which parastatals for the most part operate in Tanzania, market forces have been substantially replaced by government controls.

The price-control system, for example, is in many cases based on a cost-plus formulation which both shelters the inefficient and gives only a weak incentive to become more efficient ... The incentive-structure to which the parastatal manager responds offers little in the way of personal financial rewards and, in any case, may focus on surpluses which are more related to windfall gains from the pricing system than to productive efficiency.[13]

Thus deprived of any incentive to minimise costs, the manager turns to other goals that appear to offer greater scope for advancement in the eyes of his superiors in the planning hierarchy. In particular, he shifts his attention to initiating as many projects as possible. But the manager is constrained in pursuing this goal by the need to acquire finance (especially foreign exchange) and he is well aware that this can usually be much more easily accomplished by searching for aid-related projects than by seeking funds from the planners. 'The project which can be secured, presented, moved past the planners, delivered and staffed fastest and at the least effort to the parastatal is the one that is chosen.'[14]

The key element of this hypothesis is thus that, given the goals of the Tanzanian manager, it is the securing of a source of finance that becomes critical to the achievement of his objective. And since the technology for projects is usually very closely associated with the financial source (e.g. aid donors or export credits), it follows that 'the "choice of technique" in any particular project *is often merely a fallout from the chosen source of finance and related project inputs*'.[15] The bureaucratic man hypothesis may indeed be expressed in the even stronger form that 'the bureaucratic decision-maker attempts to achieve objectives which *eliminate* the choice of technology from the decision process'.[16]

In addition to its principal implication – that technology (in the form of alternative combinations of factor inputs) is not a decisive factor in investment projects in Tanzania – bureaucratic man embodies a number of subsidiary hypotheses. First, actual investment decisions are made by individuals 'who are not, by experience and training, in possession of special competence in the technological aspects of the industry in question'.[17] Second, 'Investment decision-makers are sometimes ignorant of the possibility of alternative technologies'.[18] Third, 'Investment decision-makers do not seek or use advice on the technological choice aspects of investments'.[19]

What can be said about the characteristics of the technological choices that emerge from this process? According to Williams, it is large-scale, turnkey projects that tend best to meet the requirements of rapidly raising finance for projects and ensuring their rapid delivery and construction. Such projects, moreover, also have the advantage of providing economies of scale in terms of scarce managerial resources at headquarters.

But while the bureaucratic process has, therefore, a systematic bias associated with *large-scale* production, it does not, according to Williams, also have a systematic factor-intensity bias. Rather, the factor-intensity of the technology that results from the bureaucratic man process is thought to be *random*.

A comparison of the technological implications of the behavioural alternatives to the neoclassical model

So far we have merely provided a sketch of the main behavioural alternatives to the simple neoclassical model in the hope that the former may have technological implications that accord more closely with the observed facts than the latter. Let us therefore derive, and compare in summary form, these technological implications with respect to scale, factor-intensity, degree of departure from cost-minimisation, and product choice. (See Table 13.1: the neoclassical model is included in the table for comparative purposes.)

TABLE 13.1 *Technology implications of alternative models*

Model	Scale	Factor intensity	Departure from cost-minimisation	Products
Bureaucratic man	Large	Random		Varies directly with degree of monopoly and/or government underwriting of activities
Engineering man	—	Capital-intensive	Varies directly with degree of monopoly	Embody a high proportion of 'high-income' characteristics
X-efficiency	—	—	Varies directly according to degree of pressure	—
Neoclassical	—	Depends on relative factor prices	None	—

NOTE: Dashes indicate no specific prediction with respect to the dimension concerned.

It appears from Table 13.1 that each model seems to be capable of explaining at least *some* element of the actual choices made by Tanzania's parastatals as these were characterised in the introduction (namely, large-scale, capital-intensive and inefficient processes producing sophisticated products). But because the policy implications of the various approaches differ, we need to have some means of identifying which of them has greater explanatory power in particular situations. Since we view technology choice as the outcome of a process, the explanatory test will consist of the ability of each model to explain the way in which these processes actually take place.

We turn now to the second component of the conceptual framework, which, as noted above concerns the relationship between the enterprise and the agencies of government.

The limits of government control of public enterprise

Apart from specific problems that vary from one country to another, there is a set of *intrinsic* difficulties in seeking to ensure that public enterprises are effectively used to implementing government policies. Much of this inherent difficulty can be explained in terms of agent/principal theory.

Raymond Vernon has expressed the basic problem in this branch of theory as follows: 'How does the principal ensure that the agent acting for him responds to the same information and the same congeries of objectives as the principal would do if acting on his own behalf?'[20] While this problem pervades, by definition, all organisations in which agents act on behalf of principals, its *severity* depends largely on the degree to which the behaviour of the former can be made accountable to the latter. For without an adequate system of accountability, control of the agent by his principal becomes extremely difficult.

Howard Raiffa has correctly observed that the problems of accountability and control are likely to much less acute in private than publicly owned firms. In the former, 'Managers usually have a bottom-line figure that holds them accountable to some extent. In private enterprise, the profit motive is strong and serves as a sieve through which gross incompetents are weeded out and others rewarded'.[21] In public enterprises, however, as is well-known, the objectives are usually far more diffuse, since these firms are formed to fulfil a variety of different functions.

In itself, however, the diversity of objectives of the public enterprise creates no particular problem for the accountability and control system.

If, as is assumed in the 'cosmic maximisation' model described above, the numerous objectives of the enterprise are combined into an unambiguous objective function, managers could be judged, and held accountable, according to this function in the same way that the private enterprise manager is held accountable in terms of profits. In practice, however, an unambiguous objective function is rarely, if ever, presented to the managers of the public enterprise and the multiplicity of goals consequently creates severe problems of enterprise accountability and control.

The difficulties involved in aggregating multiple objectives into an operational composite index have been lucidly described by Raiffa, in relation to the chief executive officer (the principal) of a public enterprise, whose problem it is to communicate the multiple conflicting objectives of the firm to his agents in such a way that they act as the principal would in the same situation. The dilemma facing the chief executive is this. On the one hand, if he is to be able effectively to control his agents he will need for formalise the trade-offs between the conflicting objectives of the firm (for only with such formalisation can an ambiguous objective function be derived).

On the other hand, because there is unlikely to be any kind of consensus among the board members about the various trade-offs, whatever formalisation of these he enunciates, will get him into 'political trouble' with at least some members of the board. 'Thus, the chief executive officer is in an uncomfortable squeeze: he is damned if he formalises his trade-offs and damned if he does not'.[22]

Raiffa's example can be readily extended to the case in which 'the government' is the principal and the public enterprise its agent, for the problem of distilling from the various agencies of government a comprehensive set of trade-offs among conflicting goals is likely to be no less serious than it is for the board of directors in the firm. Indeed, Vernon points to 'the disconcerting fact that, where conflicting and mutually inconsistent goals seem to exist, *politicians may find it undesirable – even dangerous – to try to clarify the ambiguity*'.[23]

The political difficulties of formalising trade-offs (and consequently of controlling public enterprises effectively) may perhaps be especially severe in open, participatory democracies in which there is a diffuse set of opposing interest groups. Certainly, there have been marked difficulties in the control of many types of public enterprise in the mixed West European economies. For example, 'State-owned oil companies serve multiple interests ... governments have particular difficulty providing clearly defined goals for state-owned enterprises'.[24]

Somewhat fewer difficulties may be predicted in less participatory regimes where political power is more highly concentrated among a small group of decision-makers. But even in such cases, a quite considerable amount of disagreement about fundamental trade-offs among development goals can still exist.

Managerial discretion

What we have shown so far in this section is that there are some inherent (and often seemingly intractable) difficulties of making public enterprise conform to national goals. These difficulties often confer substantial autonomy on the enterprises. Thus, 'In Italy the lack of government consensus on goals for state-owned enterprises allows ENI a high degree of independence. In France, conflicts between the Ministry of Finance and the Ministry of Industry ... have empowered SNEA to act with relative autonomy'.[25]

But there are also measures that may be *actively* pursued by managers to further this goal. The degree to which managers are successful in these endeavours is a further determinant of the likelihood that the outcomes of the behaviour of public enterprises will be at variance with what is intended by government.

According to Aharoni, a variety of variables bears on the ability of the manager to increase his autonomy.[26] Among the most important of these are finance, the legal organisation of the firm and the efficacy of the control functions exercised by government.

THE RESEARCH METHOD

The aim of the research conducted in Tanzania was to apply the above conceptual framework to the analysis of decision-making for technology in a sample of public enterprises selected from the following industries: a sample of public enterprises selected from the following industries: sugar, textiles, footwear, detergents, printing ink, grain and oil milling.

Many of the industries were selected with the intention of utilising, and building upon, the considerable data that Perkins had already collected for them (the remainder – detergents and printing ink – were chosen largely because of data availability). As a result, the industry-composition of our study bears a close similarity to the sample of ten industries chosen by Perkins. However, the firms we selected within each of the sample industries overlap to only a slight degree with those which Perkins analysed. There are two main reasons for this.

The first has to do with the two different ways in which public enterprises have been created in Tanzania, namely by nationalisation and by the formation of entirely new institutions. The majority of the public enterprises studies by Perkins came into existence by means of the former method. Because the technologies in these firms were invariably chosen by their former, *private* owners, Perkins' findings, in relation to her overall sample of public enterprises, appear to have implications for questions to firm *size* rather than *ownership*. To avoid this problem, our sample is confined to newly created public enterprises.

The second reason is that a large number of new public enterprises were created after 1975 – the year on which most of Perkins' data are based – and it is these, more recent firms which seemed better suited to an attempt to reconstruct details of the decision process that led to technology choice.

For these two reasons, most of the case studies form part of the Third Five Year Plan period, i.e. from July 1976 to June 1981. Data were sought not only from decision-makers at various levels of the planning hierarchy, but also in the form of relevant documents, such as feasibility studies, Board minutes and annual reports. In some cases the combination of these sources enabled a quite complete reconstruction of the technology decision process, but the others unavailability or lack of access to data permitted only a rather sketchy account to be drawn.

RESULTS AND ANALYSIS

In the conceptual part of this chapter it was argued that there are likely to be two main components of a valid explanation of technological choice in Tanzanian public enterprises, namely an understanding of the nature of the decision-making process on the one hand, and of the limits to government control on the other. This empirical section of the paper begins with the analysis of the latter issue.

The investment planning system and managerial discretion in Tanzania

In spite of the seemingly admirable procedure for the initiation and control of investment projects that has been developed, it is widely agreed that in practice this system has been an almost total failure. Even a recent government evaluation of the operation of parastatals, for example, concludes that 'The elaborate internal and external control system over parastatal activities, which exist on paper are in reality very weak'.[27] In similar vein, the World Bank Report of 1977 described the outcome of parastatal investment decision-making as 'unplanned socialism'.[28] What, then, has gone so badly wrong with the practice of the control system?

The major difficulties appear to be directly related to agent/principal theory and in particular to those aspects of the theory that form part of the models of Raiffa and Aharoni that were described above.

It will be recalled from our discussion of these models that among the most important problems for the government (as principal) with respect to controlling its agents (the parastatals) effectively, are its ability to provide them with an unambiguous objective function and its capacity (legal, managerial and administrative) for such a degree of control. We shall investigate the situation in Tanzania from each of these standpoints.

Difficulties in the formulation of a national objective function

Formulation of a national objective function requires, as we have seen, that decision-makers are able and willing to specify the trade-offs between multiple and conflicting goals of development. In Tanzania, however, this requirement appears to be entirely unmet. For what one finds repeatedly in official documents as well as in interviews is that the willingness to specify national goals is matched by a reluctance to formalise the extent of the trade-offs between them. Consider, for example, the Report of the Parliamentary Working Party on the Long-Term Industrial Strategy, which specifies three national goals to be met in the selection of technology (namely regional balance, growth and employment). However, 'these 3 objectives are not ordered and there is no discussion ... of which should receive priority if conflicts arise between them'.[29] Another manifestation of the problem is to be found in the nebulosity of the guidelines that are presented to the holding companies. The order establishing the Sugar Development Corporation, for example, offers merely the injunction that it should function so as 'to develop and promote the sugar industry'.[30] Because of the pervasiveness of this feature of Tanzanian planning one finds that 'both the proposing parastatals and the central planning authorities appear to lack clear criteria on which to assess the alternative projects which they develop and evaluate'.[31]

According to Loxley and Saul, the vagueness with which development goals are articulated in Tanzania is far more than a mere technical problem.[32] Rather, it is symptomatic of a fundamental political dissensus, and in particular one which centres around basic ideological questions, such as 'the nature and causes of underdevelopment and on the type of society that Tanzania wishes to create'.[33] They argue persuasively that it is because of these fundamental political divergences of opinion that the Party (TANU) 'has remained an institution capable of directing the system only on the most general plane. TANU has never developed the capacity continuously *to concretize goals and in that way both guide the bureaucracy and hold it effectively to account'*.[34] Their conclusion is that, 'Until the development policies and goals of government itself are defined more clearly there will always be ambiguity over what parastatals are supposed to be doing and therefore doubts as to what the control mechanism is designed to achieve'.[35]

The limited capacity for control

Even if there was no problem of formulating a reasonably unambiguous national objective function, it is still extremely doubtful whether the degree of managerial discretion in Tanzania parastatals would be low. For as Aharoni's model indicates, discretion is also an important function of the government's *capacity* to control. This capacity has a number of dimensions.

Most obviously, the capacity for control depends on the resources available, and in this respect Tanzania, in common with most other African countries, is severely deficient. The consequences of this state of affairs were forthrightly described to me by a senior official in the Planning Ministry where projects ought theoretically to be evaluated after being passed from the parastatal holding company and its parent Ministry. What happens instead, according to the official, is that this Ministry is inclined simply to assume that projects have been adequately screened by the parent Ministry concerned. Unfortunately, the very same assumption is made by the latter with respect to the holding company from which the project originated. The outcome of this procedure is, not surprisingly, that the technological aspects of projects conform only as a coincidence to overall development goals.

With respect to the legal environment within which parastatals operate, Mihyo has argued that the widely used company form (which vests control in the board of directors subject to any regulations and law to the contrary) 'excludes the chances of government, party, parliamentary and public operational control'.[36] In his view, the government's position as a shareholder in this type of parastatal invests it with limited control, relative to the directors who are typically authorised by the articles of association to decide on the scope and form of investments. Since the shareholders can only object if an investment is not authorised by the memorandum, it is clear that the influence of government may be quite narrowly circumscribed.

The case studies

The discussion above suggested that managerial discretion is often considerable, and sometimes nearly total in Tanzanian parastatals. In the case studies we sought to examine the directions in which this discretion is pursued in the choice of technology.

An overview of the findings is presented schematically in Table 13.2 which shows for each case the form in which the various models described above contribute to an explanation of the technology choice made by the sample of public enterprises (which, typically, is one that is based on a turnkey contract, is large-scale and capital-intensive and inefficient relative to available small-scale alternatives). Of course, such an abbreviated form of presentation represents an oversimplified view of a much more complex reality that was revealed by the attempted reconstruction of the decision processes, but it does nevertheless enable us to highlight at least some of the most important conclusions from the research.

First, in most of the seven cases shown in Table 13.2, no single approach appears to be capable of accounting entirely for the pronounced bias in the choice of technology; in general, elements of several approaches are required for a satisfactory explanation. There are several reasons for this complexity. One is that the operation of the bureaucratic man mechanism (which, as Table 13.2 shows, was revealed in most of the cases) imparts a (large) *scale* bias to the choice, and although this in itself tends to raise the degree of capital-intensity (in so far as there is a positive correlation between the two variables), there is still plenty of scope for other factors to impart an *independent* upward bias to the capital-intensity at the scale that is determined in this way. From the table it can be seen that the most important of these factors is related to choice of products (though other engineering man-type influences also play a role).[37]

The product-choice bias in the case-studies is imparted in three ways: the first is through the alleged need to produce exports to 'international standards'; the second is through the historically determined preference of some members of the society for highly specified, inappropriate products; the final source of bias originates in the fact that this same product preference is frequently held by project consultants.

TABLE 13.2 *An overview of the survey findings by industry (firms in parenthesis)*

Model	Textiles (*Musoma & Mwatex*)	Sugar (*Kilombero, Kagera and Mtibwa*)	Oil-milling (*Moproco*)	Detergents (*Sabuni Industries Ltd*)	Maize-milling (*Korogwe*)	Printing Inks (*Printpak*)	Footwear (*Morogoro*)
Cases arising from operation of bureaucratic-man mechanism	Major goal of rapid output growth ('to clothe the nation as fast as possible')	Major goal of rapid output growth ('to achieve self-sufficiency at the earliest opportunity'); managerial diseconomies of small-scale production	Major goal of rapid output growth	?	?	?	Ease of raising finance for large (vs small-scale) projects; managerial economies of scale in large (vs small-scale) production
Cases arising from product-choice	—	Choice of refined sugar (at Kilombero) which is 'a higher grade than is found in many underdeveloped countries'	Preference for product of 'uniform colour'	Desire to replicate previously imported detergent ('to produce a detergent of the same standard or even better')	Desire for 'quality products' (i.e. 'free from foreign matter' and 'more consistently uniform')	Preference for 'more sophisticated inks than the ones already in use'	Requirement to meet 'international standards' for exports

TABLE 13.2 (Continued)

Model	Textiles (Musoma & Mwatex)	Sugar (Kilombero, Kagera and Mtibwa)	Oil-milling (Moproco)	Detergents (Sabuni Industries Ltd)	Maize-milling (Korogwe)	Printing Inks (Printpak)	Footwear (Morogoro)
Engineering-man biases	—	—	Bias against second-hand equipment; preference for well-known suppliers; British standards for plant construction	—	Exaggerated view of the efficiency of modern roller milling	Simplification of managerial problems through use of modern machinery	—
Elements of X-efficiency theory	Cybernetic mechanism (i.e. pressure to reduce costs by more effective use of chosen inputs within loss-making enterprises)	Cybernetic mechanism (i.e. pressure to reduce costs by more effective use of chosen inputs within loss-making enterprises)	—	—	—	—	—

The recently established Morogoro Shoe Company may be cited as an instance of the predominance of the first factor. The choice of product for this project – which was financed by the World Bank – was dictated almost entirely by its orientation to exports, as is made quite clear in the Bank's Appraisal Report. Thus,

> One fairly modern shoe factory presently produces leather and canvas shoes for the internal market. The output is of acceptable quality within Tanzania, but does not meet international standards. The new shoe factory ... would produce about 4 million pairs of shoes to international standards, primarily for export, but it is expected that a small part of the production will be sold internally.[38]

The same Report also makes explicit the link between production for export and the nature of the technology that is required. To quote again from this documents, 'During the detailed engineering design phase, efforts will be made to substitute labour for capital without compromising product style, quality and cost competitiveness *but the extent to which this can be done is limited in export-oriented industries'*.[39]

The case of Sabuni Industries Limited – the only parastatal in Tanzania which produces powdered laundry detergent – is perhaps the clearest example of the second main influence on product choice which emerged from the case studies, namely that which originates in historically determined tastes. The Sabuni project was conceived in the 1960s, when, following the break-up of the East African Community, supplies of the detergent 'OMO' from Kenya were discontinued. It seemed clear to the National Development Corporation, at the time the holding company responsible for the detergent industry, that local production of a substitute was required. In the decision merely to replicate, or even improve, the brand that previously had been imported, what appears to have been crucial was the consideration that 'since most of the people in the country had used the Kenyan brand of detergent ('OMO'), which is of very high quality, it was envisaged to produce a detergent *of the same standard or even better*, in order to capture the market previously supplied by the Unilever Company in Kenya'. The intention was also to produce a product that could be exported to neighbouring countries by competing effectively with other high quality brands.[40]

That the influence of consultants serves to impart the same type of bias to the characteristics of products can be illustrated with reference to the proposed maize mill at Korogwe in the Tanga region. In the report of the feasibility study that was conducted for this project by the

Tanzanian Industrial Studies and Consulting Organisation (TISCO), one is confronted at the very outset with a revealing *non-sequitur*. Thus,

> the demand for maize flour whether in a household or in a restaurant or in the other industrial uses is ever present and increasing due to the increase in population. *To produce quality products, it is necessary to have quality maize flour manufactured under scientific and hygienic conditions* ... There is no modern roller flour mill in Tanga region producing quality maize flour.[41]

In other words, the consultants simply take it as axiomatic that any increase in demand has to be met by 'quality products'. There is no discussion of whether different types of flour, of varying qualities, may be more appropriate to the incomes and needs of different groups in the population. Nor is there any allusion to the possibility that alternative varieties might be better suited to the different purposes for which they are used (e.g. industrial versus household uses).

The second main reason why a multi-faceted explanation of technological choice is required has to do with the nature of the decision process on which these choices are based. Much of the existing literature implicitly assumes that technology choice is a single 'one-shot' transaction, or, to the extent that it recognises the staged nature of the choice, tends to focus on only a *single* stage. In either case, the result is a predisposition to search for a single-factor explanation of the problem. Our research, in contrast, points to the fact that there are numerous stages in the decision, among the most important of which are the feasibility study, the search for finance, the choice of consultants, the floating of the tender and the evaluation of the tender bids, and that at each such stage more or less subtle biases in the choice of technology can, and often do, arise.

The case of Moproco, the multi-purpose oil-mill at Morogoro (see Table 13.2) is a particularly good illustration of this important point. Although the scale of this operation, as well as its highly packaged form, appears to derive largely from the workings of the bureaucratic man mechanism, a further set of factors, operating at different stages of the decision process, exacerbated the capital-intensive bias of the technology that was chosen.

First, the tender documents specifies that all the equipment should be new.[42] This prohibition against second-hand equipment is not unique to the process of acquisition of oil-milling equipment; on the contrary, it is a practice that is endorsed in the bidding rules of the World Bank and by the government of Tanzania itself.

In a second respect as well – which concerns the link between products and techniques – the specification of the tender document appears to have imparted a bias against the use of more appropriate techniques. Specifically, the document embodies requirements for buildings which have necessarily to be met by relatively sophisticated products and techniques. Thus, to quote from the document, 'Building and construction work must meet local building and hygienic requirements and standards, *which to a great extent are of British origin*'.[43] Or, to take another example, the use of locally produced roofing tiles is precluded by 'the minimum requirements for roofing materials – corrugated aluminium sheets or corrugated asbestos sheets'.[44]

If there were therefore biases in the manner in which the tender document was specified, it is also true that in the next stage – the evaluation of the tenders received – engineering man-type factors further reduced the pressures for cost minimisation in the choice of technology. At the very outset of the evaluation procedure, for example, we find that most of the many quotations were rejected on the grounds that they had not come 'from potentially competent and internationally-known companies'.[45] And in the selection from among the five contractors that did conform to this description, 'considerable emphasis' was laid on the following factors (in addition, of course, to costs): 'goodwill of the bidder in his country and abroad', 'competence and capability of the bidder to successfully complete the project', 'quality of the end products', and 'experience in export and establishment of plants in foreign countries'.[46]

One of the major technological issues that appears to have confronted the sub-committee formed by Moproco to evaluate the bids was the choice between a batch and a continuous refining process. Despite the relatively high cost of the latter this was nevertheless the method selected. With respect to the bleaching component of the refining process, the sub-committee motivated its choice with what amounts to a nearly complete statement of the engineering man hypothesis. Thus,

> Continuous bleaching plants have gained wide acceptance as they are now feasible, but they are relatively costly owing to their expensive control instruments ... Continuous bleaching units are favoured by processors *because of their independence of human operation*, because they permit savings in bleaching earth and oil loss in it, finally *because they render a finished product of uniform colour.*[47]

In the opinion of the general manager of Moproco, who was a member of the sub-committee for evaluating the tenders, the last reason – the uniformity of product quality associated with continuous refining – was perhaps most influential in the choice of this process.

CONCLUSIONS

The point of departure for this study was earlier research findings that the technology choices made by public enterprises in Tanzania appear to be only tenuously related to the major development goals of the country. In an effort to throw more light on these seemingly puzzling findings, we began by relaxing both major assumptions of the traditional economic model, namely that public enterprises maximise according to an objective function that is given to them unambiguously by the government. In place of these assumptions, two different sets of models were presented. The first set deals with a more complex relationship between the government and the public enterprise than is posited in the traditional model. The second set of models offer behavioural alternatives to the simple neoclassical theory of the enterprise. Taken together, the two sets of models allow for the possibility that the public enterprise is able to pursue goals other than those of the government.

In the empirical section of the paper it was shown that this framework is able to provide considerable insight into some of the most recent technological choices made by public enterprises in Tanzania. What emerged from the case studies was, among other things, the finding that the pronounced tendency towards the selection of large-scale, capital-intensive and highly packaged technologies is the result of biases arising at different stages of the decision process.

In general, the main policy implication of the study is that improvements in the choice of technology need to be sought in the way decisions are actually made in the public enterprise, rather than in the enterprise is assumed to behave according to the tenets of neoclassical micro-theory. In particular, measures will be required, on the one hand, to reduce the large-scale bias that results from the operation of the bureaucratic man mechanism, and on the other, to eliminate the biases that arise independently of this mechanism, most notably from the choice of inappropriate products. Success in the pursuit of the former objective will demand reform of the price control system (in the direction of specifying the extent to which any cost reductions are allowed to accrue to the enterprise as profits), a greater emphasis on profitability, and institutional change which provides a focus for the technological choice aspects of projects (e.g. a technology unit that offers guidance to public enterprise managers in the various stages of the selection of technology). Policies to correct the product choice bias should seek, first, to counter historically conditioned consumer tastes for advanced-country imports (through, for example, promotional campaigns for local goods based on appeals to nationalism), and secondly, to draw to the attention of consulting groups (especially the Tanzania Industrial Studies and Consulting Organisation) the economic advantages that are afforded by the choice of more appropriate products. Finally, while product policies may be the major means of combating engineering man-type biases, attention also needs to be paid to other areas of this problem – for example, to lifting the effective prohibition of used equipment.

NOTES

1. This is a revised version of a World Employment Programme Research Working Paper, Number 125, Technology and Employment Programme, International Labour Office, Geneva, October 1983.
2. J.K. Nyerere, *South-South Option*, Third World Lecture, 1982, Third World Foundation, Monograph 10.
3. W.E. Clark, *Socialist Development and Public Investment in Tanzania 1964–73* (University of Toronto Press, 1978), p. 140.
4. F. Perkins, 'Technological Choice, Industrialisation and Development: the Case of Tanzania', D. Phil thesis, University of Sussex, July 1980, p. 408.
5. F. Perkins, 'Technology Choice, Industrialisation and Development Experiences in Tanzania', *Journal of Development Studies*, Vol. 19, January 1983, p. 211. As we show below, however, the significance of these results is weakened by the inclusion of public enterprises whose technologies were chosen by the former,
6. M. Gillis, 'The Role of State Enterprises in Economic Development', *Harvard Institute for International Development*, Discussion Paper No. 83, February 1980, p. 3.
7. The most complete exposition of the theory is to be found in H. Leibenstein, *Beyond Economic Man* (Harvard University Press, 1976). The theory is applied to development problems in H. Leibenstein, *General X-efficiency Theory and Economic Development* (London: Oxford University Press, 1978).
8. H. Leibenstein, 'X-efficiency Theory and the Analysis of State Enterprises', paper prepared for the Second Boston Area Public Enterprise Group Conference, 1980.
9. *Ibid.*, p. 8
10. Louis T. Wells, 'Economic Man and Engineering Man: Choice of Technology in a Low-Wage Country', in C.P. Timmer *et al.*, *The Choice of*

Technology in Developing Countries, Harvard Studies in International Affairs, No. 32, 1975, p. 85.
11. F. Stewart, *Technology and Underdevelopment* (London: Macmillan, 1977).
12. D. Williams, 'National Planning and the Choice of Technology: The Case of Textiles in Tanzania', Economic Research Bureau Paper No. 75.12, Dar-es-Salaam, June 1975.
13. *Ibid.*, p. 7.
14. *Ibid.*, p. 7–8.
15. *Ibid.*, p. 8.
16. *Ibid.*
17. *Ibid.* p. 9.
18. *Ibid.*
19. *Ibid.*
20. R. Vernon, 'Introduction', in R. Vernon and Y. Aharoni (eds), *State-Owned Enterprise in the Western Economies* (St. Martin's Press, 1981), p. 10–11.
21. H. Raiffa, 'Decision Making in the State-Owned Enterprise', in Vernon and Aharoni, *op. cit.*, p. 57.
22. *Ibid.*, p. 62.
23. Vernon, *op. cit.*, p. 12.
24. O. Noreng, 'State-Owned Oil Companies: Western Europe', in Vernon and Aharoni, *op. cit.*, p. 142.
25. *Ibid.*, p. 142.
26. Y. Aharoni, 'Managerial discretion', in Vernon and Aharoni, *op. cit.*
27. The United Republic of Tanzania, *Structural Adjustment Programme for Tanzania* (Dar-es-Salaam: Ministry of Planning and Economic Affairs, June 1982), p. 42. The nominal control system is based on a hierarchical structure, at the base of which producing parastatals are located. They are, in effect, subsidiaries of parastatal holding companies, which in turn are responsible to a parent ministry. In theory, the relations between the different layers of the structure are such as to ensure that national objectives are closely incorporated in all decisions for technology.
28. IBRD, *Tanzania: Basic Industry Report*, Annex V, December 1977, p. 121.
29. Perkins, 'Technological Choice, Industrialisation and Development: the Case of Tanzania', p. 133.
30. Sugar Development Corporation, *Annual Report and Accounts*, 1976–7.
31. Perkins, 'Technology Choice, Industrialisation and Development Experiences in Tanzania', p. 236.
32. John Loxley and John S. Saul, 'Multinationals, Workers and the Parastatals in Tanzania', *Review of African Political Economy*, No. 2, 1975.
33. *Ibid.*, p. 65
34. *Ibid.*, p. 62.
35. *Ibid.*, p. 71
36. P. Mihyo, 'The Legal Enivronment and the Performance of Public Enterprises in Tanzania', mimeo, University of Dar-es-Salaam, p. 13.
37. The operation of Leibenstein's cybernetic mechanism in the loss-making enterprises of the textile and sugar industries (see Table 13.2) is a further indication that the bureaucratic man hypothesis is not a sufficient explanation of the Tanzanian problem. For in this formulation, X-inefficient technology choices are tolerated (even encouraged) by the price control

system, which operates on a cost-plus basis. Yet, in the case of the Musoma textile mill, for example, whose costs of production were well above those of the established textile mills, the systems did *not* protect its inefficiency. The Price Controller allowed a selling price that was based not upon costs of production at Musoma, but rather upon the average costs of other established mills. A similar story appears to be true of the sugar mill at Mtibwa.

38. IBRD, *Tanzania: Appraisal of th Morogoro Industrial Complex*, Industrial Projects Department, March 1977, p. ii.
39. *Ibid.*, p. 29 (emphasis added).
40. From a document prepared by the present Holding Company of Sabuni, namely the National Chemical Industries, at the request of the author (emphasis added).
41. Tanzania Industrial Studies and Consulting Organisation, *Maize Mill at Korogwe: A Feasibility Study for the German Agency for Technical Cooperation Ltd*, Dar-es-Salaam, 1978, p. 1:8 (emphasis added).
42. Industrial Studies and Development Centre, Dar-es-Salaam,*Tender Document for a Turnkey Project for a Multi-Purpose Oil Mill Company*, 25 April 1975, p. 14.
43. *Ibid.*, p. 13
44. *Ibid.*
45. Industrial Studies and Development Centre, *Evaluation of Tender Bids for a Multipurpose Oilseed Processing Plant for Morogoro*, Dar-es-Salaam, October 1975, p. 2.
46. *Ibid.*, p. 3.
47. *Ibid.*, p. 14.

14 East–South Trade[1]

DEEPAK NAYYAR

INTRODUCTION

The literature on international economics makes two sets of distinctions between nation states in the contemporary world. The first distinction between rich and poor countries, North and South, is based on differences in levels of income and development. The second distinction between socialist and capitalist countries, East and West, is based on differences in political and economic systems. Such a division of the world into North and South or East and West is not adequate, since the categories are neither mutually exclusive nor exhaustive. The somewhat old-fashioned distinction between the First, Second and Third Worlds is perhaps more appropriate. This enables us to divide the world into three groups of countries: the West constituted by the OECD countries, the East made up of the USSR and Eastern Europe, and the South comprising the less developed world. Such a division of the world economy into East, West and South is not without its conceptual problems, but it is preferable from the viewpoint of analysis in so far as it uses both sets of distinctions mentioned above.

For some time now, it has been fashionable for scholars interested in problems of international trade and development economics to study the economic interaction between countries. More often than not, however, these studies focus attention either on North and South or on East and West. Surprisingly enough, the subject of East and South has received much less attention. This relatively unexplored theme is extremely important, as it relates to the interaction between two sets of countries at different levels of development and characterised by different political and economic systems. It need hardly be stressed that for both the East and the South, interaction with the West is an overwhelmingly important part of the same picture.

There is a somewhat controversial question that arises in the context of the triangular relationship between East, West and South in the world economy: to what extent can the East be equated with the West and be treated as part of the North? In the perception of the South, the East is very much a part of the industrialised world, and that is borne out by the position of the Group of 77 in international fora where similar claims apropos official development assistance, market access for manufactured exports and so on, are addressed not only to the West but also to the East.[2] The perception of the East is, however, very different; the socialist countries do not accept that the East is part of the North, as it implies equating East and West *vis-à-vis* the South.[3] In terms of conventional development indicators – whether GNP per capita, the proportion of the workforce engaged in manufacturing activities, or the share of manufactures in total exports – it is reasonable to infer that the East is part of the industrialised North even if it is not at the same level of development as the West.[4] Yet in terms of the fundamental differences in political and economic systems, the East is distinct from the West. Thus, for the analyst interested in examining the position and prospects of the South in the world economy, it is important to distinguish between East and West in the industrialised world. For this reason, wherever possible, I shall attempt to explore the similarities and differences between East and West in their interaction with the South.

In this chapter, the 'East' refers to Bulgaria, Czechoslovakia, the German Democratic Republic, Hungary, Poland, Romania and the USSR; for brevity, the six European member countries of the Council for Mutual Economic Assistance (CMEA), other than the USSR, are referred to as Eastern Europe. The 'West' is used to describe the developed market economies or the industrialised OECD countries. The 'South' refers to the developing market economies, that is, Africa (excluding South Africa), Asia (excluding Japan and the centrally planned economies), Oceania (excluding Australia and New Zealand), and Latin America. The centrally planned economies of Asia – China, Mongolia, the Democratic Republic of Korea and Vietnam – are not included in either the East or the South, for two reasons. First, in terms of levels in income and development, these countries constitute an integral part of the South, while in terms of their political and economic system, they may plausibly be considered as part of the East. Second, economic relations between the East and the centrally planned economies of Asia constitute a somewhat special case and are, therefore, not analysed here.

At the outset, it must be recognised that neither the East nor the South represent homogeneous entities as both are made up of countries whose characteristics and interests might diverge significantly from one another. It is difficult enough to generalise about the East with the USSR on the one hand and the six smaller European CMEA countries on the other. It is well nigh impossible to consider the South as a homogeneous group of countries, with the oil-exporting countries and the newly industrialising countries at one end of the spectrum and some of the poorest countries in the world at the other. Nevertheless, there is enough in common among countries within each of the two groups for us to consider issues at the aggregated levels of East and South.

This chapter attempts to focus on East-South trade, which is the principal medium of interaction between the two sets of countries.[5] A complete economic analysis of East-South trade is beyond the scope of the present exercise. The object of my paper is a limited one. It attempts to sketch a profile of East-South trade, to examine some of the key issues that arise in this context, and to explore the problems associated with he implicit division of labour between the East and South. The next section outlines the dimensions of, and trends in, East-South trade over the period 1955–82. I then examine the changes in the structure and composition of East-South trade during the period under review. The following section analyses the factors underlying the growth in East-South trade and the sources of gains from such trade. I go on to consider the issue of the distribution of gains from trade between the two sets of countries on the basis of available evidence. The final section explores briefly the division of labour revealed by the pattern of trade between East and South, in retrospect and prospect.

DIMENSIONS AND TRENDS

Economic relations between the East and the South began to develop in the mid- 1950s when several newly independent nations emerged from the colonial era in Asia and Africa. Thus the empirical evidence presented here treats 1955 as the base year for comparisons. A complete time series would make for cumbersome tables. In order to reduce the volume of data to manageable proportions, therefore, I have selected six years at quinquennial intervals as benchmark years. This method is by no means perfect, but it is reasonable in so far as international trade transactions are not characterised by sharp fluctuations from year to year during the period under review. Wherever possible, data for 1982 have also been incorporated into the evidence presented as that is the latest year for which international trade statistics are available.

Table 14.1 outlines the trends in trade between the East and the South during the period 1955–82. It shows that the expansion in East-South trade, from less than $ 7 billion in 1970 to $ 44 billion in 1980, was indeed quite remarkable; the level dropped to $ 43 billion in 1982 as there was a contraction in world trade in the early 1980s. Over the quarter century from 1955 to 1980, trade between the USSR and the South increased from $ 0.3 billion to $ 25 billion, while trade between Eastern Europe and the South increased somewhat less from $0.6 billion to $ 19 billion. Starting from a small base, however, the growth in trade valued at current prices is almost bound to appear impressive. To place these magnitudes in perspective, therefore, we must compare this trade expansion with (a) the growth in trade between the East and other segments of the world economy, and (b) the growth in the total trade of the East and the South.

Table 14.2, which outlines the trends in the share of selected components of international trade flows in world trade, reveals that, from 1955 to 1965, trade between the USSR and Eastern Europe on the one hand and the rest of the world on the other, whether East, West or South, increased at a pace greater than total world trade. Over this period, the growth in trade between the East and the South exceeded that of both intra-East trade and East-West trade. Thereafter, the growth in East-South trade roughly kept pace with the expansion in

TABLE 14.1 *Trends in East-South trade, 1955–82 (in US $ million at current prices)*

	USSR			Eastern Europe		
Year	Imports	Exports	Total trade	Imports	Exports	Total trade
1955	165	150	315	250	330	580
1960	639	411	1050	501	559	1060
1965	1158	1498	2656	863	928	1791
1970	1789	2688	4477	1158	1396	2554
1975	6178	6188	12366	3395	4303	7698
1980	10916	14106	25022	9664	9553	19217
1982	12985	11847	24832	7578	10670	18248

NOTES
(a) The figures for 1955 are drawn from the UNCTAD *Handbook of International Trade and Development Statistics*, 1972.
(b) Eastern Europe includes Bulgaria, Czechoslovakia, the German Democratic Republic, Hungary, Poland and Romania.
SOURCE: United Nations, *Monthly Bulletin of Statistics*, June 1979 and July 1983.

TABLE 14.2 *Selected components of world trade flows (in percentages)*

Trade flows	1955	1960	1965	1970	1975	1980	1982
East–East	5.1	6.3	6.7	5.9	5.1	3.9	4.5
East–West	2.9	3.9	4.4	4.5	5.5	4.7	4.9
East–South	1.0	1.5	2.3	2.2	2.2	2.0	2.6

NOTES
(a) The figures for 1982 are derived from data in the UN *Monthly Bulletin of Statistics*, May 1984.
(b) In the table, East is constituted by the centrally planned economies of Europe, West by the developed market economies and South by the developing market economies.
(c) East–West trade flows are the sum of exports from the East to the West and from the West to the East. Similarly, East–South trade flows are the sum of exports from the East to the South and from the South to the East.
(d) The above figures have been calculated as a percentage of total world exports.
SOURCE: UNCTAD *Handbook of International Trade and Development Statistics*, 1983.

world trade, whereas the relative importance of intra-East trade declined steadily and that of East-West trade increased significantly, particularly during the 1970s. Between 1980 and 1982, as in the period 1955 to 1965, the share of intra-East, East-West and East-South trade flows in world trade registered an increase, among which the share of East-South trade registered the largest increase in proportionate terms. These increases in shares, however, were a consequence of the sharp contraction in world trade, which was greater than that in trade between the East and the rest of the world, for between 1980 and 1982 even East-South trade registered a decline in terms of absolute values.

Tables 14.3 and 14.4 trace the changes in the percentage share of the East and the South in the imports and exports of each other. An examination of the data reveals the following trends:
1. The share of the South in the total imports of the USSR rose from about 5 per cent in 1955 to a little over 15 per cent in 1970 and remained in the range 16–17 per cent thereafter, while its share in the total exports of the USSR rose from about 4 per cent in 1955 to 21 per cent in 1970 but dropped to a level of around 18 per cent in 1980 and less than 14 per cent in 1982. For imports and exports taken together, the share of the South in the foreign trade of the USSR rose from 5 per cent in 1955 to 18 per cent in 1970 but fell to 17 per cent in 1980 and 15 per cent in 1982.[6]
2. The share of the USSR in the imports of the South rose from less than 1 per cent in 1955 to 4.7 per cent in 1970, but declined to a level of about 3 per cent thereafter; its share in the exports of the South rose from less

TABLE 14.3 *The share of the South in the foreign trade of the East (in percentages)*

Year	USSR Imports	USSR Exports	Eastern Europe Imports	Eastern Europe Exports
1955	5.5	4.4	5.8	7.4
1960	11.4	7.4	6.5	7.3
1965	14.4	18.3	7.4	7.8
1970	15.2	21.0	6.3	7.7
1975	16.7	18.6	6.7	9.6
1980	15.9	18.5	11.3	11.9
1982	16.7	13.6	9.8	13.9

NOTES
(a) The figures for 1955 are derived from the UNCTAD *Handbook of International Trade and Development Statistics, 1972*, and those for 1960 from the UN *Monthly Bulletin of Statistics*, July 1979.
(b) The percentages have been computed from data on trade flows valued in US $ million at current prices.
SOURCE: United Nations, *Monthly Bulletin of Statistics*, July 1983.

TABLE 14.4 *The share of the East in the foreign trade of the South (in percentages)*

Year	USSR Imports	USSR Exports	Eastern Europe Imports	Eastern Europe Exports
1955	0.6	0.7	1.4	1.1
1960	1.5	1.9	1.8	1.6
1965	4.0	3.1	2.5	2.3
1970	4.7	3.1	2.3	2.0
1975	3.1	2.7	2.0	1.6
1980	3.1	1.8	1.9	1.2
1982	2.5	2.7	2.2	1.6

NOTES
(a) The percentages have been computed from data on trade flows valued in US $ million at current prices.
(b) The figures on imports are based on exports of USSR/Eastern Europe to the South, expressed as a proportion of total world exports to the latter.
SOURCE: For 1955–80, UNCTAD *Handbook of International Trade and Development Statistics, 1983*. For 1982, UN *Monthly Bulletin of Statistics*, July 1983 and May 1984.

than 1 per cent in 1955, to 3.1 per cent in 1970 and declined somewhat thereafter.
3. The share of the South in the imports of Eastern Europe, by contrast, did not register any significant increase during the period 1955–75, but

rose from a range of 6–7 per cent through this period to a level of about 10 per cent in the early 1980s. Similarly, the share of the South in the total exports of Eastern Europe was fairly stable at a little more than 7 per cent from 1955 until 1970, but rose sharply in the 1970s and early 1980s to almost 14 per cent in 1982. For imports and exports taken together, the share of the South in the foreign trade of Eastern Europe remained relatively stable at about 7 per cent during the period 1955–70 but increased steadily thereafter to reach a level of almost 12 per cent at the beginning of the 1980s.[7]

4. The share of Eastern Europe in the total imports of the South rose from 1.4 per cent in 1955 to 2.5 per cent in 1965 and stabilised at a slightly lower level in subsequent years, whereas its share in the total exports of the South rose from 1 per cent in 1955 to 2.3 per cent in 1965 and dropped to an average level of 1.6 per cent thereafter.

It is worth noting three important inferences from the evidence presented in Tables 14.3 and 14.4. First, for the East, the South was far more important as a source of imports and as a market for exports than the East was for the South throughout the period 1955–82. Second, trade with the South was more important for the USSR than for Eastern Europe during most of the period under review. Third, much of the evidence suggests that the growth in East-South trade accelerated from the mid-1950s, reached its peak level *circa* 1970, and slowed down thereafter whether we consider the share of the East in the foreign trade of the South or vice-versa.[8]

The above discussion has made a distinction between the USSR and Eastern Europe in the East but it has made no distinction between countries or groups of countries in the South. In this context, it is important to note that East-South trade was characterised by a high degree of concentration in a few countries. During the period 1970–80, just twelve countries accounted for more than two-thirds of the USSR's trade with the South and a slightly smaller proportion of Eastern Europe's trade with the South. In Africa, it was Algeria, Egypt and Libya; in Latin America, it was Argentina, Brazil and Cuba; in the Middle East, it was Iran, Iraq and Syria; and in Asia, it was Afghanistan, India and Pakistan. Within each region, the three specified countries accounted for as much as 70 to 90 per cent of the trade between the USSR and Eastern Europe on the one hand and the South on the other.[9] The degree of concentration was somewhat higher for the USSR than for the Eastern Europe.

The rapid growth in trade and economic co-operation between the East and the South has taken place largely in a framework of bilateral agreements, particularly for most of the twelve countries mentioned above. Economic aid, development credits, technical assistance and trade are all incorporated into long-term agreements negotiated with individual governments. In fact, bilateralism was, and to a significant extent remains, an integral part of the overall system of economic relations between East and South. Although this framework is somewhat different from the usual *modus operandi* of international trade, it is not surprising that the East would want to plan its economic relations with the rest of the world as a part of the process of planned production.

The principal features of such bilateral arrangements between a country in the East and a country in the South are as follows:[10]

1. The agreement specifies the objectives of economic co-operation for both partners and attempts to set out planned needs as accurately as possible.
2. Trade balances outstanding at the end of each period are settled in exports and imports of mutually agreed products or in inconvertible currency.
3. The socialist partner pledges to provide economic assistance in the form of capital equipment, technology or knowhow. Aid as well as debt repayments are automatically converted into trade flows; credits extended to the country in the South, for instance, can be repaid in the inconvertible domestic currency, traditional exports or the output of aid-financed projects.
4. As far as possible, all transactions are carried out in terms of world prices, except that bilateral agreements seek to eliminate short-term fluctuations. This is a typical, but by no means universal example. In several cases, trade, along with other transactions, is conducted in terms of convertible currencies. As a matter of fact, since the early 1970s there has been a trend towards an increasing use of convertible currencies instead of bilateral payments arrangements.[11] The implications of this trend for East-South trade are considered later in the chapter.

STRUCTURE AND COMPOSITION

In order to obtain a clear picture of the division of labour between the East and the South, both past and present, it is essential to consider the structure and composition of East-South trade and also the changes in it over time. For this purpose, it is appropriate to divide the trade flows into four commodity groups: food, raw materials, fuels and manufactures. While such a classification is aggregative, and merges SITC categories at one-digit level, it is sufficient from the viewpoint of the discussion that follows; wherever necessary, as in the case of manufactures, evidence at a disaggregated level is also presented.

The changes in the commodity structure of exports from the East to the South are outlined in Table 14.5. The trends are somewhat difficult to discern in the composition of exports from the USSR to the South, in part because of data problems: if we add up the USSR's exports to the South in SITC categories 0 to 9, the sum works out to be significantly lower than the figure showing USSR's total exports to the South. It would seem that, over the period 1955–80, as much as 20–50 per cent of the Soviet Union's exports to the Third World are not classified by

TABLE 14.5 *The composition of exports from the East to the South (in percentages)*

Commodity group	1955	1960	1965	1970	1975	1980
A. Exports from the USSR						
Food	7.3	11.3	9.9	8.3	9.8	4.4
Raw materials	2.0	6.4	5.7	4.6	4.9	3.4
Fuels	10.7	16.0	12.1	5.6	13.4	18.4
Manufactures	30.0	46.9	50.9	44.7	34.3	30.0
Total	100.0	100.0	100.0	100.0	100.0	100.0
B. Exports from Eastern Europe						
Food	3.9	6.6	6.9	10.0	13.4	14.9
Raw materials	10.3	7.0	6.7	3.5	3.5	4.1
Fuels	9.7	3.4	1.3	2.4	3.3	2.4
Manufactures	62.4	71.9	84.8	83.5	78.9	78.0
Total	100.0	100.0	100.0	100.0	100.0	100.0

NOTES
(a) The definitions of commodity groups are as follows: (i) food: SITC $0+1+22+4$; (ii) raw materials: SITC 2 less 22 plus 68; (iii) fuels: SITC 3; (iv) manufactures: SITC 5 to 8 less 68.
(b) For the USSR, columns add up to much less than 100 because there is a significant proportion of exports from the USSR for which the country of destination is not attributed; while such exports are included in the total to developing market economies, they are excluded from the data on exports by commodity class and destination.
(c) For Eastern Europe, columns do not add up to 100 in 1955 and 1960 possibly for the above reasons; from 1965 to 1980 columns do add up except for rounding errors.

SOURCE: UNCTAD *Handbook of International Trade and Development Statistics*, 1983.

destination and commodity group. There are two possible reasons for this discrepancy: first, all exports from the USSR are not attributed to countries of destination in Soviet trade statistics;[12] second, a significant proportion of the residual amount may be accounted for by exports of armaments (Lavigne, 1982). Unfortunately, the proportion of the 'unaccounted residual' in USSR's exports to the South was not stable over time; hence the data in Table 14.5 are not an appropriate index of the directional changes in the composition of the trade. All the same, the figures we have suggested that the share of food and raw materials in the USSR's exports to the South decreased, while the share of fuels increased, over the period under review; on the other hand, these figures reveal no clear trend in the share of manufactures. It is likely that the share of manufactures, as also fuels, during the 1970s is underestimated because of the 'unaccounted residual', the magnitude of which doubled between 1965 and 1980. Available evidence confirms this conjecture: in 1980, manufactures constituted 45.1 per cent and fuels 43.3 per cent of USSR's exports to selected developing countries, which, taken together, accounted for about two-thirds of the USSR's exports to the South.[13]

A similar, albeit smaller, 'unaccounted residual' in exports from Eastern Europe to the South poses problems of interpretation for the years 1955 and 1960; fortunately, it is negligible thereafter. It appears that the composition of exports from Eastern Europe to the South registered little change over the period 1965–80: the share of manufactures was overwhelmingly large although it decreased from 85 per cent to 78 per cent; the share of raw materials and fuels was in the range 6–8 per cent; and the share of food increased from 7 per cent to 15 per cent.

Consider now the changes in the commodity structure of exports from the South to the East that are outlined in Table 14.6. The data reveal that at least 85 per cent, if not more, of the South's exports, both to the USSR and Eastern Europe, were constituted by primary commodities – food, raw materials and fuels – throughout the period 1955–80. In the case of exports to the USSR, the share of food ranged from one-half to two-thirds, the share of raw materials dropped from one-third in 1970 and earlier to one-eighth in 1980, while the share of fuels rose from a negligible level in the late 1960s to more than one-tenth in the late 1970s. In the case of exports to Eastern Europe, the share of food was about 30 per cent in 1955 and in 1980 (although it reached a level of around 50 per cent during the late 1960s), the share of raw materials dropped sharply from two-thirds until 1960 to one-fifth in 1980, while the share of fuels rose from a negligible level in 1965 to more than two-fifths in 1980. The trend in the share of manufactures in exports from the South was similar

TABLE 14.6 *The composition of exports from the South to the East (in percentages)*

Commodity group	1955	1960	1965	1970	1975	1980
A. Exports to the USSR						
Food	62.4	43.7	55.2	49.9	62.5	69.6
Raw materials	35.8	52.2	35.1	31.4	12.7	12.6
Fuels	1.2	—	0.1	2.0	12.3	9.4
Manufactures	0.6	3.7	9.3	16.7	12.5	7.8
Total	100.0	100.0	100.0	100.0	100.0	100.0
B. Exports to Eastern Europe						
Food	28.0	22.7	50.2	44.5	28.9	29.3
Raw materials	68.6	70.4	40.7	36.5	28.4	20.0
Fuels	—	—	0.4	4.1	31.0	41.2
Manufactures	2.8	6.8	8.5	14.3	11.5	9.0
Total	100.0	100.0	100.0	100.0	100.0	100.0

NOTES
(a) The definitions of the commodity groups are as follows (i) food items: SITC 0+1+22+4; (ii) raw materials: SITC 2 less 22 plus 68; (iii) fuels: SITC 3; (iv) manufactures: SITC 5 to 8 less 68.
(b) The columns may not add up to 100 as the figures have been rounded off.
SOURCE: UNCTAD *Handbook of International Trade and Development Statistics*, 1983.

for the USSR and Eastern Europe over the period under review: between 1955 and 1970, it increased rapidly from less than 1 per cent to almost 17 per cent in the case of the USSR, and from nearly 3 per cent to about 14 per cent in the case of Eastern Europe; thereafter, in both cases, it declined to a level of less than 10 per cent by 1980.

There is a striking asymmetry when we compare the share of manufactures in exports from the East to the South with that in exports from the South to the East. The division of labour implicit in such a composition of trade flows needs to be placed in perspective. For this purpose, it is worth making two comparisons: (a) the share of manufactures in the South's exports to the West as compared to the East; and (b) the share of manufactures in exports from the centrally planned economies of Asia to the centrally planned economies of Europe as compared to that in exports from the South to the East.

Table 14.7, which makes the first comparison, shows that the diversification in the South's exports to the East, in particular the USSR, was more rapid than that in exports from the South to the West during

TABLE 14.7 *The share of manufactures in exports from the South to the East, the West and the world (in percentages)*

Year	USSR	Eastern Europe	Developed market economies	World
1955	0.6	2.8	4.9	7.7
1960	3.7	6.8	6.9	9.2
1965	9.3	8.5	8.1	11.7
1970	16.7 (18.0)	14.3 (14.9)	14.6 (22.2)	17.3 (25.9)
1975	12.5 (14.2)	11.5 (16.7)	12.4 (34.2)	15.0 (37.1)
1980	7.8 (8.6)	9.0 (15.1)	15.0 (45.5)	18.0 (47.1)
1982	9.7 (10.1)	5.6 (11.9)	20.8 (53.6)	22.9 (53.3)

NOTES
(a) Manufactures are defined as SITC categories 5 to 8 less division 68.
(b) The percentages have been calculated from the data on trade flows valued in US $ million at current prices.
(c) The figures in parentheses denote the share of manufactures in non-fuel exports.
SOURCE: For 1955–80, UNCTAD *Handbook of International Trade and Development Statistics*, 1983. For 1982, UN *Monthly Bulletin of Statistics*, May 1984.

the period 1955–70, so that by 1970 the proportion of manufactures in total exports to the East and the West was about the same. Thereafter, the share of manufactures in the South's exports to the East decreased steadily, whereas the corresponding share in the South's exports to the West registered an increase from the mid-1970s, as a result of which the latter at a little over 20 per cent was more than double the former by 1982. The contrast is even sharper if we consider the share of manufactures in non-fuel exports from the South. During the 1970s, this proportion rose rapidly in case of the West and fell sharply in case of the East, particularly the USSR; so much so that, in 1982, the share of manufactures in the South's non-fuel exports to the West was more than 50 per cent as compared to just over 10 per cent in non-fuel exports to the East.

The second comparison, outlined in Table 14.8, reveals that the composition of exports from the centrally planned economies of Asia to the East – both the USSR and Eastern Europe – was notably less traditional, in so far as manufactured goods accounted for approximately 50 per cent of exports. For trade with the USSR, this proportion was attained as early as 1960, although it declined a little thereafter; in the case of trade with Eastern Europe it was reached *circa* 1970. As compared to the situation in the mid-1950s, the diversification in exports

TABLE 14.8 *The share of manufactures in exports from the centrally planned economies of Asia to the East and the West (in percentages)*

Year	USSR	Eastern Europe	Developed Market economies
1955	17.2	10.0	10.5
1960	49.9	5.8	16.1
1965	44.6	8.7	26.6
1970	52.8	54.2	31.4
1975	43.2	54.5	31.5
1980	44.1	55.0	38.5
1982	54.8	49.4	41.1

NOTES
(a) Manufactures are defined as SITC categories 5 to 8 less divison 68.
(b) The percentages have been calculated from data on trade flows valued in US $ million at current prices.
(c) The figures for 1982 have been derived from the UN *Monthly Bulletin of Statistics*, May 1984.
SOURCE: UNCTAD *Handbook of International Trade and Development Statistics*, 1983.

from the Asian socialist countries to the East was not only impressive but also rapid: this is in sharp contrast with the pattern of East-South trade. Interestingly enough, the share of manufactures in exports from the centrally planned economies to the West also rose rapidly from about 10 per cent in 1955 to more than 40 per cent in 1982. *Inter alia*, these trends suggest that industrialisation in the Asian socialist countries enabled them to transform their structure of production and pattern of trade.

The discussion so far has considered the composition of trade at an aggregate level and treated manufactured goods as one composite group. An examination of the structure of East-South trade within the category of manufactures reveals a further asymmetry. Using the SITC categories at one-digit level, manufactures can be divided into the following product-groups: (a) chemicals (SITC 5), mostly intermediates; (b) machinery and transport equipment (SITC 7), largely investment goods; and (c) goods classified by material (SITC 6) plus miscellaneous manufactured articles (SITC 8), mainly resource-based products or consumer goods, excluding non-ferrous metals (SITC 68). During the period 1960-80, the composition of manufactured exports from the USSR to the South was quite stable: chemicals accounted for a mere 5 per cent, machinery and transport equipment for as much as 75-80 per cent, and SITC categories 6 and 8 for 15-20 per cent; in the case of manufactured exports from Eastern Europe to the South, these proportions were 10-15 per cent, 50 per cent and 35-40 per cent respectively.

The composition of manufactured exports from the South to the East, both the USSR and Eastern Europe, was just the opposite: chemicals contributed 10–15 per cent, machinery and transport equipment accounted for less than 5 per cent, while SITC categories 6 and 8 constituted an overwhelming 80–90 per cent; two-thirds of the exports in the third product group were accounted for by textiles and clothing.[14]

In other words, the South exchanged simple domestic resource-based or labour-intensive manufactures for capital goods or products based on more sophisticated technology from the East. It might be argued that such a structure of trade is not unexpected between two sets of countries at different levels of development. However, it needs to be recognised that the composition of East-South trade in manufactures did not match the structure of exports either from the East to the rest of the world or from the South to the rest of the world.[15] In trade flows from the East to the South, the share of machinery and transport equipment in manufactured exports was very high and that of SITC 6 and 8 somewhat low as compared with Eastern exports of manufactures to other parts of the world.[16] On the other hand, in trade flows from the South to the East, the share of SITC 6 and 8 in manufactured exports was very high and that of SITC 7 extremely low as compared with Southern exports of manufactures to the rest of the world.[17]

The evidence considered above suggests that the composition of East-South trade is not significantly different from the conventional (i.e. pre-1970s) pattern of North-South trade in so far as the South exports largely raw materials and primary commodities to the East mostly in exchange for manufactured goods. A comparison of the proportion of manufactures in total exports from the South to the East with the corresponding proportion in total exports from (a) the East to the South, (b) the South to the West, and (c) the centrally planned economies of Asia to the East, reveals asymmetries which need to be recognised. The composition of East-South trade in manufactures is skewed in as much as Eastern exports are concentrated in investment goods whereas Southern exports are concentrated in resource-based or labour-intensive goods.

THE GAINS FROM TRADE

From the mid-1950s to the early 1970s, there was a remarkable expansion of trade between the East and the South, during which period East-South trade was among the most dynamic components of world trade. There were two basic factors underlying this remarkable trade expansion.

First, in a situation where scarcities of foreign exchange were a constraint on international trade, bilateralism made possible a much higher turnover of trade. Multilateral trade might have been superior in principle but, in the period 1955–70, it was not an option available to the East, nor was it a feasible option for many countries in the South. Although one cannot be certain, it is extremely unlikely that the East would have increased its trade with the South to the extent that it did in the absence of special payment arrangements which eliminated the use of convertible currencies in trade. For the South, too, without bilateralism the East might not have emerged as an alternative source of imports and as an alternative outlet for its traditional exports.

Second, complementarities of demand between the two sets of countries were fundamental to the expansion in trade. In the East, the relative isolation from the world economy, and the prevalent levels of consumption, meant that income elasticities of demand for primary commodities exported by the South were high – in sharp contrast with the near-saturated markets in the West. At the same time, in the South, the needs of industrialisation meant high income elasticities of demand for intermediate and capital goods exported by the East. During the 1960s, therefore, trade expansion was indeed remarkable; it began to taper off in the early 1970s and a threshold was reached when the growth potential stemming from complementarities was exhausted.

These two factors were also the principal source of mutual benefit, for the scarcity of foreign exchange and the constraints on exports in both sets of countries meant that gains from trade were ensured. The principle of bilateralism, which governed a substantial proportion of such trade flows, had several virtues in this phase. Most important, given the extreme shortage of foreign exchange, it enabled both the East and the South to avail themselves of the international trade opportunities which might not have been possible otherwise. For the East, the South was a useful source of imports and an obvious market outlet for exports; the USSR and Eastern Europe sold machinery and other manufactured goods, which were probably difficult to sell in Western markets, in exchange for primary products which would otherwise have involved an expenditure in convertible currencies. For the South, the East provided welcome new markets for a large number of traditional commodity exports which faced near-saturated markets and rather low income elasticities of demand in the West. At the same time, imports from the East were constituted by capital goods and intermediate products which were essential to the industrialisation programmes in the South.[18]

It is worth noting that both factors ran out of steam by the mid-1970s. For one thing, as we shall see a little later, the *modus operandi* of East-South trade shifted markedly from bilateral payments arrangements to transactions in convertible currencies. For another, the growth potential of complementary trade patterns between East and South was significantly reduced, as the import requirements and the export prospects of both sets of economies changed rapidly by the late 1970s. In spite of the loss of dynamism attributable to these developments, it should be pointed out that the growth in East-South trade was sufficient to keep pace with the expansion in global trade flows.

It need hardly be stressed that an expansion of trade *per se* is no index of the gains from such trade. After all, it is perfectly possible that a part of the increase in exports to bilateral agreement markets was illusory in so far as it represented a diversion of exportable commodities away from traditional markets. Alternatively, the prices received for exports might not have been favourable. Even if they were, the real benefit of bilateral trade would also depend upon the choice of imports offered by the partner and the import prices charged. In principle, therefore, an evaluation of the gains from trade must be based on some assessment of (a) the net increase in exports, (b) the composition of imports, and (c) the terms of trade obtained. I have discussed these issues from the viewpoint of countries in the South at some length elsewhere (Nayyar, 1977a), and to avoid repetition I shall not elaborate on the same points here. Suffice it to say that the net export growth in trade between the East and the South might have been less than the apparent increase if the latter met a part of its commitment under bilateral agreements by diverting exports away from convertible currency markets, or if the East re-exported goods imported under special arrangements to the rest of the world. While such occurrences would have diminished the gains from trade for the South, their incidence was probably not significant,[19] and the existence of the East as an alternative outlet for exports might have offered two special advantages to the South, if it improved terms of trade *vis-à-vis* the rest of the world, or if it reduced export instability.[20]

It is worth pointing out that the USSR and Eastern Europe might have derived a special benefit from their trade with the South on account of their trade surplus with the latter, which emerged in the 1960s and increased steadily from the mid-1970s. There is a view that the East used its surplus in trade with the South to finance its mounting deficit in trade *vis-à-vis* the West.[21] For the 1960s, however, this argument does not have much force primarily because (a) a very large proportion of the trade was conducted through bilateral clearing arrangements in convertible currencies, so that the surplus was not quite usable in the West; and (b) the economic and military aid extended by the East, particularly the USSR, which reached a peak during this period, was bound to result in such a trade surplus. My reservations are confirmed by existing research on the subject. After careful consideration of available evidence, Chandra (1977, p. 355) concludes that the USSR could not have financed its trade deficit with the West from its trade surplus with the South in the period from the mid-1950s to the late 1960s.

The picture is somewhat different for the 1970s. There was a steady shift from bilateral payments arrangements to transactions in convertible currencies, in trade between the East and the South. The share of trade conducted through clearing arrangements, in the case of the USSR, declined from 78.6 per cent in 1965 to 73.0 per cent in 1970 and 67.1 per cent in 1975; for Eastern Europe, the same proportion remained unchanged at about 75 per cent between 1965 and 1970, but dropped sharply to 42.5 per cent in 1975;[22] there was, of course, a corresponding increase in the share of convertible currency transactions. More important, perhaps, a very large proportion of the trade surplus which became substantial in the 1970s was attributable to trade in convertible currencies. This is confirmed by the data in Table 14.9, which outlines the trade balances of the East with the South in 1965, 1970 and 1975; unfortunately, data for intervening or subsequent years are not available. It is therefore perfectly possible that during the 1970s, the East used its trade surplus with the South, in so far as it was in convertible currencies, to finance its deficit in trade with the West. This issue has also been examined by Lavigne (1982), who argues that such an inference should be drawn with caution as it can only be based on certain assumptions regarding the precise division between trade flows in convertible and clearing currencies in each bilateral relation.

While a definite conclusion is not possible on the basis of available evidence, it is necessary to place these magnitudes in perspective. First, the convertible currency surplus in favour of the East *vis-à-vis* the South constituted about 10 per cent of the total trade turnover with the latter. Second, in 1975, the trade surplus with the South in convertible currencies was sufficient to finance 14 per cent of the trade deficit with the West for both the USSR and Eastern Europe.[23] It must be stressed that this possible gain for the East did not entail a loss for the South which, presumably, entered into such convertible currency transactions with the former on an entirely commercial basis.

DISTRIBUTION OF GAINS

For any evaluation of East-South trade, it is essential to assess the distribution of gains from such trade. Clearly, it is a complex and

TABLE 14.9 *Trade balances of the East with the South (in US $million)*

Year	USSR Under clearing agreements	In convertible currencies	Total trade balance	Eastern Europe Under clearing agreements	In convertible currencies	Total trade balance
1965	132.5	165.5	298.0	−66.4	103.4	37.0
1970	228.6	708.4	937.0	184.0	40.0	224.0
1975	−659.2	699.2	40.0	116.9	898.1	1015.0

NOTES

(a) Eastern Europe includes Bulgaria, Czechoslovakia, the German Democratic Republic, Hungary, Poland and Romania.
(b) Figures for 1975 do not include the German Democratic Republic, as data were not available.
(c) The USSR's trade deficit of $425 million with Cuba was responsible for a significant proportion of its total deficit with the South under clearing agreements in that year.

SOURCE: UNCTAD (1977), p.12

debatable question where precise answers are difficult to formulate. All the same, I shall attempt to provide a tentative answer on the basis of available evidence, with particular reference to the terms of trade.

For the South, trade with the East and trade with the West, or the South, are not mutually exclusive possibilities. To a limited extent, however, they do provide alternative sources of imports or markets for exports. In so far as that is the case, a comparison of the terms of trade obtained by the South in the two sets of countries should throw some light on the distribution of gains from trade, at least from the viewpoint of the Third World. *Ceteris paribus*, terms of trade are directly dependent on prices received for exports and prices paid for imports. Therefore, in order to compare the terms of trade obtained by the South from the East with those obtained from the rest of the world, price comparisons are unavoidable.

It need hardly be stressed that prices of traded goods are notoriously difficult to compare because of quality variations, which are present not only in manufactured goods but also in apparently homogeneous primary commodities. Nevertheless, to the extent that it is possible to indulge in price comparisons, evidence available from Egypt, India, Pakistan, Bangladesh, Sri Lanka, Tanzania, and Ghana suggests that the East offered terms which were sometimes better and, at any rate, no worse than those offered by the rest of the world.[24] If one thinks about this statement, it stands to reason. After all, East-South trade is carried out on a commercial basis. State trading corporations from the USSR and Eastern Europe conduct transactions with individuals or firms in the South; relatively few countries in the South have state trading agencies, and even where these exist, the bulk of foreign trade is carried out by private firms and individuals. There is no reason why individual exporters should sell for less than prices obtainable elsewhere or individual importers should pay more than the going prices. If anything, it is likely that the East, attempting to establish trade relations with countries in the South, to begin with had to offer small premiums in order to break into long-established market channels.

It has been argued that price comparisons of the sort mentioned above are neither adequate nor appropriate if the object is to examine the distribution of gains. In a paper on this subject, Chandra (1977) has shown that, during the period 1971–4, the USSR charged the South considerably higher prices than it was able to obtain in the West for comparable goods, whereas for exports from the South it paid prices which were only slightly higher than those paid by the West. From this asymmetry, he concludes that the distribution of gains from trade between the USSR and the South was unequal. In my view, this hypothesis is not convincing because of statistical and methodological problems. The empirical evidence must be treated with caution for two reasons. First, Chandra's statistical analysis hinges on price comparisons of manufactured goods, particularly machinery; such a procedure is fraught with difficulties on account of quality variations, and average unit values derived from trade statistics might be deceptive. Second, in so far as such price comparisons require an exact correspondence between goods sold in different markets, or an overlap in the USSR's exports to the West and to the South, the data are likely to relate only to a small proportion of the total trade. Even if we were to ignore these weaknesses, however, there remain methodological problems with the argument. It is not clear that just a difference between Soviet export prices charged in the West and in the South establishes the fact of price discrimination against the latter. It must also be shown that the USSR paid the West higher prices than it paid the South for comparable imports. Even if both these propositions are established beyond reasonable doubt, which they are not, the occurrence might be a reflection of Western discrimination against the East rather than of Eastern discrimination against the South.

As an aside, it might be recalled that a similar argument was advanced regarding the alleged Soviet exploitation of Eastern Europe. The work of Mendershausen (1959) pointed to price discrimination in trade by the

USSR *vis-à-vis* Eastern Europe, when compared to USSR-West trade, from which it was inferred that the Soviet Union was exercising its monopoly power in trade against the smaller CMEA countries. But further research on the subject cast serious doubts on the validity of this inference. It has been shown by Holzman (1974) that: (a) West European countries did, in fact, practise price discrimination in trade against the USSR; and (b) intra-CMEA trade prices were higher than world market prices, so that Eastern Europe and the USSR charged each other higher prices for exports (and paid each other less for imports) compared to similar transactions with the West.

Hence there is no *a priori* reason why prices in trade between the USSR and the West represent a norm of fairness against which intra-CMEA trade or East-South trade should be judged. To establish such a norm, it would have to be argued that the prices of Soviet exports in Western markets are a more accurate index of domestic resource costs or opportunity costs than either intra-CMEA trade prices or domestic prices in the USSR. This, in turn, raises a wide range of questions about the pricing of foreign trade transactions in centrally planned economies; it would be too much of a digression to enter into a discussion of those issues here. For the present, suffice it to say that there are a number of reasons, such as market entry barriers or tariff discrimination, why manufactured exports from the USSR and Eastern Europe might have to be sold at significant price discounts in the West.[25] On the other hand, it seems to me that a comparison of intra-CMEA trade prices with prices of transactions between the East and the South might be more appropriate. If it were shown that the USSR and Eastern Europe charged the South higher than CMEA prices for their exports, or paid lower than CMEA prices for their imports, or both, the distribution of gains from trade might indeed be unequal. However, Chandra (1977, p. 367) found that the USSR charged intra-CMEA prices for its exports to the South; unfortunately, he did not investigate the differences in the prices of comparable USSR imports from different sources.

It is apparent that serious data problems preclude a systematic and comprehensive analysis of the point at issue. Nonetheless, available evidence on the terms of trade obtained by the South compared with (a) those obtained from the West, or (b) those prevalent in intra-East trade, suggests that the terms were approximately the same and, at any rate, no worse. From the viewpoint of the South, therefore, it would be reasonable to infer that the distribution of gains from trade with the East was no worse than that in the case of trade with the West, and probably as favourable as that in the case of intra-East trade.

DIVISION OF LABOUR BETWEEN EAST AND SOUTH

The evidence presented earlier in the chapter suggests that the composition of East-South trade is not significantly different from the historical pattern of trade between the industrialised countries and the developing world, in so far as the South exports largely raw materials and primary commodities to the East mostly in exchange for manufactured goods. This division of labour between East and South provides a sharp contrast with other aspects of Eastern participation in world trade. For instance, the commodity composition of trade between the USSR and Eastern Europe on the one hand and the centrally planned economies of Asia on the other was notably less traditional. As a contrast, it is also worth noting that almost two-thirds of total world exports to the East were constituted by manufactured goods (Grosser and Tuitz, 1982). Indeed, it has been observed that, in terms of trade patterns, the South is to the East what the East is to the West.[26] Such traditional patterns of trade, however, can neither transform the structure of production in the South nor make for a new international division of labour. Admittedly, the patterns of production and trade that have evolved in the South over a long period of time could not have been changed overnight and, during the 1960s, there was a discernible increase in the share of manufactures in exports from the South to the East. However, this trend did not continue in the 1970s and was, in fact, reversed, whereas in the case of South exports to the North the share of manufactures went up sharply.

In this context it is worth pointing out that generalisations are difficult and sometimes misleading if we treat the South as one composite group. The pattern of trade with a few countries in the South such as India, Pakistan, Egypt, Syria and Bangladesh, did undergo a significant change over the period under review; this was mainly due to agreements which specified an increase in the share of manufactured exports from the country in the South to its socialist partner (Lavigne, 1982). For example, in the case of India, the share of manufactures in exports to the USSR rose from 20 per cent in 1960 to 50 per cent in 1980.[27] On balance, nevertheless, it needs to be recognised that the diversification in the pattern of East-South trade, with the possible exception of a few countries, has not been very significant. Even as late as 1980, there were only ten countries in the South from which manufactured imports constituted more than 25 per cent of total imports by the USSR.[28]

Thus it would seem that the claims made by the East, such as the passage below, are not borne out by available evidence:

> The successful promotion of economic relations of the USSR and other socialist countries with the developing states has given rise to a new sphere of the international division of labour – between socialist and developing states – that differs fundamentally from the existing division of labour between the imperialist countries and their former colonial possessions. (Skachkov, 1974, p. 11)

Indeed, whether we consider the composition of trade or the terms of trade, the similarities between East-South trade and West-South trade appear to be far greater than the differences, although there may be some qualitative differences implicit in the long-term trade agreements which envisage economic co-operation on a wider nexus.

It is obvious enough that the division of labour implicit in such patterns of specialisation and trade is not consistent with the objectives of rapid industrialisation in the South. What is more, it cannot facilitate structural change in the world economy which is required for the establishment of a new international economic order. But that is not all. It would also limit the pace and extent of East-South co-operation since the growth potential of inter-sectoral trade between East and South is now far more limited, as compared with the period until the early 1970s. At the present juncture, it might appear that oil imports by Eastern Europe, which is switching sources from the USSR to OPEC, might be a new bonanza for East-South trade. In my view, however, this new complementarity might not provide a net boost to trade between the East and the South. It would probably mean that one set of primary commodities is replaced by another, while one group of countries in the South is replaced by another. It would, of course, do little to change the division of labour.

Most observers are somewhat pessimistic about the prospects of a structural change in the composition of East-South trade during the 1980s. In a paper which deals with the prospects of economic co-operation between the East and the South, Dobozi and Inotai (1981) have provided a set of projections on East-South trade for the period 1977–90. The composition of this trade at the end of the projected period is revealing: manufactures would account for 80 per cent of exports from the East to the South, while the diversification in exports from the South to the East would not be very significant, except that primary commodities would be replaced by minerals and fuels. Similarly, Lavigne (1982) has argued that the growing needs for raw materials and primary commodities in the East, particularly imports of fuels in Eastern Europe and imports of food in the USSR, would leave little room for a parallel expansion of imports of manufactures from the South; the author concludes that no significant shift in the structure and composition of East-South trade can be expected during the 1980s. A detailed study by Grosser and Tuitz (1982), on structural change in manufacturing industries in the European CMEA countries and the pattern of East-South trade in manufactures, arrives at roughly the same conclusion.

Given such perceptions, any significant change in the composition of trade would require a mechanism for structural adjustment which would have to be reciprocal and simultaneous: a programmed, negotiated process which can emerge from planned changes in international specialisation through long-term bilateral agreements between countries in the East and the South (Paszynski, 1981). There are two problems with his approach (Nayyar, 1981). Is it possible even in principle to plan the integration of production capacities between the centrally planned economies of the East on the one hand and the market economies of the South on the other? In practice, the experience of centrally planned economies at different levels of development – say in the CMEA – attempting planned economic integration through trade and specialisation, highlights the problems that are likely to arise; the process would be all the more difficult in relations with market economies of the South.

In this context, it is worth noting some structural constraints which might limit not only the diversification but also the expansion in East-South trade (Nayyar, 1982). First, the nature and pace of technical progress in the East is bound to push in the direction of more East-West trade in the 1980s, rather than East-South trade, as there is a growing need in the industrialised CMEA countries to import Western technology and thereby increase productivity. Second, the worsening trade balance and the increasing international indebtedness of the East *vis-à-vis* the West would only squeeze the prospects of convertible currency trade with the South further.[29] Third, the stipulated objectives of reducing raw material intensity and increasing value-added in industrial production within the European CMEA economies would also adversely affect the prospects of exports from the South to the East, whether of primary commodities or processed products.

For a proper assessment, it is important to recognise the structural constraints outlined above. There can be little doubt that sustained growth and dynamism in East-South trade would depend on a successful transition from a complementary to a competitive pattern of trade. In other words, inter-sectoral trade must be replaced by intra-sectoral or intra-industry trade and specialisation. While the scope for such a new international division of labour between East and South appears limited in the short run, or even the medium term, in the long run the situation has to be transformed, as part of the process of structural change in the world economy brought about by a changing international division of labour. Otherwise, East-South trade would simply be bypassed in a rapidly changing scenario. There is, however, a silver lining to the cloud. For in principle the East should be much better equipped to cope with structural change than the West. After all, in the OECD countries the ability of governments to mould the direction of trade and specialisation in accordance with their priorities is limited, as it is individuals or firms who trade and whose decisions are determined by market forces rather than by planning authorities. On the other hand, the economies in the East can plan for structural change, as indeed Japan has done in a completely different context, and thus minimise the problems or costs associated with the process.[30]

It is obviously not sufficient to enunciate a general principle about planning for structural change in the European CMEA countries. A consideration of future prospects must go further, simply because it would be idle to pretend that the potential for change is uniform across the board. The possibility of bringing about a change in the division of labour between East and South would vary considerably across sectors and countries. For the purpose of analysis, therefore, it would be useful to identify sectors where manufactured exports from the South to the East might be developed, and to distinguish between groups of countries in the South for an assessment of the prospects.

If the object is to change the composition of East-South trade, the main avenues for increasing manufactured exports from the South are likely to be: (a) the processing of natural resources such as non-ferrous metals or petroleum, which would increase value-added before export; (b) domestic resource-based manufactures, such as wood products, leather goods, textiles and processed foods; or (c) labour-intensive manufactured goods, such as clothing, carpets, travel goods, footwear, toys, sports goods, simple electronic products, metal manufactures, and so on. A diversification of trade in these directions, which are by no means exhaustive, would also yield gains for the East. First, it would release scarce domestic resources, particularly labour, which have alternative uses. Second, it would increase the range and volume of consumer goods available, which is now a priority in the European CMEA economies. There would, of course, be corresponding costs, such as the absorption of convertible foreign exchange or the redundance of established production capacities, but these are an inevitable price of structural change.

In order to explore the possibility of changing the division of labour between East and South, it would also be useful to distinguish between three groups of countries in the South: the oil-exploring countries, the newly industrialising countries, and the other developing countries. It need hardly be stressed that there would be significant variations even within these groups of countries; but some degree of aggregation is essential for analysis. Consider each set of countries in turn. For the oil-producing and exporting countries in the Middle East, the prospects of trade with the East are bright because of the latter's emerging need for oil imports from sources other than the USSR, but the pattern of trade would remain as traditional as ever, unless OPEC exports petroleum products instead of crude oil. For the NICs in Latin America, South Asia and South East Asia, as argued earlier, the complementarities between the East and South as a source of trade expansion are almost exhausted; if anything, there is an increasing degree of competitiveness between the two sets of economies, which is likely to pose some problems A diversification of trade patterns which leads to an absorption of labour-intensive and domestic resource-based manufactured exports from the South would be absolutely essential here. For the remaining countries in the South, whether in Africa, Asia or Latin America, the complementarities of East-South trade might remain an important force for some time to come. But the objectives of industrialisation in these economies require a change in the traditional division of labour; for this component of East-South trade, the processing of natural resources and agricultural produce in the South holds the greatest promise for diversification.

CONCLUSIONS

From the mid-1950s to the early 1970s, the growth in trade between the East and the South was extremely rapid; it experienced a deceleration thereafter. Bilateral payments arrangements and complementarities in demand between the East and the South were the principal factors underlying the growth in trade, as well as the major sources of the gains from such trade for both sets of countries. Available evidence suggests that, from the viewpoint of the South, the distribution of gains from trade with the East was no worse than that in the case of trade with the West and probably as favourable as that in the case of intra-East trade.

The composition of East-South trade was not significantly different from the traditional pattern of trade between the industrialised and developing countries in so far as the South exported largely raw materials and primary commodities to the East mostly in exchange for manufactured goods. In the phase from the mid-1950s to the early 1970s, there was a significant diversification in the composition of East-South trade, but this trend was reversed thereafter; the share of manufactures in exports from the South to the East was much less than the corresponding proportion in total exports from the South to the West, or from the centrally planned economies of Asia to the East, at the beginning of 1980s. Such traditional patterns of trade, it should be recognised, can neither transform the structure of production in the South nor make for a new international division of labour.

Sustained growth and dynamism in East-South trade over the next decade would also depend on a successful transition from a complementary to a competitive pattern of trade, so that inter-sectoral trade is gradually replaced by intra-sectoral or intra-industry trade and specialisation. The scope for such a new international division of labour between East and South appears limited in the short run, but there is a potential that can be realised by planning for structural change possibly through bilateral arrangements. The prospects for structural change in the composition of East-South trade would, of course, depend not only on how trade is incorporated into the wider sphere of economic cooperation, but also on political factors in East-South relations.

NOTES

1. Some of the ideas developed in this essay were first presented to seminars at the University of Sussex and the University of Oxford. These were subsequently outlined in my contributions to the Sixth Workshop on 'East-West Economic Interaction' organised by the Vienna Institute of Comparative Economic Studies at Dubrovnik in May 1980, and a UNIDO Research Seminar on 'Structural Change in Industry in the CMEA Countries' at Budapest in March 1982. Questions and comments from participants in these discussions led me to further research on the subject. I recall, in particular, helpful suggestions from Amit Bhaduri, Nirmal Chandra, Reg Green and Paul Streeten. The views expressed in this paper are entirely personal and do not necessarily reflect the views of the Ministry of Commerce, or the Government, with which I am associated at present.

2. See, for example, the *Manila Declaration and Programme of Action*, the *Arusha Programme for Collective Self-Reliance and Framework for Negotiations*, and the *Buenos Aires Platform*, adopted by the Third, Fourth and Fifth Ministerial Meetings of the Group of 77 respectively, which were held in Manila from 27 January to 7 February 1976, in Arusha from 6 to 16

February 1979, and in Buenos Aires from 28 March to 9 April 1983. These have been reproduced as UNCTAD documents TD/195, TD/236 and TD/285 respectively.
3. The position of the socialist countries on this issue is reflected clearly in the following statement by the Foreign Minister of the USSR at the Sixth Special Session of the United Nations General Assembly in 1974: 'We shall never accept, either in theory or in practice, the fallacious concept of the division of the world into 'poor' and 'rich' countries, a concept which puts the socialist states on the same footing as certain other states which extracted so much wealth from the countries which were under the colonial yoke'; this passage is cited in Lavigne (1982), p. 130.
4. The proposition equating the East with the North is examined at length in a recent paper by Lavigne (1982).
5. For a discussion on the other aspects of economic interaction between the East and the South, see Nayyar (1977a).
6. The figures on the share of the South in the total trade turnover of the USSR and Eastern Europe cited here are not set out in the tables but are calculated from the same sources.
7. The increase in the share of the South in Eastern European trade, from the mid-1970s, was attributable to the increased trade between OPEC and Eastern Europe following the oil price increases in 1973–4 and 1979–80.
8. It does appear, however, that the growth in trade between Eastern Europe and the South was an exception to this inference in so far as the share of the South in the foreign trade of Eastern Europe registered an increase starting around the mid-1970s.
9. The regional composition of East-South trade is also worth noting. For the USSR, in 1970, the shares were as follows: Africa 30 per cent, Latin America 35 per cent, Middle East 15 per cent and other Asia 20 per cent; in 1980, these proportions were 15, 45, 15 and 25 per cent respectively. For Eastern Europe, in 1970, foreign trade with the South was divided in an approximately equal manner between the four regions; in 1980, the shares were 24, 20, 45 and 11 per cent respectively (these percentages are calculated from data in the UN *Monthly Bulletin of Statistics*, July 1983). The relatively high and rising share of Latin America and Asia in USSR's trade with the South was attributable to the large trade turnover with Cuba and India respectively. The sharp increase in the share of the Middle East in the trade of Eastern Europe with the South was, of course, attributable to developments in the wake of the oil price hikes.
10. For a detailed discussion, see a study prepared for the United Nations by the Moscow Institute of Economics of the World Socialist System, UNCTAD (1970), pp. 8–11.
11. For a description of the evolution in payments arrangements between the East and the South during the 1970s, see UNCTAD (1977).
12. See UNCTAD *Handbook of International Trade and Development Statistics, 1983*, p. A138.
13. For the selected developing countries, USSR foreign trade statistics provide a complete commodity-wise classification; see UNCTAD (1982) Addendum 1, p. 18.
14. The figures on the composition of East-South trade in manufactured goods, cited in this paragraph, have been calculated from data published in the

UNCTAD *Handbook of International Trade and Development Statistics, 1983.*
15. For discussion on the composition of trade in manufactures between East and South, as also for an analysis of its implications, see Grosser and Tuitz (1982).
16. In 1980, for example, SITC 7 accounted for 80 per cent of the USSR's manufactured exports to the South, while SITC 6 and 8 constituted 13 per cent; by contrast, only 60 per cent of the USSR's manufactured exports to the world were accounted for by SITC 7, whereas 30 per cent were constituted by SITC 6 and 8. The composition of manufactured exports from Eastern Europe to the South, on the other hand, was approximately the same as that to the rest of the world. (Calculated from the UN *Monthly Bulletin of Statistics*, May 1984).
17. It is worth citing the exact proportions. In 1980, SITC categories 6 and 8 less division 68 accounted for 76 per cent of manufactured exports from the South to the USSR and for 86 per cent of those to Eastern Europe, as compared to 63 per cent for the world as a whole. The contrast was even more pronounced in the case of exports of machinery and transport equipment. The proportions of SITC 7 in manufactured exports from the South, in 1980, were 4.6 per cent for the USSR, 2.4 per cent for Eastern Europe and 27.4 per cent for the world. These percentages have been computed from data published in th UN *Monthly Bulletin of Statistics*, May 1984.
18. The above discussion, on the factors underlying the growth in East-South trade and the sources of gains from this trade, draws upon my earlier work on the subject (Nayyar, 1981).
19. The likelihood of implicit diversion on the part of countries in the South is an empirical question about which generalisations are rather difficult. But it appears that re-exports by countries in the East, notwithstanding stray instances, could not have been significant or widespread; see Nayyar (1977a), pp. 7–8.
20. For a further discussion and elaboration on these issues, see Nayyar (1977a), p. 9.
21. This view was first put forward by Vassilev (1969). It has subsequently been reiterated by Frank (1977) and, in a qualified manner, by Chandra (1977).
22. These percentages have been calculated from the data in UNCTAD (1977), p. 9. The aggregate figures for Eastern Europe conceal important variations between countries in the group. In 1975, for instance, the share of clearing agreements in total trade with the South declined to 28.9 per cent in Hungary, 23.9 per cent in Poland, 39.1 per cent in Romania, 44.9 per cent in Bulgaria, but was significantly higher at 56.2 per cent in the German Democratic Republic and 61.1 per cent in Czechoslovakia.
23. Calculated from the data in UNCTAD (1978), Addendum 1, p. 6. It is also worth pointing out that, in 1970, the USSR's convertible currency trade surplus with the South was about 75 per cent larger than its trade deficit with the West.
24. For evidence on Egypt, see Mabro (1977), pp. 68–70; on India, Nayyar (1977b), pp. 130–5; on Pakistan, Kidron (1972), pp. 47–54; on Bangladesh, Khan (1975), pp. 331–2; on Sri Lanka, Fernando (1979); on Tanzania, Bienefeld (1977), pp. 43–5; and on Ghana, Stevens (1977), pp. 85–7 and 91.

25. For a lucid discussion on this point, see Holzman (1976), pp. 84–5.
26. For an explicit statement of this view, see Frank (1977), p. 305; see also Portes (1981), Lavigne (1982) and Grosser and Tuitz (1982).
27. These percentages have been calculated from India's foreign trade statistics published by the Director General of Commercial Intelligence and Statistics, Calcutta, and relate to the fiscal years 1960–1 and 1980–1. Trade between India and the USSR, however, is a somewhat special case in so far as the share of manufactures in imports from the USSR was only 15 per cent in 1980–1, as compared to about 75 per cent in 1960–1. This dramatic change is attributable almost entirely to the overwhelming share of crude oil and petroleum products in India's imports from the USSR during the past few years.
28. These countries were Bangladesh, Egypt, India, Iran, Lebanon, Nepal, Pakistan, Singapore, Syria, and Tunisia; see UNCTAD (1982), Addendum 1, pp. 19–21.
29. Apropos this point, it is worth noting that the steady shift from bilateral payments arrangements to transactions in convertible currencies in East-South trade might also limit the possibilities of a sustained growth in trade between the two sets of countries.
30. The discussion in the following paragraphs draws upon my earlier work on the subject (Nayyar, 1982).

REFERENCES

Bienefeld, M., 'Special Gains from Trade with the Socialist Countries: The Case of Tanzania', in Nayyar (1977), pp. 18–52.

Chandra, N. K. 'USSR and the Third World: Unequal Distribution of Gains', *Economic and Political Weekly*, Annual Number, February 1977.

Dobozi, I. and Inotai, A., 'Prospects of Economic Cooperation between CMEA Countries and Developing Countries', in Saunders (1981), pp. 48–65.

Fernando, L., *Bilateral Trade and Payments Agreements in Sri Lanka's Foreign Trade*, unpublished D. Phil. thesis, University of Sussex, 1979.

Frank, A. G., 'Long Live Transideological Enterprise: Socialist Economies in Capitalist International Division of Labour', *Economic and Political Weekly*, Annual Number, February 1977.

Grosser, I. and Tuitz, G., 'Structural Change in Manufacturing Industries in the European CMEA Area and Patterns of Trade in Manufactures between CMEA Countries and Developing Countries', paper presented at the UNIDO Research Seminar on Structural Changes in Industry in the European CMEA Countries, ID/WG 357/5, Budapest: 22–26 March 1982.

Holzman, F. D., *Foreign Trade Under Central Planning* (Cambridge, Mass: Harvard University Press, 1974).

Holzman, F. D., *International Trade Under Communism: Politics and Economics* (London: Macmillan, 1976).

Khan, A. R., 'Bangladesh's Trade and Economic Relations with the Socialist Countries', *World Development*, Volume 3, Number 5, 1975.

Kidron, M., *Pakistan's Trade with Eastern Bloc Countries* (New York: Praeger, 1972).

Lavigne, M., 'Consequences of Economic Developments in Eastern Europe for East-West and East-South Relations', *Trade and Development*, an UNCTAD Review, Number 4, 1982, pp. 129–148.

Mabro, R., 'Egypt's Economic Relations with the Socialist Countries', in Nayyar (1977), pp. 53–77.

Mendershausen, H., 'Terms of Trade between the Soviet Union and Smaller Communist countries', *Review of Economics and Statistics*, May 1959.

Nayyar, D. (1977a) (ed.), *Economic Relations between Socialist Countries and the Third World* (London: Macmillan, 1977).

Nayyar, D. (1977b) 'India's Trade with the Socialist Countries', in Nayyar (1977), pp. 105–142.

Nayyar, D., 'East-West-South: Interests and Prospects: A Comment', in Saunders (1981), pp. 78–84.

Nayyar, D., 'Some Reflections on East-South Trade and the Division of Labour', paper presented at the UNIDO Research Seminar on Structural Changes in Industry in the European CMEA Countries, ID/WG 357/7, Budapest: 22–26 March 1982.

Paszynski, M., 'The Economic Interest of the CMEA Countries in Relations with Developing Countries', in Saunders (1981), pp. 33–47.

Portes, R., 'East, West and South: the Role of the Centrally Planned Economies in the International Economy', in S. Grassman and E. Lundberg (eds), *The World Economic Order* (London: Macmillan, 1981), pp. 319–57.

Saunders, C. T. (ed.), *East-West-South: Economic Interactions between Three Worlds* (London: Macmillan, 1981).

Skachkov, S., 'Economic Cooperation of the USSR with Developing Countries', *Social Sciences*, No. 3, 1974, Moscow, USSR Academy of Sciences.

Stevens, C., 'Entente Commerciale: The Soviet Union and West Africa', in Nayyar (1977), pp. 78–104.

UNCTAD, *Innovations in the Practice of Trade and Economic Cooperation between the Socialist Countries of Eastern Europe and the Developing Countries*, a study prepared by the Moscow Institute of Economics of the World Socialist System (New York: United Nations, 1970).

UNCTAD, 'Review of the Present State of Payments between Developing Countries and the Socialist Countries of Eastern Europe' (Geneva: TD/B/AC. 22/2, October 1977).

UNCTAD, 'Review of Trends and Policies in Trade among Countries having different Economic and Social Systems' (Geneva: TD/B/708, July 1978).

UNCTAD, 'Trade Relations among Countries having different Economic and Social Systems and all Trade Flows resulting therefrom' (Geneva: TD/B/912, July 1982).

Vassilev, V., *Policy in the Soviet Bloc on Aid to Developing Countries* (Paris: OECD, 1969).

Publications by Paul Streeten

BOOKS (AUTHOR OR EDITOR)

The Political Element in the Development of Economic Theory, by Gunnar Myrdal. Translated, edited and appendix, 1953 (German edition 1963) (London: Routledge & Kegan Paul).

The Great Economists, by R.L. Heilbroner, revised, edited and two additional chapters, 1955.

Economic Integration: Aspects and Problems, 1961 (Sythoff second edition, 1964).

Value in Social Theory, by Gunnar Myrdal, edited and foreword by Paul Streeten, 1958 (Germa edition 1964).

The Crisis of Indian Planning, edited with M. Lipton (Royal Institute of International Affairs, Oxford University Press, 1968).

Unfashionable Economics (editor) (Weidenfeld & Nicolson, 1970).

Commonwealth Policy in a Global Context, edited with Hugh Corbet, with two chapters and introduction by Paul Streeten (Frank Cass, 1971).

Diversification and Development: The Case of Coffee (with Diane Elson) (Praeger, 1971).

Capital for Africa: The British Contribution, with Helen Sutch (Africa Publications Trust, 1971).

The Frontiers of Development Studies (Macmillan, 1972). (Spanish edition 1982).

Aid for Africa (Praeger, 1972).

The Limits of Development Research (Pergamon Press, 1974).

Trade Strategies for Development (Macmillan, 1973) edited by Paul Streeten

Foreign Investment, Transnationals and Developing Countries, with Sanjaya Lall (Macmillan, 1977).

Recent Issues in World Development, edited with Richard Jolly (Pergamon, 1981).

Development Perspectives (Macmillan, 1981).

First Things First: Meeting Basic Human Needs in Developing Countries, with S. J. Burki, Mahbub ul Haq, Norman Hicks, Frances Stewart (Oxford University Press, 1981).

Human Resources, Employment and Development, Volume 2, *Concepts, Measurement and Long-Run Perspective*, edited by Paul Streeten and Harry Maier for the International Economic Association (Macmillan, 1983).

SOME CONTRIBUTIONS TO BOOKS

Vollbeschäftigung (Cologne, 1950), 'Mangel des Preismechanismus'.
'Keynes and the Classics', in *Post-Keynesian Economics*, edited by K. Kurihara, 1954.
Studi in Memoria di Benevenuto Griziotti: 'The Taxation of Overseas Profits' (Milano: Guiffre, 1959).
Theorie et Politique de l'Expansion Régionale (Brussels, 1961). Contribution on regional problems in developed countries.
'Commercial Policy', in *The British Economy in the Nineteen-fifties*, edited by Worswick and Ady (Oxford University Press, 1962).
'Values, Facts and the Compensation Principle', in *Probleme der normativen Ökonomik und der wirtschaftspolitischen Beratung*, edited by von Beckerath and Giersch (Berlin, 1963).
Economic Growth in Britain, edited by P.D. Henderson (Weidenfeld & Nicolson, 1966), contributed two chapters: 'The Objectives of Economic Policy and 'Rich and Poor Nations'.
'The Use and Abuse of Models in Development Planning', in *The Teaching of Development Economics*, edited by K. Martin and J. Knapp (Cass, 1967).
'Counselling in British Stabilisation Policy', in *Grundsatzprobleme wirtschaftspolitischer Beratung* (Berlin: Duncker & Humbolt, 1968).
Gunnar Myrdal, *Asian Drama, an Inquiry into the Poverty of Nations* (Twentieth Century Fund, March 1968).
'International Capital Movements', *Essays in Honour of Antonio de Viti de Marco*, edited by Ernesto d'Albergo.
'Education and Development', in Festchrift for Professor Dr Friedrich Edding, *Economics of Education in Transition*, edited by K. Hufner and Jens Naumann (Klett, 1969).
'Aid to India', *Year Book of World Affairs 1970* (Stevens & Sons).
'Trade and Liquidity in India and Pakistan', with Akbar Noman, in *The Widening Gap*, edited by Barbara Ward, Lenore d'Anjou and J.D. Runnals (Columbia University Press, 1971).
'Costs and Benefits of Multinational Enterprises in Less Developed Countries', in *The Multinational Enterprise*, edited by John H. Dunning (Allen & Unwin, 1971).
'New Approaches to Private Overseas Investment', in *Private Foreign Investment and the Developing World*, edited by Peter Ady (Praeger, 1971).
'Economic Development and Education', in *Essays on Modernization of Underdeveloped Societies*, editor: A.R. Desai (Bombay, 1971).
'The Political Economy of the Environment: Problems of Method', in *Uncertainty and Expectations in Economics*, Essays in Honour of G.L.S. Shackle, edited by C.F. Carter and J.L. Ford (Blackwell, 1972).
Comments in *Reconstruction and Development in Nigeria*, Proceedings of a National Conference, edited by A.A. Ayida and H.M.A. Onitra (Oxford University Press, 1971).
'Overseas Development Policies' (with Dudley Seers) in *The Labour Government's Economic Record 1964-1970*, edited by Wilfred Beckerman (Duckworth, 1972).
'International Capital Movements', in *Studi in memoria di Antonio de Viti de Marco* (Bari, 1972).

'A New Look at Foreign Aid', in *Foreign Resources and Economic Development*, a Symposium on the Report of the Pearson Commission, edited by T.J. Byres (Cass, 1972).

'Some Comments on the Teaching of Economics' and 'An Institutional Critique of Development Concepts', in *The Teaching of Economics in Africa*, edited by I. Livingston, G. Routh, J.F. Rweyemamu, K.E. Svendsen (Chatto & Windus, 1973).

'Probleme internationaler Kooperation in Forschung und Technologie aus der Sicht der Europäischen Gemeinschaften', in *Technischer Fortschrift und Unternehmensgrosse*, edited by Burkhardt Roper (Düsseldorf, 1973).

Preface to *Earned International Reserve Units*, by Chris Economides (*World Development*, Oxford, 1973).

Summary Report on Six Country Studies for UNCTAD and policy conclusions (with Sanjaya Lall).

'World Trade in Agricultural Commodities and the Terms of Trade with Industrial Goods', in *Agricultural Policy in Developing Countries*. Proceedings of a Conference held by the International Economic Association at Bad Godesberg, West Germany, edited by Nurul Islam (Macmillan, 1974).

'The Multinational Enterprise and the Theory of Development Policy', in *Economic Analysis and the Multinational Enterprise*, edited by John Dunning (Allen & Unwin, 1974).

ARTICLES

'The Theory of Pricing' *Jahrbücher für Nationalökonomic und Statistik*, Band 161, Heft 3/4, October 1949.

'The Theory of Profit' *Manchester School*, Vol. XVII, No. 3, September 1949.

'Economics and Value Judgments', *Quarterly Journal of Economics*, November 1950.

'Reserve Capacity and the Kinked Demand Curve', *Review of Economic Studies*, 1950–1.

'The Inappropriateness of Simple "Elasticity" Concepts in the Theory of International Trade' and 'Exchange Rates and National Income', both with T. Balogh in *Banca Nazionale del Lavoro*, October–December 1950, and *Bulletin of the Oxford University Institute of Statistics*, March and April 1951.

'The Modern Theory of Welfare Economics' (French), *Economie Appliquée*, Tome V, No. 4, October–December 1952.

'The Effect of Taxation on Risk-Taking', *Oxford Economic Papers*, Vol. V, No. 3, September 1953.

'Programs and Prognoses', *Quarterly Journal of Economics*, LXVIII, No. 3, August 1954 (translated into German and Spanish).

'Elasticity Optimism and Pessimism in International Trade', *Economia Internazionale*, Vol. VII, No. 1, 1954.

'Two Comments on the Articles by Mrs Paul and Professor Hicks', *Oxford Economic Papers*, Vol. 7, No.3, October 1955.

'Productivity Growth and the Balance of Trade', *Bulletin of the Oxford University Institute of Statistics*, Vol 17, No. 1, February 1955.

'Some Problems Raised by the Report of the Royal Commission on the Taxation of Profits and Income', *Bulletin of the Oxford University Institute of Statistics*, Vol. 17, No. 4, 1955.

'The Taxation of Overseas Profits', *Manchester School*, January 1957.
'Government and the Economy in the USA', *Rivista di diritto finanziario e scienzo delle finanze*, March 1957.
'The Economic Consequences of Overseas Trade Concessions', *Bulletin*, August 1957.
'Growth, the Terms of Trade and the Balance of Trade', *Economie Appliquée*, April/September 1957 (with J. Black).
'Sviluppo economico Stabilita e altri fini della politica fiscale', *Rivista internazionale di scienze sociali*, October 1957.
'A Reconsideration of Monetary Policy', *Bulletin*, November 1957 (with T. Balogh).
'A Note on Kaldor's Speculation and Economic Stability', *Review of Economic Studies*, Vol. XXVI, No. 1, October 1958.
'Taxation and Enterprise', *University of Toronto Quarterly*, January 1958.
'Tassazione e iniziativa privata', *Revista internazionale di scienze sociali*, February 1958.
'Principio de Compensacion', *Rivista de Economia Politica*, April 1959.
'Unbalanced Growth', *Oxford Economic Papers*, June 1959 (translated into Spanish).
'Desequilibre et croissance', *Cahiers de l'institut économique appliquée*, July 1959.
'Tax Policy for Investment', *Rivista di diritto finanziario e scienza delle finanze*, June 1960. Shortened reprint in *Mercurio*.
'Domestic v. Foreign Investment', *Bulletin of Institute of Statistics*, August 1960 (with T. Balogh).
'Wages, Prices and Productivity', *Kyklos*, October 1962. Reprinted in *Inflation*, Penguin Modern Economics, edited by R.J. Ball and Peter Doyle (1969).
'Socialist Economics' in *Collier's Encyclopaedia*, New York, 1963.
'Common Fallacies about the Common Market' and 'Problems of Economic Integration', in *Weltwirtschaftliches Archiv*, Band 90, Heft 2, 1963.
'Balanced versus Unbalanced Growth', *Economic Weekly*, 20 April 1963.
'The Coefficient of Ignorance' (with T. Balogh), *Bulletin of the Oxford University Institute of Statistics*, Vol. 25, No. 2, 1963. Reprinted in *Economics of Education*, 1, Penguin Modern Economics, edited by Mark Blaug (1968) and *Human Capital Formation and Manpower Development*, edited by Ronald Wykstra, Vol. 28, Nov. 76, No. 3.
'More Care about Capital Use', *Yojana* (Delhi), 17 March 1963.
'Unbalanced Growth: A Reply', *Oxford Economic Papers*, March 1963 (translated into Spanish).
'The Case for Export Subsidies', *All India Congress Committee Economic Review*, April 1963.
UNESCO Dictionary of Political and Social Terms; articles on 'Welfare', 'Wealth', and 'Economic Equilibrium'.
'Programmes and Prognoses, Unbalanced Growth and the Ideal Plan', *Banca Nazionale del Lavoro*, June 1964.
'Bergedorfer Protokolle: Economic Aid – a Way to growth or Decline?', published in German 1964 and paperback 1965 (contribution).
'Hilfe, Handel and Entwicklung', *Schmollers Jahrbuch*, Heft 6, 1964.
'Educational Planning for Development', *Overseas Universities*, August 1965.

'Studying to Make Overseas Aid More Effective', *The Times*, 16 September 1966.
'International Monetary Reform and the Less Developed Contries', *Banca Nazionale del Lavoro Quarterly Review*, June 1967.
'Development and the Institute of Development Studies', *Journal of Administration Overseas*, October 1967.
'The Frontiers of Development Studies', *The Journal of Development Studies*, October 1967.
'A Poor Nation's Guide to Getting Aid', *New Society*, 1 February 1968 (reprinted in several places).
'Economic Development and Education', *Educational Encyclopaedia*, published by the Ministry of Education and Culture and the Bialik Institute, Israel. Reprinted in Essays in Honour of Friedrich Edding, edited by Hellmut Becker.
'European Development Policy and Development Concepts', *Rivista Internazionale di Scienze Economiche e Commerciali*, March 1968, Anno XV, n. 5.
'Improving the Climate', *Ceres* (FAO Review), Vol. 2, No.2, 8, March-April 1969.
'EEC Membership: Impact on the British Balance of Payments', *Intereconomics*, No. 10, October 1968.
'Die EWG ist gar nicht so anziehend, *Wirtschaftsdienst*, No. 12, December 1968.
'The Case for Export Subsidies', *The Journal of Development Studies*, Vol. 5, No. 4, July 1969.
Several contributions to the *Bulletin* of the Institute of Development Studies, Vol. 1, No. 4, May 1969.
'A New Commonwealth', *New Society*, 3 July 1969.
'Linking Money and Development', *International Affairs*, Vol. 46, No. 1, January 1970.
'Nouvelles manières d'aborder le probleme de l'investissement privé dans les pays en voie de développement', *Revue de la Société d'Etudes et d'Expansion*, No. 238, Novembre-Decembre 1969 Reprinted in *Mercurio*, Anno XIII, No. 9, September 1970.
'The Role of Private Investment', *Venture*, January 1970.
'Principles and Problems of a Liberal Order of the Economy', *Weltwirtschaftliches Archiv*, Band 104, Heft 1, 1970.
'Obstacles to Private Foreign Investment in the LDCs', *Columbia Journal of World Business*, Vol. V, No. 3, May-June 1970.
'Two Worlds: Problems of Integration', *History of the 20th Century*, Vol. 8, Chapter 121, One World.
'Enoch Powell, the Churches and Aid', *Study Encounter*, Vol. VI, No. 2, 1970.
'An Analysis of the Factors that Militate Against or are Conducive to the Formation of International Trade Groupings', in *International Trade Groupings* (Ministry of Overseas Development, 1970).
'An Institutional Critique of Development Concepts', *European Journal of Sociology*, XI, 1970, pp. 69–70.
'The Developing Countries in a World of Flexible Exchange Rates', *International Currency Review*, January/February 1971, Vol. II, No. 6.
'Development Investment', *Venture*, June 1971.

'Conflicts between Output and Employment Objectives', with Frances Stewart, *Oxford Economic Papers*, July 1971, Vol. 28, No. 2. Reprinted in *Prospects for Employment Opportunities in the Nineteen Seventies*, edited by Richard Jolly, Emanuel de Kadt, Hans Singer and Fiona Wilson (Penguin, 1973).

'Regional Integration in Asia', *Foreign Trade Review* Annual Number, January/March 1972.

'The Effects of Asian Economic Integration on Private Overseas Direct Investment', *Foreign Trade Review*, April/June 1972.

'Terms of Trade are not Made on Paper', *Ceres* (FAO Review), Vol. 5, No 2 March/April 1972. Also reprinted in shortened version, 'Self-Help for Poor Nations', *New Society*, 13 April 1972.

'Economic, and Social Rights and the Developing Countries', *Mondes en Développement* (2, 1972) *Revue européenne des sciences sociales*, Tome X, No. 26, 1972.

'Little-Mirrlees Methods and Project Appraisal', with Frances Stewart, *Bulletin of the Oxford University Institute of Economics and Statistics*, Vol. 34, No. 1, February 1972.

'Santiago in Retrospect', *Third World*, Vol. 1, No. 2, October 1972.

'To Back Moral Appeals by Power', *Bulletin of Peace Proposals*, Vol. 3, 1972.

'Cambridge Conference on Trade and Development', *Journal of World Trade Law*, Vol. 6, No. 6, November/December 1972.

'Technology Gaps between Rich and Poor Countries', *Scottish Journal of Political Economy*, November 1972. A shorter version is in *Royal Central Asian Journal* and in *Kajian Ekonomi Malaysia*, June 1971.

'Trade Strategies for Development: Some Themes for the Seventies', *World Development*, Vol. 1, No. 6, June 1973.

'Money: Root of All Good?', *Third World*, Vol. 2, No. 7, July/August 1973.

'Research', in *Food Research Institute Studies in Agricultural Economics, Trade and Development*, Vol. XII, No. 1, 1973, edited by Guy Hunter.

'The Multinational Enterprise and the Theory of Development Policy', *World Development*, Vol. 1, No. 10, October 1973.

'Alternatives in Development', *World Development*, Vol. 2, No. 2, February 1974.

'The Limits of Development Research', *World Development*, Vol. 2, Nos 10-12, October-December 1974. Reprinted in *Scientific Cooperation for Development: Search for New Directions*, edited by P.J. Lavakare, Ashok Parthasarathi, B.M. Udgaonkar Vikas (New Delhi, 1980).

'Social Science Research on Development: Some Problems in the Use and Transfer of an Intellectual Technology', *Journal of Economic Literature*, December 1974.

'Industrialization in a Unified Development Strategy', in *Employment, Income Distribution and Development Strategy*, Essays in Honour of H. W. Singer, edited by Sir Alec Cairncross and Mohinder Puri (Macmillan, 1976), and in *World Development*, Vol. 3, No. 1, January 1975, pp. 1–9.

'Policies Towards Multinationals', *World Development*, Vol. 3, No. 6, June 1975, and in *Essays in Honour of Felipe Pazos, Politica economica en centro e periferia*, edited by Diaz-Alejandro, Teitel and Tokman, 1976.

'The Dynamics of the New Poor Power', in *A World Divided: the Less Developed Countries in the International Economy*, edited by G. K. Helleiner (Cambridge

University Press, 1975); expanded version in *Resources Policy*, June 1976. Spanish translation, 1979.

'Why Interdisciplinary Studies?', in *What We Can Do for Each Other, An Interdisciplinary Approach to Development Anthropology*, edited by Glynn Cochrane, B.R. Gruner (Amsterdam, 1976).

'The Meaning and Purpose of Interdisciplinary Studies',. *Interdisciplinary Science Reviews*, Vol. 1, No. 2, 1976.

'Bargaining with Multinationals', *World Development*, Vol. 4, No. 3, March 1976.

'The Meaning and Purpose of Interdisciplinary Studies as Applied to Development Economics', *Interdisciplinary Science Reviews*, June 1976.

'It *is* a Moral Issue', *Crucible*, July-September 1976.

'New Strategies for Development: Poverty, Inequality and Growth', with Frances Stewart, *Oxford Economic Papers*, Vol. 28, November 1976, No. 3. Reprinted in *The Political Economy of Development and Underdevelopment* edited by Charles K. Wilber (1979).

'Labour-intensive Technologies for the Caribbean Area', with Jeffrey James, *The Seoul National University Economic Review*, Vol. XI, No. 1, December 1977, pp. 147–76.

'The Distinctive Features of a Basic Needs Approach to Development', *International Development Review*, Vol. XIX, No. 3, 1977.

'Changing Perceptions of Development', *Finance and Development*, Vol. 14, No. 3, September 1977, reprinted in *Challenge*, November/December 1977.

'Basic Needs: Some Issues', with S. J. Burki, *World Development*, March 1978, Vol. 6, No. 3, pp. 411–21.

Editor's Introduction to issue on 'Poverty and Inequality', *World Development*, March 1978, Vol. 6, No. 3, pp. 241-3.

'Basic Needs: Premises and Promises', *Journal of Policy Modelling*, Vol. 1, No. 1, January 1979.

'Indicators of Development: the Search for a Basic Needs Yardstick', with Norman Hicks, *World Development*, Vol. 7, June 1979, pp. 567–80.

'Multinationals Revisited', *Finance and Development*, June 1979.

'From Growth to Basic Needs', *Finance and Development*, June 1979. Reprinted in *Poverty and Development* (World Bank).

'Growth, Redistribution and Basic Human Needs', in *Beiträge zur Diskussion und Kritik der neoklassichen Ökonomie; Festschrift für Kurt W. Rothchild und Josef Steindl*, edited by K. Laski, E. Matzner, E. Nowotny (Springer Verlag, 1979), pp. 105–21.

'Transnational Corporations and Basic Needs', in *Growth with Equity: Strategies for Meeting Human Needs*, edited by Mary Evelyn Jegen and Charles K. Wilber (New York: Paulist Press, 1979).

'Development Ideas in Historical Perspective', in *Toward a New Strategy for Development*, Rothko Chapel Symposium, (Pergamon Press, 1979). Reprinted in Internationales Asienforum 1/2, 9. Jahrgang, May 1978; and *Regional Development Dialogue*, Autumn 1980, Vol. 1., No. 2. Also in *Changing Perceptions of Development Problems*, edited by R.P.Misra and M. Honjo, (Japan: Nagoya, 1981).

'Basic Needs and Human Rights', *World Development*, Vol. 8, February 1980, pp. 107–11.

'The Choices before Us', *International Development Review*, Vol. XXII, Nos. 2-3, 1980.
'Self-reliant Industrialization', in *The Political Economy of Development and Underdevelopment*, by Charles K. Wilber (1979) and 'Eisentandige Industrialisierung', in Khushi M. Khan (ed.), *Self-reliance als nationale und kollektive Entwicklungsstrategie* (Munchen: Weltforum Verlag, 1980) and in *Strategies of Planning and Development*, edited by Saeed Ahmad Qureshi and Dr Muhammad Arif, Planning and Development Board, Punjab, Pakistan.
Conferencia Internacional sobre economia Portugesa, Lisboa, 26-28 Setembro 1979 (Lisboa, 1980), pp. 483-8.
'Reply', with Norman Hicks, *World Development* Vol. 9, No. 4, April 1981.
'Constructive Responses to the North-South Dialogue', in *The Challenge of the New International Economic Order*, edited by Edwin F. Reubens, (Boulder, Colorado: Westview Press, 1981), pp. 71-89.
'Comment' on Benjamin Higgins, 'The Disenthronement of Basic Needs', *Regional Development Dialogue*, Vol. 1, No. 1, Spring 1980.
The United States and World Development: Agenda 1980, John Sewell and the staff of the Overseas Development Council (contributor) (New York: Praeger, 1980).
'Basic Needs in the Year 2000', *The Pakistan Development Review*, Vol. XIX, No. 2, (Summer 1980), pp. 129-41.
'The New International Economic Order: Development Strategy Options', in *Development and Peace*, Vol. 1, No. 2, Autumn 1980, Budapest, pp. 5-25.
'Development: What Have We Learned?', in *The Relevance of Economic Theories*, Proceedings of a Conference held by the International Economic Association at Warsaw, Poland, edited by Jozef Pajestka and C.H. Feinstein (Macmillan, 1980).
Foreword to Danny M. Leipziger (ed.), *Basic Needs and Development*, (Cambridge, Mass: Oelgeschlager, Gunn & Hain, 1981).
'Issues for Transnational Corporations in World Development', *CTC Reporter*, Vol. 1, No. 10, Spring 1981.
'The New International Economic Order: Development Strategy Options', in *East-West-South Economic Interactions between Three Worlds*, edited by Christopher T. Saunders (Macmillan, 1981).
'New Strategies for Development: a Comment', with Frances Stewart, in *Hommage à Francois Perroux* (Presses Universitaires de Grenoble, 1977).
International Responses to the Brandt Report. Towards One World? edited by Friedrich Ebert Foundation (London: Temple Smith, 1981), contribution.
'Growth, Redistribution and Basic Human Needs', *Development Strategies and Basic Needs in Latin America*, edited by Claes Brundesius and Mats Lundahl (Westview Press, 1982).
'Approaches to a New International Economic Order', *World Development*, Vol. 10, No. 1, January 1982, pp. 1-17.
'The Limits of Development Research', in *Social Sciences and Public Policy in the Developing World*, edited by Laurence D. Stifel, Ralph Davidson and James S. Coleman (Lexington Books, 1982).
'The Conflict between Communication Gaps and Suitability Gaps', *Communication Economics and Development*, edited by Meheroo Jussawalla and D.M. Lamberton (Pergamon Policy Studies, 1982).

'Commentary on Cancun', *Third World Quarterly*, July 1982.

'Environmental Aspects of Development', in *Expansion, Stagnation and Demokratie*, Festschrift für Theodor Prager und Philipp Rieger, *Wirtschaft und Gesellschaft*, 8. Jahrhang, Number 2/82.

'Basic Needs and the New International Economic Order', *Perspectives on Economic Development Essays in the Honour of W. Arthur Lewis*, edited by T.E. Barker, A.S. Downes, J.A. Sackey (University Press of America, 1982). Also in *Monde en Developpement*, No. 39, Tome 10, 1982.

'The New International Economic Order', *International Review of Education*, Vol. 28, No. 4, 1982. Special Issue: 'Education and the New International Economic Order', edited by John Oxenham, UNESCO Institute for Education, Martinus Nijhoff.

'A Cool Look at "Outward-Looking" Development Strategies', *The World Economy*, Vol. 5, No. 2, September 1982, pp. 159-69. Also in *Essays in Honour of A.N. Damaskenides*, 1982.

'What New International Economic Order?' in *Ordnungspolitische Fragen zum Nord-Süd-Konflikt*, edited by U.E. Simonis, Schriften des Vereins für Sozialpolitik, Bd 129, pp. 79-112 (Berlin: Duncker & Humbolt, 1983), and *Pakistan Journal of Applied Economics*, Vol. I, No. 2, Winter 1982.

'Trade as the Engine, Handmaiden, Brake or Offspring of Growth?', *The World Economy*, Vol. 5, No. 4, December 1982.

'Food Prices as a Reflection of Political Power', *Ceres*, March-April 1983, No. 92 (Vol. 16, No. 2).

'Twentyone Arguments for Public Enterprise', in *Global Development: Issues and Choices*, edited by Khadija Haq, North-South Roundtable of SID (Washington DC, 1983).

'Development Dichotomies', *World Development*, Vol. 11, No. 10, October 1983, pp. 875-89.

'Direct Private Foreign Investment, Transnational Corporations and Development', in *Commonwealth Economic Paper* No. 18, *Towards a New Bretton Woods*, Challenges for the World Financial and Trading System, selected background paper prepared for a Commonwealth Study Group, Volume 2, Commonwealth Secretariat, November 1983.

'Why Development Aid?', *Banca Nazionale del Lavoro Quarterly Review*, December 1983; also in *International Journal of Development Banking*, Vol. 2, No. 1, January, 1984.

'E Possibile uno sviluppo independènte?', *Politica Internazionale* N. 11-12, November-December 1983.

'La Interdepedendencia desde una perspectiva Norte-Sur', *Informacion Commerical Espanola*, No. 605, Enero, 1984.

'The New International Economic Order', Occasional Paper No. 3, Michigan State University Center for Advanced Study of International Development, 1983.

'Development Dichotomies' and comments on Albert O. Hirschman's chapter in *Pioneers in Development*, edited by Gerald Meier and Dudley Seers (World Bank Publication, Oxford University Press, 1984).

'Basic Needs: Some Unsettled Questions', *World Development*, September 1984.

Index

Africa, 241
　building of 'super-highways', 74
African countries
　growth: data on, 151–2; from 1960 to 1980, 148; imports' importance to, 150; poor countries', 147, 149; relation of export instability to, 142–4
　import instability 143, 146: need to overcome, 149, 150
　included and excluded from survey, 145, 151–2
　need for greater foreign exchange reserves, 149–50: paucity of international loans, 149, 150
　relation of outward orientation to growth, 139–40: alternative approaches, 140–4; little evidence for, 140–1, 146; theoretical case for, 141, 142
　sources of data, 144–6
Afghanistan, trade with Eastern bloc, 246
Aharoni, Y., model *re* managerial discretion, 226, 228, 229
Albania, 173
　agriculture: growth of labour productivity, 171; international trade, 174, 175; production growth rate, 167, 168
　communal land tenure, 165
　health, education and life expectancy, 1980s, 184
　population growth rate, 1960–81, 169
Algeria
　communal land tenure, 166
　self-managed farms, 187
　trade with Eastern bloc, 246

Amsden, A., 131
Andean Pact states, success of collective action by, 105
Argentina, 162
　depressions in 1930s and 1980s compared, 155–9 *passim*
　export of technological services, 133
　propped up by Latin American loan, 1984, 108
　trade with Eastern bloc, 246
Aristotle, 29
Arusha Declaration, 1967, 217
ASEAN, trade skirmish with Australia, 104
Asia, 241
　exported manufactures from centrally planned economies in, 250, 251–2, 265
Asian Wall Street Journal, 108
Athabaskan tar sands, 75
Australia, 241
　cereal exports, 194
　trade skirmish with ASEAN countries, 104
　yield variability in cereals, 194

Bagehot, Walter, 67
　Lombard Street, 78
Balassa, B., 127, 140
Balogh, Thomas, Lord, 3, 10, 15, 16, 27
　Irrelevance of Conventional Economics, The, 5
　relations with Paul Streeten, 4–5
　Unequal Partners, 8
　view of neoclassical theory, 5, 25
Banca Nationale de Lavoro, 8, 16
Bangladesh, trade with Eastern bloc, 257, 260

Bank of International Settlements (BIS), 101
Banking
 crisis of 1980s, 101
 lending to developing countries, 78–9, 81: 'development debts', 79–80; recessionary effect, 60, 65, 78
 nineteenth-century, 78
Baran, P. A., 15
Basic needs strategy, 23–5
 successes, 26
Beckerman, Wilfred, 38
Bhagwati, Jagdish N., 116, 117
 and Brecher, Richard A., 115, 118
Boston University, 14
Brandt Commission, 100, 102, 104
 reforms proposed by, 96
 Reports, 95, 103, 106
Brazil
 debtor-power, 107, 110
 depressions of 1930s and 1980s compared, 155–60 *passim*
 export of technological services, 133
 'gasohol', 134
 market dependence on USA, 110
 Petrobas, 133
 success of individual land tenure, 187
 trade with Eastern bloc, 246
Brecher, Richard A., 115
 and Choudhri, E. U., 115, 117
 and Diaz-Alejandro, C. F., 117
 and Feenstra, R. C., 117, 119
Bretton Woods Conference, 87, 94
Britain
 food deficit, 174
 neo-*laissez-faire* ideology, 1980s, 162
 Reform Act, 100
 shipping services, 129
 stops servicing US First World War loans, 1930s, 161
 trade liberalisation, nineteenth c., 99–100
 trade skirmishes with Indonesia, Malaysia and India, 103
Bulgaria, 241
 agriculture: growth of labour productivity, 171; international trade, 175; production growth rate, 167, 168
 centralised decision-making, 178
 communal land tenure, 165
 population growth rate, 1960–81, 169
Bulletin of the Oxford University Institute of Statistics, 8
Burki, Shavid Javed, 23

Canada
 cereal exports, 194
 cereal stockholding, 209, 210
 yield variability in cereals, 194
Caribbean, depressions of 1930s and 1980s compared, 162, 163
Carr, Edward Hallett, *What is History?*, 9
Central America, depressions of 1930s and 1980s compared, 162, 163
Chandra, N. K., 256, 258, 259
Chile
 asentamientos, 186, 187
 depressions of 1930s and 1980s compared, 155, 156, 158, 159
China, 111, 241
 agriculture: cereal imports, 194; cereal reserves, 194; growth of labour productivity, 171, 173; international trade, 175, 176–7; production growth rate, 167, 168; production teams, 178; 'production responsibility system', 179; yield variability in cereals, 194
 capital accumulation in Hebei province, 181–2, 182
 communal land tenure, 165, 186
 fuel exports, 176
 health, education and life expectancy, 1980s, 184
 population growth rates, 1960–81, 169, 170
 trade skirmish with USA, 103
Chipman, J. S., 119
Clark, W. E., on inconsistency of public investment with Tanzanian ideology, 217, 218

Cline, William, 90
  on effects of deflation by OECD countries, 40–1
Colombia, depressions of 1930s and 1980s compared, 155, 156, 158, 163
Commodity prices, see Third World
Commonwealth Secretariat, 150 Group, 102
Communal land tenure, 165–6
  collectivisation, 185–6
  countries practising, 165, 166
  'free rider' issue, 180
  growth of labour productivity in agriculture under, 170–3: compared with individual tenure, 171–2, 173
  growth of output per head under, 168–70: compared with individual tenure, 169
  growth of production under, 166–8: compared with individual tenure, 167, 168
  international trade in agricultural products and, 173–7
  peasants' attitude to, 185, 186
  problem of vested interests developing, 186–7
  question of advantages in promoting development, 180–8: creation of equality, 181; full employment, 181; potential for capital accumulation, 181–2, 188; providing framework for industrialising countryside, 182; providing framework for local political participation, 183, 185, 187; providing social framework, 182–3, 187; providing welfare, 183, 184
  question of efficiency, 177–80: managerial problems, 179–80
  socialist policies and, 188
Cooke, Peter, 101
Corn Laws, 65, 66, 68, 100
Council for Mutual Economic Assistance (CMEA), 241, 262, 263
Cuba
  agriculture: growth of labour productivity, 171, 173; international trade, 174, 175; production growth rate, 167, 168
  communal land tenure, 165
  health, education and life expectancy, 1980s, 184
  land reforms, 185
  population growth rate, 1960–81, 169, 170
  situation in 1930s and 1980s compared, 162
  trade with Eastern bloc, 246
Czechoslovakia, 241
  agriculture: growth of labour productivity, 171; international trade, 175; production growth rate, 167, 168
  centralised decision-making, 178
  communal land tenure, 165
  population growth rate, 1960–81, 167, 168

Department of Overseas Development, 14
Development Studies Association, 58
Diaz-Alejandro, Carlos F., 154, 155
Dick, R. and Dicke, H., on comparative advantage in services, 124–5, 127
Dobozi, I. and Inotai, A., on East–South trade, 261
'Dornbusch Report', 43

East Germany (GDR), 241
  agriculture: growth of labour productivity, 171; international trade, 175; production growth rate, 167, 168
  centralised decision-making, 178
  communal land tenure, 165
  population growth rate, 1960–81, 169
East–South trade, 240–2
  definitions of North, East, South and West, 240–1
  dimensions and trends, 1955–82, 242–7: bilateral agreements as trade basis, 246–7; compared with E–W and E–E trade, 243–4; expansion, 243, 253, 254, 264;

East–South trade—*continued*
  greater importance for E than S, 246; greater importance for USSR than E. Europe, 246; share of E in foreign trade of S, 244–6; share of S in foreign trade of E, 244–6; southern countries most concerned, 246
  division of labour between E and S, 260–4, 265: avenues for increasing southern manufactures, 263, 264: no help to southern industrialisation, 261; similarity of E–S to W–S trade, 261; similarity of S–E and E–W trade relations, 260; structural constraints on trade, 262; trade pattern's likely permanence, 261–2, 263
  gains from, 253–6: advantages and disadvantages of bilateral trading, 253–4, 254, 255; distribution of gains, 256–60, 264; Eastern bloc's, 255, 256; effect of complementarities of demand, 254, 263, 264; reduction of S export instability, 255; trade balances, 1965–75, 256, 257; USSR trade surplus, 256
  move from bilateral to convertible payments, 1970s, 247, 254–5, 256
  structure and composition, 1955–82, 247–53: E exports, 248–9, 252; food, 248, 249; fuels, 248, 249, 261; manufactures, 248–53 *passim*, 260, 265; raw materials, 248, 249; similarity to N–S trade, 253, 260, 264–5; S exports, 249–51, 253; Soviet armament exports, 249
Eastern bloc, 240, 241
  part of industrialised North, 241
Eastern Europe, 240, 241, 242
  see also East–South trade
ECA 'Transport and Communications Decade' for Africa, 74
Economist, The, 42
Edgeworth, F. Y., 34
Egypt, trade with Eastern bloc, 246, 257

Engel's Law, 72
Epicurus, 30
Ethiopia, communal land tenure in, 166
European Economic Community (EEC), 198, 211
  Common Agricultural Policy (CAP), 46
  yield variability in cereals, 194
Exchange rate, use in combating inflation, 52, 53

Feder, G. 144
  case for export expansion leading to growth, 141, 142
Federal Deposit Insurance Corporation, 78
Food Aid Convention, 213–14
Food and Agriculture Organisation (FAO), estimates safe level of world cereal reserves, 203–7
France
  failure of expansionary policies during recession, 42
  managerial discretion in SNEA, 226
  shipping deficit, 129
  stops servicing US First World War loans, 1930s, 161
Frank, A. G., 21

Galbraith, J. K., 27
Gandhi, Mrs Indira, 103, 107
General Agreement on Tariffs and Trade (GATT), 92, 94, 115, 122, 161
George, Henry, 75
German Democratic Republic (GDR), *see* East Germany
Germany, suspends reparations, 1930s, 161
Ghana, trade with Eastern bloc, 257
Gillis, M., 218
Gold standard, 9–10
Goldstein, Morris and Khan, Mohsin, on effect of slowdown in OECD countries on non-oil LDCs, 43–4
Griffin, Keith, 165
Grosser, I. and Tuitz, G., on E–S trade, 260, 262

Group of 77 (G77), 102, 106, 109, 241
  'New International Economic Order' (NIEO), 95, 97, 103, 109
  reforms proposed by, 96
Guatemala, success of individual land tenure, 187

Helleiner, G. K., 139, 149
Heller, Joseph, 67
Heller, P. S. and Porter, R. C., on export–orientation and growth, 141
Hicks, Norman, 17, 23
Hicks, Sir John, 39
Hirschman, Albert O., 15, 16
Holzman, F. D., 259
Hume, David, 30
  on Adam Smith's 'curious facts', 34
Hungary, 241
  agriculture: growth of labour productivity, 171; international trade, 174, 175; production growth rate, 167, 168
  communal land tenure, 165
  population growth rate, 1960–81, 169
  progress of collectivisation, 185

India, 111, 174, 183, 198
  agriculture: cereal reserves, 202; growth in labour productivity, 172, 173; growth of production, 167
  export of technological services, 131, 133
  IDA flows to, 109
  population growth rate, 1960–81, 169
  trade skirmish with Britain, 103
  trade with Eastern bloc, 246, 257, 260
Indonesia, trade skirmish with Britain, 103
Institute of Commonwealth Studies, Oxford, 14
Institute of Development Studies, Sussex, 14

Institutional economists
  dilemma of economic values for, 7–13
  reformist left among, 12–13
Inter-American Development Bank, 164
International debt problem
  amount of developing countries' debt, 89
  essential elements in solution: adjustment of trading patterns to aid repayment, 91; assurance of repayment, 91; need for institutional intermediary, 91
  fallacies concerning, 88–91: case-by-case approach, 89–90; collective approach, 89, 90; costless answers, 90; costs of adjustment must be paid by debtors, 90; financial response only needed, 89; insolvency of debtor nations, 88; irresponsibility of debtor nations, 88; postponement of payment the answer, 89
  Latin American, 160–1, 163–4
  present problems 87–8
  proposals for solving 90–1: international response, 101
  see also IMF, proposal for debt refinancing subsidiary
International Encyclopedia of the Social Sciences, 6, 8
International Grains Agreement, 211
International investment
  extending free trade to include, 115–19: conflicting-interest outcome, 115, 116; effects, 116–19; under GATT 115
International Labour Organisation (ILO), 23
  'basic needs strategy' concept, 23
International Monetary Fund, 79, 89, 90, 139, 149, 150, 161
  cereal financing facility, 212–13
  finance for African countries, 150: form needed, 150
  optimism about world economy, 1984, 58

Index

International Monetary Fund—*continued*
  proposal for debt financing subsidiary, 92–4: funding of, 93; role of, 93
  response to banking crises, 1980s, 101
International Wheat Agreement, failure to negotiate, 210
Iran, trade with Eastern bloc, 246
Iraq, trade with Eastern bloc, 246
Islam, Nurul, 192
Israel, communal land tenure in, 166
Italy
  managerial discretion in ENI, 226
  shipping deficit, 129

Jahrbücher für Nationalökonomie und Statistik, 2
James, Jeffrey, 217
Japan, 102, 241
  motivational factors behind success, 34
  shipping services, 129
Jenkinson, Tim, 51
Johnson, D. Gale, 177
Johnson, H. G., 117
Jones, R. W., 117
Junginger-Dittel, K. O. and Reisen, H., 143

Kaldor, Lord, 3, 53
  distinguishes 'price' in primary production from industrial prices, 48
Kampuchea, communal land tenure in, 166
Katouzian, H., on competitive advantage in services, 125, 127, 129
Kemp, M. C., 117
Kendrick, John, 40
Kenen, Peter, 90, 92
Keynes, J. M., 59, 61
  General Theory of Employment, Interest and Money, 1
  gloss on Ricardo's rent theory, 63
Krueger, Anne, 141
Kuhn, Thomas, 18
Kuwait, 60
  current account surpluses, 1981, 79

Lal, D., 96
Lall, Sanjaya, 122, 133, 134
  Foreign Investment, Transnationals and Developing Countries (with Paul Streeten), 20
Laos, communal land tenure in, 166
Latin America, 241
  booms of 1920s and 1970s, 155–6: comparison of export sectors, 159
  contrasts in depressions of 1930s and 1980s, 159–62: in climate of international political economy, 161–2; in foreign investment and loans, 160–1; in export sector, 159; in import sector, 159–60
  external debt, 163
  similarities in depressions of 1930s and 1980s, 154–5: decline in capital inflows, 156–7; deterioration in commodity terms of trade, 156; devaluations, 157–8; exchange controls, 158–9; import cuts, 157; soaring interest rates, 156
  success of conservative programmes, 163
Lavigne, M., on E–S trade, 249, 256, 260, 261–2
Lehrer, Tom, 22
Leibenstein, H., X-efficiency theory, 219–20
Lenin, V. I., 21
Lévy-Bruhl, Lucien, 18
Libya, trade with Eastern bloc, 246
Lim, D., 143
Lindbeck, Assar, 40, 41
Lindblom, C. E., 16
Lipsey, R. G., 26
Lipton, Michael, 58
Loxley, J. and Saul, J. S., on vagueness of Tanzanian development goals, 228–9

MacBean, A. I., 142
McNamara, Robert, 23, 88
Mahbub ul Haq, 23, 87
  on basic needs strategy, 24

Maizels, A., 142
Malaysia, trade skirmish with Britain, 103
Malthus, Thomas, 59, 71, 76
Malvinas/Falklands War, 157
Manchester School, 2
Mannheim, Karl, 18
Marshall, A., gloss on Ricardo's rent theory, 63
Mendershausen, H., 258
Mexico
 collective *ejido* in, 186
 communal land tenure, 166
 depressions of 1930s and 1980s compared, 155, 156, 158
 export of technological services, 133
 HYL steel process, 133
Michaely, Michael, 44
 on relation between export expansion and growth, 141
Mihyo, P., on limited government control of Tanzanian public enterprises, 229–30
Mongolia, 241
 agriculture: growth of labour productivity, 171, 173; international trade, 174, 175; production growth rate, 166, 167, 168
 health, education and life expectancy, 1980s, 184
 population growth rate, 1960–81, 169, 170
Moran, C., 142
Morishima, Michio, 34
Mozambique, communal land tenure, 166
Multinational companies, Code of Conduct, 96, 97
Myrdal, Gunnar, 4, 5–6, 10, 15, 16, 19, 26, 27
 American Dilemma, An, 6
 Asian Drama, 6, 13, 15, 17
 'Logical Crux of All Science, The', 6
 Political Element in the Development of Economic Theory, The, 5, 6
 relations with Paul Streeten, 5–6, 8–9
 Value in Social Theory, 6, 7

Nayyar, Deepak, 240, 255, 262
Nestlé's, boycotted by ten countries, 104
Netherlands, shipping deficit, 129
New Zealand, 241
Nicaragua, communal land tenure in, 166
North Korea, 241
 agriculture: growth of labour productivity, 171; international trade, 175; output per head, 170; production growth rate, 166, 167, 168, 170
 collectivisation, 185–6
 communal land tenure, 165
 health, education and life expectancy, 1980s, 184
 land reform, 185
 population growth rate, 1960–81, 169
North–South negotiations
 alternative strategies, 101–6: bargaining, 103–5, 112; concentrating on modest reforms, 102; identifying reforms to promote development, 102; maximising performance within present rules, 102–3; power of collective action, 105–6, 113
 areas for negotiation, 106–12: buyer-power of South, 106–7; countries' political sensitivity and aid, 108; debtor-power of South, 107–8; investment and technology transfer by MNCs, 107; issue linkage, 109; power, for South, in large contracts, 107; problems for least developed countries, 109–10; seller-power of South, 107
 barter deals, 104
 debt crisis and, 101
 differences between North and South, 240
 need for freer trade, 98–9: examples of national interest supporting, 99–100; gains for weakly represented consumers, 98–9; political opposition to, 99; producer opposition to, 99

North–South negotiations—*continued*
  proposed reforms of international economic system, 95–6: moral basis of, 96, 97; challenges to, 96; little action of, 97, 101, 112; mutual interest basis, 97, 98
  question of aid, 100
  question of commodity price stabilisation, 100
  'rules' of the game, 95
  strengthening southern countries' negotiating position, 110–12: collective self-reliance, 111–12; concentration of purchases and borrowing, 110; diversification of selling outlets, 110; reduced dependence on external world, 110–11
Nott, John, 103
Norway, shipping services, 129

Oceania, 241
Ohlin, B. and Samuelson, Paul, development of free trade theory, 8
Oil
  advantages of producers over earlier food-and-fibre producers, 75
  E–S trade in, 248, 249, 261
  easy to restrain output, 71
  effect of price increases on OECD countries, 41, 50, 65
  expenditure on compared with expenditure on food in Ricardo's day, 75
  price inelasticity, 71
Okun, Arthur, 39
Organisation of Economic Cooperation and Development (OECD) countries, 240, 241, 263
  comparative advantage in trade and services, 124–5
  effect of fall in imported commodity prices on wages, unemployment and inflation, 48–9: statistical verification, 50–2, 56–7
  effect of unemployment on wage rates, 47
  individual land tenure compared with communal, *see* Communal land tenure
  inflation, 1979–83, 47
  internal commodity production, 46
  recession, profit recovery and real wage falls, 72, 77
  recessionary effect of bank lending to developing countries, 60, 75
  slowdown in growth from 1973, 39–44: conflicting theories on, 42–3; effect of oil price increases, 40, 41, 50, 65; effect on Third World countries, 38–9, 40–1, 43–4, 53; growth rates, 1960–83, 39; part played by deflationary policies, 40–1; role of anti-inflationary policies, 41, 42, 60; role of reduction in investment, 41
  wage increases reduced by unemployment, 49
Organisation of Petroleum Exporting Countries (OPEC), 47, 65–8 *passim*, 72, 79, 107, 261, 264
  class unity of landlord and entrepreneur under, 71
  difficulty of rentiers financing entrepreneurship, 72
  rental income, 76
  world losses through 1970s' actions of, 105

Pakistan, trade with Eastern bloc, 246, 257, 260
Paszynski, M., 262
Perkins, F.
  on inconsistency of technological choice with Tanzanian development goals, 218
  Tanzanian public enterprise studies, 226, 227
Peru, depressions of 1930s and 1980s compared, 156, 157, 158
Philippines, 183
  debtor-power, 108
Pickett, J., 219
Pinochet, Gen., 187
Poland, 241
  communal land tenure, 166
  dissolution of co-operatives in, 185
Popper, K., 76
Prebisch, Raùl, 15

Index

Quarterly Journal of Economics, 2, 7
Queen Elizabeth House, Oxford, 14

Raiffa, Howard, 228
  on accountability and control in firms, 224
  on trade-offs between conflicting objectives, 225
Raphael, D. D. and Macfie, A. L., 29
Recession, the continuing
  caused by monetary flows, 59: effect of bank lending to developing countries, 60
  caused by public policy, 59: effect of withdrawal of investment, 60
  caused by transfer of Ricardian rent from entrepreneurs to oil rentiers, 60–1, 62–3, 64–5, 80–1: effect of income redistribution on demand, 64; farmland rents not analogous to oil rents, 65–6; oil-rent threat compared to Ricardo's food-rent threat, 66–74; parameters today compared to Ricardo's day, 73, 74; problem of no alternative to oil, 66, 68, 76; Third World demand compared to 'colonial' demand of Ricardo's day, 73, 74; today's rentiers, 60
  false dawn of recovery, 1980s, 58
Ricardo, David, 65, 68, 71, 76, 100
  behaviour of rentiers in time of, 78
  faith in Say's Law, 64
  notion of wage share, 77
  Principles, 62, 63
  rent theory, 59, 61, 67: fall in profit and, 61–2, 63, 64, 68, 70, 76; invalidated by grain imports into Britain, 66; squeeze on accumulation under, 62
  sees food as crucial to rent squeeze on growth, 69, 70
Rohatyn, Felix, 90, 92
Romania
  agriculture: growth of labour productivity, 171; international trade, 174, 175; production growth rate, 167, 168
  communal land tenure, 165
  health, education and life expectancy, 1980s, 184
  population growth rate, 1960–81, 169

Samuelson, Paul A., 1–2, 10, 21, 26
  gains-from-trade theorem, 115
Sapir, A. and Lutz, E., on comparative advantage in services, 125–7, 129, 135
Saudi Arabia, 60, 75
  current account surpluses, 1981, 79
Say, Jean-Pangloss, 61
Say's Law, 59, 63, 64
Schumer, Charles, 90
Seers, Dudley, 13, 96
Sen, Amartya, 28
Singer, H. W., 116
Skachkov, S., on E–S trade, 261
Smith, Adam, 21, 100
  'Adam Smith Institute', 28
  fascination with curious facts, 34–5
  pluralism and sympathy in theories of, 29–31
  policies claiming descent from, 28–9
  prudence and common motivation in theories of, 31–2, 33, 35–6: on rules of conduct, 31, 32, 34
  Theory of Moral Sentiments, The, 28, 34
  view of self-interest, 32, 33–4
  view of the rich, 32–3
  view of usefulness and virtue, 32–3, 34
  Wealth of Nations, The, 28, 29, 34
South Korea, 102, 111
  agriculture: growth of labour productivity, 172, 173; growth of production, 167, 168; output per head, 170
  equitable distribution of income in countryside, 187
  export of technological services, 133
  indices of real exchange rates, 1976–82, 158
  'political' aid to, 108
  population growth rate, 169

Soviet Union, 198, 240, 241, 242
  agriculture; growth of labour productivity, 171; growth of production, 167, 168; international trade, 175
  centralised decision-making, 178
  cereals: fluctuation in production, 207; imports, 194; yield variability, 193, 194
  communal land tenure, 165
  peasant coercion, 1930s, 185
  population growth rate, 1960–81, 169
  see also East-South trade
Sri Lanka
  success in providing basic needs and services, 187
  trade with Eastern bloc, 257
Stewart, Frances, 17, 23, 95, 221
  'Conflict between Output and Employment Objectives' (with Paul Streeten), 19
  'New Strategies for Development: Poverty, Income Distribution and Growth' (with Paul Streeten), 21
Stigler, George, 'Smith's Travel on the Ship of the State', 31
Streeten, Paul, viii–ix, 95, 140
  birth, 1
  'Changing Perceptions of Development', 17
  'Conflicts between Output and Employment Objectives' (with Frances Stewart), 19
  contributions to development economics, 13–27
  'Development Dichotomies', 17
  'Development Ideas in Historical Perspectives', 17, 26
  Development Perspectives, 6, 12, 14, 15, 18, 20, 23
  'Development: What have we learned?', 17
  dilemma of economists' values and, 7–13
  'Economics and Value Judgements', 2, 6
  First Things First: Meeting Basic Human Needs in Developing Countries (with Burki, Mahbub, Hicks and Stewart), 23, 24, 25
  Foreign Investment, Transnationals and Developing Countries (with Sanjaya Lall), 20
  Frontiers of Development Studies, The, 6, 10, 16, 17, 28
  'Institutional Critique of Development Concepts, An', 17
  'Limits of Development Research, The', 18–19
  'New Strategies for Development: Poverty, Income Distribution and Growth' (with Frances Stewart), 21
  on Adam Smith's belief in education, 29
  on development, 11–12
  'Programmes and Prognoses, Unbalanced Growth and the Ideal Plan', 16
  'Programs and Prognoses', 3, 6, 7, 10, 26
  publications, ix, 3, 270–8
  relations with Gunnar Myrdal, 5–6, 8–9
  relations with Thomas Balogh, 4–5
  sceptical about orthodox economic theory, 2, 3
  'Social Science Research and Development: Some Problems in the Use and Transfer of an Intellectual Technology', 18
  style, 1, 2
  teaching at Balliol, 1948–64, 2–3
  'Theory of Pricing, The', 2
  'Theory of Profit, The', 2
  'Value in Social Theory', 26
  'Values, Facts and the Compensation Principle', 3
Stretton, Hugh, 1
Syria, trade with Eastern bloc, 246, 260

Taiwan, 111
  economic success, 187

'political' aid to, 108
Tanzania
communal land tenure, 166, 178
difficulties in formulation of national objective function, 228–9: Report... on Long-Term Industrial Strategy, 228
National Development Corporation, 233
state-owned enterprises: case studies, 230–6; conceptual framework of analysis of, 218–26, 236; failure of investment planning, 227–8; Kagera (sugar), 231, 232; Kilombero (sugar), 231, 232; Korogwe (maize-milling), 231, 232, 233–4; limited capacity for government control, 229–30; managerial discretion, 229, 230; method of research into, 226–7; Moproco (oil-milling), 231, 232, 234; Morogoro (footwear), 231, 232, 233; Mtiba (sugar), 231, 232; Musoma (textiles), 231, 232; Mwatex (textiles), 231, 232; Printpak (inks), 231, 232; Sabuni Industries Ltd, 231, 232, 233; technology inconsistent with national objectives, 217–18, 230–6
Sugar Development Corporation, 228
TANU party, 229
Tanzanian Industrial Studies and Consulting Organisation (TISCO), 234, 236
Third Five Year Plan, 1976–81, 227
trade with Eastern bloc, 257
ujamaa villages, 178
Thailand, power of large contract illustrated by, 107
Third World, 240
commodity prices in: Latin American in 1930s and 1980s compared, 156; OECD countries' recession and fall in, 38–9, 43–4, 53; question of price stabilisation in N–S negotiations, 100; relation to stabilisation in OECD area, 47–50
comparative advantage in trade services, 122, 132–6: advantage of specific skills, 133; determinants, 128–32; existing studies, 124–8; in insurance, 126–7; in shipping and transportation, 123, 126, 128–9, 132; in technological services, 123, 129–31, 132; specialisation and, 134, 135; trade services defined, 122–4
large proportion of income spent on food, 73
larger use of fossil energy than developed countries, 73
neo-Ricardian oil-rent-induced 'limits to growth' and, 73
relation of public enterprises to governments: 'bureaucratic man' hypothesis and, 221–3, 231, 236; 'engineering man' hypothesis and, 220–1, 223, 232; limits of government control, 224–6; managerial discretion, 226; neoclassical model, 219, 223, 225; technological implications of alternatives to neoclassical model, 223–4; X-efficiency theory and, 219–20, 223, 232
seasonal unemployment, 181
see also East–South trade and North–South negotiations
Trade services, 122–4
Tyler, W. G., on export orientation and growth, 141

Uekawa, Y., 119
United Arab Emirates, 60
current account surpluses, 1981, 79
United Nations, 87, 155
Committee for Development Planning, 102
Conference on Trade and Development (UNCTAD), 92, 94, 122, 123, 145, 146
Development Decades, 95, 102: International Development

United Nations—*continued*
  Strategies (IDS), 95, 97, 100, 101, 104; reforms proposed, 96
United States of America
  banking failures, 1930s, 161
  cereals: exports, 194; price changes, 197; stockholding, 209, 210; yield variability, 193, 194
  International Emergency Food Reserve, 214
  Marshall Plan, 100
  opposed to international cereal agreement, 211, 212
  shipping deficit, 129
  trade skirmish with China, 103
  vigour of 1980s, 162, 163
Uruguay, depreciation of currency, 1930s, 157

Venezuela, depressions of 1930s and 1980s compared, 155–8 *passim*
Vernon, Raymond
  on principal's problem in controlling agent, 224
  on problem of conflicting goals, 225
Vietnam, 241
  agriculture: growth of labour productivity, 171, 173; international trade, 175, 176; production growth rate, 167, 168
  communal land tenure, 165
  health, education and life expectancy, 1980s, 184
  'political' aid to, 108
  population growth rate, 1960–81, 169

Weber, Max, 19
  on scientific freedom, 19
Wells, L. T., 'engineering man' hypothesis, 219, 220–1
Wheeler, D., 143
Whorf, Benjamin Lee, 18
Williams, D., 'bureaucratic man' hypothesis, 219, 221–3
World Bank, 14, 25, 92, 139, 144, 167, 170, 228, 234
  appraisal of Tanzanian footwear enterprise, 233

'Berg Report', 140
disbursements, 89
IDA, 87, 92
studies on basic needs, 23
World Development Report, 145, 146
World Development, 14, 17
World Food Conference, 1974, 202, 213
  International Undertaking on World Food Security, 215
World food security in cereals, 192–3
  alternative measures for promoting, 212–15: Food Aid Convention, 213–14; IMF cereal financing facility, 212–13; long-term contracts, 214; preferential access for developing countries, 214–15
  different countries' share of stocks, 206
  international grains negotiations, 207–10: insufficiency of private stockholding, 208: need for stockholding subsidies, 209–10; plan for international price-stabilising buffer stocks, 207–8, 208–9, 210; reasons for breakdown, 210–12
  international measures for, 202–3
  interrelated instability in cereals and feed sectors, 195–7: disease problems, 196; effect of feed prices, 196; problems generated by monetary sector, 196–7
  major exporters, 194
  major importers, 194
  national measures for stabilising supplies, 199–202: holding of reserves in food or foreign exchange, 200–1; improved agricultural techniques, 200; improved marketing and distribution, 200; irrigation, 199–200; problems of importing, 200–1, 202
  price instability, 197–8, 212: disadvantages, 198; from 1950s to 1980, 197; national policies and, 197–8; reasons for, 197
  production variability, 193, 195

Index

scientific advance and, 195
sources of consumption instability in developing countries, 198–9: fluctuations in domestic food production, 199; variability in import price, 199
world carry-over stocks as % of total utilisation, 206
world reserves, 203–7: estimating safe level, 203–7; problems of distribution and price, 207; reserve stocks, 203, 205; working stocks, 203, 205
yield variability, 193–4, 195

Yugoslavia
communal land tenure, 166
dissolution of co-operatives, 185